PIECES FOR PRIZE SPEAKING

PIECES FOR PRIZE SPEAKING

*A collection of over one hundred new pieces
which have taken prizes in Prize Speaking Contests*

COMPILED AND EDITED BY

A. H. CRAIG

AND

BINNEY GUNNISON

Granger Index Reprint Series

BOOKS FOR LIBRARIES PRESS
FREEPORT, NEW YORK

First Published 1899
Reprinted 1972

Library of Congress Cataloging in Publication Data

Craig, Asa Hollister, 1847-1934, comp.
  Pieces for prize speaking.

  (Granger index reprint series)
  First published in 1899 under title: Pieces for
prize speaking contests.
    1. Recitations. I. Gunnison, Binney, 1863-
joint comp. II. Title.
PN4201.C8 1972   808.85'4   72-5592
ISBN 0-8369-6371-7

PRINTED IN THE UNITED STATES OF AMERICA

PREFACE

VERY few books of declamations and recitations contain selections especially suited for Prize Speaking Contests. The compilers have spent nearly three years in collecting the pieces contained in this volume, nearly every one of which has taken a prize at some Prize Speaking Contest. Several pieces have been especially adapted for this book. A glance at the list of contents will show how great care has been exercised in making the selection.

The courtesy of those who have responded so willingly to the request for permission to use selections from their speeches and writings is gratefully acknowledged. We wish particularly to thank the teachers of Elocution in the Northern, Southern, Eastern and Western Colleges, who have assisted us in collecting the material for the book, and for their many valuable suggestions.

A. H. CRAIG.
BINNEY GUNNISON.

iii

CONTENTS

PIECES

FOR

PRIZE SPEAKING

———

A HARVARD–YALE FOOTBALL GAME

THE day for the contest that was to decide whether the Crimson or the Blue would wave triumphant over the gridiron had come. Before the sun was fairly up, the van of the great army of Harvard-Yale enthusiasts had entered the city. Special trains from New York, New Haven, Boston and Albany had been pouring their heavy loads into Springfield for hours.

Hampden Park was to be the field of battle. On the north the Crimson forces were banked ten thousand strong; on the south were stationed the Blues, while at each end the hostile colors intermingled. Never was loyalty more strong. Around the standards, waiting for the advance of the skirmish lines, were governors, men whose faces were well known in the halls of. Congress; sober, calm-minded judges who had laid aside their robes to rally around the old flag and shout for their Alma Mater. The graduates of only a year or two were omnipresent, while the gentler sex, with countenances all aglow, stood ready, like the Amazons of old, to advance to the defence of the flag they loved.

About half past two o'clock, a great cheer, at first indistinct, but gradually growing louder and louder like a roll of thunder, rolled simultaneously along both sides of the field, until, when it seemed as though the very heavens would be rent, there trotted into the arena twenty-two brawny specimens of this "dyspeptic, ice-water-drinking" nation.

Stripping off their sweaters, both elevens lined up against each other. Yale had won the toss. Harvard had the ball. For a moment they stood there, all crouching, their heads well down, their great limbs tense, all straining for the word to spring at each other. There was not a sound around the vast field save the slight rustle of the wind. Both sides were waiting for the word that should precipitate the awful onslaught.

"Play!" called the referee, and the Harvard wedge shot forward and crashed with a sound of grinding canvas into the mass of blue-legged bodies that rushed to meet it.

For nearly three quarters of an hour the mimic battle was fought back and forth along the white-barred field. All the tactics of war were employed; the center was pierced, the flanks were turned, heavy columns were simultaneously massed against any weak spot. It was even, very even; but at last a long punt and a fumble gave Harvard the ball on Yale's twenty-five-yard line. A well supported run around the right end by Jarvis, the famous half-back, two rushes by Blake, the terrible line-breaker, and a flying wedge through the center drove the ball to Yale's five-yard line. Another gain was made by the tall Rivers. Then another! Then, with their backs on their own goal line, the Yale team rallied. The next attempt resulted in no gain. Now for one good push or drop kick! Too late! The umpire had called time, and the first half of the game had ended — neither side had scored.

During the fifteen minutes intermission, the Giants were surrounded by their coaches and supporters, and each side girded itself for the fray that was to win or lose the day. A strong wind was blowing when the referee called, "Play!" Jarvis, the runner, who had been saved a good deal in the first half, was now used with telling effect. In a short time an exchange of punts brought the ball to Yale's thirty-yard line.   After three downs, Spofford dropped back, as though for a kick, and the Yale full-back retreated for a catch. Instead of the expected kick, Rivers, the guard, charged for the left end, and the Blue line concentrated at that point to meet him, when suddenly Jarvis, with the ball tucked under his arm, was seen going like a whirlwind around the right, well protected by the quarter and half-back.   The Yale left-end was knocked off his legs, and the whole Crimson bank of spectators rose to its feet with a roar as it realized that Jarvis had circled the end.

The Yale halfs had been drawn to the right, and everyone knew that with Jarvis once past the rush-line no one could run him down.   On he went at full speed for the longed-for touch-down.   The full-back, however, was heading him off; he had outrun his interferers, and a Yale Varsity full-back is not apt to miss a clear tackle in the open field.

They came together close to the line.   Just as his adversary crouched for his hips, Jarvis leaped high from the ground and hurled himself forward, head first.   The Yale man, like a hawk, "nailed" him in the air, but his weight carried him on and they both fell with a fearful shock — over the line. The next minute they were buried under a pile of men.

Then for fully five minutes did all the sons of "Fair Harvard" shout with a mighty shout that made the very air tremble. For five long minutes old gray-haired sires and young freshmen cheered as they never cheered before; even the sedate judges for once forgot their dignity and hugged each other.

Suddenly from the midst of the little group of battle-scarred warriors a limp form was brought. Instantly the pandemonium ceased. All faces looked aghast, fearing lest in that awful charge the poor fellow had been seriously injured.

"It's Jarvis," anxiously murmured the crowd. A substitute ran out to the grand stand, and shouted: "Nothing serious, only broken his collar bone!" Those near the place where the plucky half-back was borne off the field could see that his face was pale, but supremely happy, and he smiled faintly as he heard the cheers of thousands, and his own name coupled with that of his Alma Mater.

The touch-down had been made almost at the corner, too far aside for the try for goal to succeed. Spofford's kick was a splendid attempt, but the ball struck the goal post and bounded back into the field.

The battle began again with increased fury. Although the Crimson team had suffered an irreparable loss in the injury to their comrade,

Jarvis, yet as the score was 4 to 0 in their favor, all they needed now was to keep Yale from scoring. Already the ten thousand Harvard supporters were proclaiming victory. The Yale men closed up and went in for the last chance. It wasn't safe to punt now because the wind had changed and was against them; but they had the heavier weight and well they used every ounce of it. Steadily, as the Old Guard trod over its slain at Waterloo, did the Blue wedge drive its way, rod by rod, toward the Harvard line. And as the fierce red Britons tore at Napoleon's devoted column, so did the Crimson warriors leap upon that earth-stained phalanx. The rushers strained against it; Blake would plunge into and stagger it; Rivers and Spofford would throw their great bodies flat under the tramping feet and bring the whole mass down over them. As often as Yale advanced toward the Harvard line, just so often was she driven back.

It was now growing dark and the excitement was so intense on both sides that hardly a cheer was heard. All were breathlessly watching the maneuvers of the opposing forces, for a bad pass by the Crimson quarter-back, a slip, a fumble by Spofford, might turn the tide and "Fair Harvard's" banners be trampled under foot.

Yale got the ball and made a short gain.

"Second down!" called the umpire. Once

more they lined up. Only ten yards away lay the
coveted goal. The halfs dropped back, the signal
was given, and the ball came flying from the hands
of the quarter-back. The left-half took it and,
guarded by quarter, right-half and full-back, dashed
for right end. The end braced himself, but the
shock was too severe and he and the little quarter-
back went rolling on the ground. But the ball
was past the end, and with two men in the interference and only Harvard's full-back to pass, they
could not possibly fail to score. The full-back
plunged bravely into the interference, but, alas, it
was too late! Yale's half shot by him and was
over the line, touching the ball down directly
behind the goal posts. The yell that went up from
the assembled crowd will never be forgotten. The
ball was brought out to the twenty-five-yard line
and the little quarter-back, lying down upon the
ground, took it between his hands. After a
minute's pause the full-back kicked it. The ball
shot forward, and describing a lofty parabola,
passed between the goal posts, winning for Yale
the greatest football contest of the year, with a
score of 6 to 4.

COMMENCEMENT

SARAH WINTER KELLOGG

IT was Commencement at one of our colleges. The people were pouring into the church as I entered it, rather tardy. Finding the choice seats in the center of the audience room already taken, I pressed forward, looking to the right and to the left for a vacancy. On the very front row of seats I found one.

Here a little girl moved along to make room for me, looking into my face with large gray eyes, whose brightness was softened by very long lashes. Her face was open and fresh as a newly-blown rose before sunrise. Again and again I found my eyes turning to the rose-like face, and each time the gray eyes moved, half-smiling, to meet mine. Evidently the child was ready to "make up" with me. And when, with a bright smile, she returned my dropped handkerchief, and I said "Thank you," we seemed fairly introduced. Other persons, now coming into the seat, crowded me quite close up against the little girl, so that we soon felt very well acquainted.

"There's going to be a great crowd," she said to me.

"Yes," I replied; "people always like to see how school-boys are made into men."

Her face beamed with pleasure and pride as she said :

" My brother's going to graduate ; he's going to speak ; I've brought these flowers to throw to him."

They were not greenhouse favorites; just old-fashioned, domestic flowers, such as we associate with the dear grandmothers ; " but," I thought, "they will seem sweet and beautiful to him for his little sister's sake."

"That is my brother," she went on, pointing with her nosegay.

" The one with the light hair?" I asked.

"Oh, no," she said, smiling and shaking her head in innocent reproof ; not that homely one ; that handsome one with brown, wavy hair. His eyes look brown, too, but they are not — they are dark blue. There ! he's got his hand up to his head now. You see him, don't you?"

In an eager way she looked from me to him, and from him to me, as if some important fate depended upon my identifying her brother.

" I see him," I said. " He's a very good-looking brother."

"Yes, he is beautiful," she said, with artless delight ; "and he's so good, and he studies so hard ! He has taken care of me ever since mamma died. Here is his name on the programme. He is not the valedictorian, but he has an honor, for all that."

I saw in the little creature's familiarity with these technical college terms that she had closely identified herself with her brother's studies, hopes, and successes.

"His oration is a real good one, and he says it beautifully. He has said it to me a great many times. I 'most know it by heart. Oh! it begins so pretty and so grand. This is the way it begins," she added, encouraged by the interest she must have seen in my face: "'Amid the permutations and combinations of the actors and the forces which make up the great kaleidoscope of history, we often find that a turn of Destiny's hand——'"

"Why, bless the baby!" I thought, looking down into her bright, proud face. I can't describe how very odd and elfish it did seem to have those sonorous words rolling out of the smiling, infantile mouth.

As the exercises progressed, and approached nearer and nearer the effort on which all her interest was concentrated, my little friend became excited and restless. Her eyes grew larger and brighter, two deep-red spots glowed on her cheeks.

"Now, it's his turn," she said, turning to me a face in which pride and delight and anxiety seemed about equally mingled. But when the overture was played through, and his name was called, the child seemed, in her eagerness, to for get me and all the earth beside him. She rose to her feet and leaned forward for a better view of her beloved, as he mounted to the speaker's stand. I knew by her deep breathing that her heart was throbbing in her throat. I knew, too, by the way her brother came up the steps and to the front that he was trembling. The hands hung limp; his face was pallid, and the lips blue as with cold. I felt anxious. The child, too, seemed to discern that things were not well with him. Something like fear showed in her face.

He made an automatic bow. Then a bewildered, struggling look came into his face, then a helpless look, and then he stood staring vacantly, like a somnambulist, at the waiting audience. The moments of painful suspense went by, and still he stood as if struck dumb. I saw how it was; he had been seized with stage fright.

Alas, little sister! She turned her large, dismayed eyes upon me. "He's forgotten it," she said. Then a swift change came into her face; a strong, determined look ; and on the funeral-like silence of the room broke the sweet, brave, child-voice :

"'Amid the permutations and combinations of the actors and the forces which make up the great kaleidoscope of history, we often find that a turn of Destiny's hand ——'"

Everybody about us turned and looked. The

breathless silence; the sweet, childish voice; the childish face; the long, unchildlike words, produced a weird effect.

But the help had come too late; the unhappy brother was already staggering in humiliation from the stage. The band quickly struck up, and waves of lively music rolled out to cover the defeat.

I gave the little sister a glance in which I meant to show the intense sympathy I felt; but she did not see me. Her eyes, swimming with tears, were on her brother's face. I put my arm around her, but she was too absorbed to heed the caress, and before I could appreciate her purpose, she was on her way to the shame-stricken young man sitting with a face like a statue's.

When he saw her by his side the set face relaxed, and a quick mist came into his eyes. The young men got closer together to make room for her. She sat down beside him, laid her flowers on his knee, and slipped her hand into his.

I could not keep my eyes from her sweet, pitying face. I saw her whisper to him, he bending a little to catch her words. Later I found out that she was asking him if he knew his "piece" now, and that he answered yes.

When the young man next on the list had spoken, and while the band was playing, the child, to the brother's great surprise, made her way up the stage steps, and pressed through the throng of professors and trustees and distinguished visitors, up to the college president.

"If you please, sir," she said with a little courtesy, "will you and the trustees let my brother try again? He knows his piece now."

For a moment the president stared at her through his gold-bowed spectacles, and then, appreciating the child's petition, he smiled on her, and went down and spoke to the young man who had failed.

So it happened that when the band had again ceased playing, it was briefly announced that Mr. —— —— would now deliver his oration — "Historical Parallels."

A ripple of heightened and expectant interest passed over the audience, and then all sat stone still, as though fearing to breathe lest the speaker might again take fright. No danger! The hero in the youth was aroused. He went at his "piece" with a set purpose to conquer, to redeem himself, and to bring the smile back into the child's tear-stained face. I watched the face during the speaking. The wide eyes, the parted lips, the whole rapt being said that the breathless audience was forgotten, that her spirit was moving with his.

And when the address was ended, with the ardent abandon of one who catches enthusiasm in the realization that he is fighting down a wrong judgment and conquering a sympathy, the effect was really thrilling. That dignified audience broke into rapturous applause ; bouquets intended for the valedictorian rained like a tempest. And the child who had helped to save the day — that one beaming little face, in its pride and gladness, is something to be forever remembered.

———

THE FIGHT WITH THE AUROCHS

Lygia, daughter of a foreign king, and Ursus, a giant slave of her father's household (who are both Christians), are in prison, awaiting punishment by torture for the burning of Rome, of which crime the Christians were accused by Nero. Vinicius, a Roman tribune, who has fallen in love with Lygia, finds no other way of obtaining her hand in marriage than by renouncing his gods and becoming a Christian.

EVENING exhibitions, rare up to that period and given only exceptionally, became common in Nero's time, both in the circus and amphitheater. Though the people were sated already with blood-spilling, still, when the news went forth that the end of the games was approaching, and that the last of the Christians were to die at an evening spectacle, a countless audience assembled in the amphitheater. The Augustians came to a man, for they understood that it would not be a common spectacle; they knew that Caesar had determined to make for himself a tragedy out of the suffering of Vinicius. Tigellinus had kept secret the kind of punishment intended for the betrothed of the young tribune; but that merely roused general curiosity. Those who had seen Lygia at the house of Plautius told wonders of her beauty.

Uncertainty, waiting, and curiosity had mastered all spectators. Caesar arrived earlier than usual; and immediately at his coming people whispered that something uncommon would happen, for besides Tigellinus and Vatinius, Caesar had with him Cassius, a centurion of enormous size and gigantic strength, whom he summoned only when he wished to have a defender at his side.

Every eye was turned with strained gaze to the place where Vinicius was sitting. He was exceedingly pale, and his forehead was covered with drops of perspiration; he was in as much doubt as were other spectators, but alarmed to the lowest depth of his soul. Petronius knew not what would happen; he was silent, except that, while turning from Nerva, he asked Vinicius whether he was ready for everything, and next, whether he would remain at the spectacle. To both questions Vinicius answered "Yes," but a shudder passed through his whole body. Hitherto he had not supposed that that moment when present would be so terrible.

But his weakness did not last long.   After a while he roused himself, or rather the stamping of the impatient multitude roused him.

"Thou art ill," said Petronius; "give command to bear thee home."

Caesar was looking through his great emerald at Vinicius, studying his pain with satisfaction to describe it afterward, perhaps, in pathetic strophes, and win the applause of hearers.

Vinicius shook his head.   He might die in the amphitheater, but he could not go out of it.   Moreover the spectacle might begin any moment.

In fact, at that very instant almost, the prefect of the city waved a red handkerchief, the hinges opposite Caesar's podium creaked, and out of the dark gully came Ursus, Lygia's giant servant, into the brightly-lighted arena.

He blinked, dazed evidently by the glitter of the arena; then he pushed into the center, gazing around as if to see what he had to meet.   In Rome there was no lack of gladiators larger by far than the common measure of man, but Roman eyes had never seen the like of Ursus.   Senators, vestals, Caesar, the Augustians, and the people gazed with the delight of experts at his mighty limbs as large as tree-trunks, at his breast as large as two shields joined together, and his arms of a Hercules.

He was unarmed, and had determined to die as became a confessor of the "Lamb," peacefully and patiently. Meanwhile he wished to pray once more to the Saviour; so he knelt on the arena, joined his hands, and raised his eyes towards the stars, which were glittering in the lofty opening of the amphitheater.

That act displeased the crowds. They had had enough of those Christians who died like sheep. They understood that if the giant would not defend himself the spectacle would be a failure. Here and there hisses were heard. Some began to cry for scourgers, whose office it was to lash combatants unwilling to fight. But soon all had grown silent, for no one knew what was waiting for the giant, nor whether he would not be ready to struggle when he met death eye to eye.

They had not long to wait. Suddenly the shrill sound of brazen trumpets was heard, and at that signal a grating opposite Caesar's podium was opened, and into the arena rushed, amid shouts of beast-keepers, an enormous German aurochs, bearing on his head the body of a woman.

"Lygia! Lygia!" cried Vinicius.

Then he seized his hair near the temples, squirmed like a man who feels a sharp dart in his body, and began to repeat in hoarse accents —

"I believe! I believe! O Christ, a miracle!"

He did not even feel that Petronius covered his head that moment with the toga. It seemed to him that death or pain had closed his eyes. He did not look, he did not see. The feeling of some awful emptiness possessed him. In his head there remained not a thought; his lips merely repeated, as if in madness —

"I believe! I believe! I believe!"

This time the amphitheater was silent. The Augustians rose in their places, as one man, for in the arena something uncommon had happened. That Lygian, obedient and ready to die, when he saw his queen on the horns of the wild beast, sprang up as if touched by living fire, and bending forward he ran at the raging animal.

From all breasts a sudden cry of amazement was heard, after which came deep silence.

The Lygian fell on the raging bull in a twinkle, and selzed him by the horns.

"Look!" cried Petronius, snatching the toga from the head of Vinicius.

The latter rose and bent back his head; his face was as pale as linen, and he looked into the arena with a glassy, vacant stare.

All breasts ceased to breathe. In the amphitheater a fly might be heard on the wing. People could not believe their own eyes. Since Rome was Rome, no one had seen such a spectacle.

The Lygian held the wild beast by the horns. The man's feet sank in the sand to his ankles, his back was bent like a drawn bow, his head was hidden between his shoulders, on his arms the muscles came out so that the skin almost burst from their pressure; but he had stopped the bull in his tracks. And the man and the beast remained so still that the spectators thought themselves looking at a picture showing a deed of Hercules or Theseus, or a group hewn from stone. But in that apparent repose there was a tremendous exertion of two struggling forces. The bull sank his feet as well as did the man in the sand, and his dark, shaggy body was curved so that it seemed a gigantic ball. Which of the two would fall first, which would fall first? — that was the question for those spectators enamored of such struggles; a question which at that moment meant more for them than their own fate, than all Rome and its lordship over the world. That Lygian was in their eyes then a demigod worthy of honor and statues. Nero himself stood up as well as others. He and Tigellinus, hearing of the man's strength, had arranged this spectacle purposely, and said to each other with a jeer, "Let that slayer of Croton kill the bull which we choose for him"; so they looked now with amazement at that picture, as if not believing that it could be real.

In the amphitheater were men who had raised their arms and remained in that posture. Perspiration covered the faces of others, as if they themselves were struggling with the beast. In the circus nothing was heard save the sound of flame in the lamps, and the crackle of bits of coal as they dropped from the torches. Their voices died on the lips of the spectators, but their hearts were beating in their breasts as if to split them. It seemed to all that the struggle was lasting for ages. But the man and the beast continued on in their monstrous exertion; one might have said that they were planted in the earth.

Meanwhile a dull roar resembling a groan was heard from the arena, after which a brief shout was wrested from every breast, and again there was silence. People thought themselves dreaming till the enormous head of the bull began to turn in the iron hands of the barbarian. The face, neck, and arms of the Lygian grew purple; his back bent still more. It was clear that he was rallying the remnant of his superhuman strength, but that he could not last long.

Duller and duller, hoarser and hoarser, more and more painful grew the groan of the bull as it mingled with the whistling breath from the breast of the giant. The head of the beast turned more and more, and from his jaws came a long, foaming tongue.

A moment more, and to the ears of spectators sitting nearer came as it were the crack of breaking bones; then the beast rolled on the earth with his neck twisted in death.

The giant removed in a twinkle the ropes from

the horns of the bull, and, raising the maiden, he stood for a moment as if only half conscious; then he raised his eyes and looked at the spectators.

The amphitheater had gone wild.

The walls of the building were trembling from the roar of tens of thousands of people. Everywhere were heard cries for mercy, passionate and persistent, which soon turned into one unbroken thunder. That giant had become dear to those people enamored of physical strength; he was the first personage in Rome.

He looked around awhile; then approached Caesar's podium, and, holding the body of the maiden on his outstretched arms, raised his eyes with entreaty, as if to say:

"Have mercy on her! Save the maiden! I did that for her sake!"

Pity burst forth suddenly, like a flame. The people had had blood, death, and torture in sufficiency. Voices choked with tears began to entreat mercy for both.

Now Vinicius started up from his seat, sprang over the barrier which separated the front places from the arena, and, running to Lygia, covered her body with his toga.

Then he tore apart the tunic on his breast, laid bare the scars left by wounds received in the Armenian war, and stretched out his hands to the audience.

At this the enthusiasm of the multitude passed everything seen in a circus before. Voices calling for mercy grew simply terrible. People not only took the part of the athlete, but rose in defense of the soldier, the maiden, their love. Thousands of spectators turned to Caesar with flashes of anger in their eyes and with clenched fists.

But Nero hesitated.

Now rage began to possess the multitude. Dust rose from beneath the stamping feet and filled the amphitheater. In the midst of shouts were heard cries, "Ahenobarbus! Matricide! Incendiary!"

Nero was alarmed.

He looked once more at Subrius Flavius, at Scevinus, the centurion, a relative of the Senator, at the soldiers; and seeing everywhere frowning brows, angry faces, and eyes fixed on him, he gave the sign for mercy.

————

THE WOUNDED SOLDIER
J. W. WATSON

STEADY, boys, steady! Keep your arms ready,
God only knows whom we may meet here.
Don't let me be taken; I'd rather awaken,
To-morrow, in — no matter where,
Than lie in that foul prison-hole, over there.
Step slowly! Speak lowly! The rocks may have life;
Lay me down in the hollow; we are out of the strife.

By heaven! the foeman may track me in blood,
For this hole in my breast is outpouring a flood.
No! no surgeon for me; he can give me no aid;
The surgeon I want is a pickaxe and spade.
What, Morris, a tear? Why, shame on you, man!
I thought you a hero; but since you began
To whimper and cry, like a girl in her teens,
By George! I don't know what the devil it means!

Well! well! I am rough, 't is a very rough school,
This life of a trooper — but yet I'm no fool!
I know a brave man, and a friend from a foe;
And, boys, that you love me I certainly know.
            But was n't it grand,
When they came down the hill over sloughing and
        sand?
But we stood — did we not? — like immovable
        rock,
Unheeding their balls and repelling their shock.
Did you mind the loud cry, when, as turning to fly,
Our men sprang upon them, determined to die.
            Oh, was n't it grand?
God help the poor wretches who fell in the fight;
No time was there given for prayers or for flight.
They fell by the score, in the crash, hand to hand,
And they mingled their blood with the sloughing
        and sand.

Great heavens! this bullet-hole gapes like a grave;
A curse on the aim of the traitorous knave!

Is there never a one of you knows how to pray,
Or speak for a man as his life ebbs away?
>> Pray! Pray!

Our Father! Our Father!—why don't you proceed?
Can't you see I am dying? Great God, how I bleed!
Our Father in heaven — boys, tell me the rest,
While I stanch the hot blood from the hole in my
>> breast.
There's something about the forgiveness of sin;
Put that in! put that in! — and then
I'll follow your words and say an "Amen."

Here, Morris, old fellow, get hold of my hand,
And, Wilson, my comrade — oh! was n't it grand
When they came down the hill like a thunder-
>> charged cloud,
And were scattered like mist by our brave little
>> crowd? —
Where's Wilson, my comrade? Here, stoop down
>> your head,
Can't you say a short prayer for the dying and dead?

>> "Christ-God, who died for sinners all,
>>> Hear Thou this suppliant wanderer's cry;
>> Let not e'en this poor sparrow fall
>>> Unheeded by Thy gracious eye;
>> Throw wide Thy gates to let him in,
>>> And take him pleading to Thine arms;
>> Forgive, O Lord, his lifelong sin,
>>> And quiet all his fierce alarms."

God bless you! my comrade, for singing that hymn,
It is light to my path, now my sight has grown dim.
I am dying! Bend down, till I touch you once
      more;
Don't forget me, old fellow — God prosper this
      war!
Confusion to enemies! — keep hold of my hand —
And float our dear flag o'er a prosperous land!

———

BURGOYNE'S SURRENDER

On the morning of October 7, at ten o'clock, fifteen hundred of the best troops in the world, led by four of the most experienced and accomplished generals, moved in three columns toward the left of the American position into a field of wheat. They began to cut forage. Startled by the rattling picket fire, the American drums beat to arms, and the British approach was announced at headquarters.

The Americans dashed forward, opened to the right and left, flanked the enemy, struck him with a blasting fire, then closed, and, grappling hand to hand, the mad mass of combatants swayed and staggered for half an hour, five times taking and re-taking a single gun. At the first fire upon the left, the Virginia sharpshooters shouting and blazing with deadly aim, rushed forward with such fury that the appalled British right wavered and recoiled. While it yet staggered under the blow of Virginia, New England swept up, and with its flaming muskets broke the English line, which wildly fled. It reformed and again advanced, while the whole American force dashed against the British center, held by the Germans, whose right and left had been uncovered. The British General Fraser hurried to their aid. With fatal aim an American sharpshooter fired and Fraser fell. With him sank the British heart. The whole American line, jubilant with certain victory, advancing, Burgoyne abandoned his guns and ordered a retreat to his camp.

The British, dismayed, bewildered, overwhelmed, were scarcely within their redoubts when Benedict Arnold came spurring up — Benedict Arnold, whose name America does not love, who, volunteering to relieve Fort Stanwix, had, by the mere terror of his coming, blown St. Leger away, and who, on September 19, had saved the American left — Benedict Arnold, whom battle stung to fury, now whirled from end to end of the American line, hurled it against the Great Redoubt, driving the enemy at the point of the bayonet. He then, flinging himself to the extreme right and finding there

the Massachusetts brigade, swept it with him to
the assault and, streaming over the breastworks,
scattered the Brunswickers who defended them,
killed their colonel, and gained and held the point
which commanded the entire British position. At
the same moment his horse was shot under him,
and he sank to the ground, wounded in the leg
that had been wounded at Quebec.

Here, upon the Hudson, where he tried to betray
his country — here, upon the spot where, in the
crucial hour of the Revolution, he illustrated and
led the American valor that made us free and
great, let us recall, for one brief instant of infinite
pity, the name that has been justly execrated for
a century.

Night fell, and the weary fighters slept. Before
day dawned Burgoyne, exhausted and overwhelmed,
drew off the remainder of his army, and the Americans occupied his camp. At evening, in a desolate
autumn rain, Burgoyne, who, in the splendid hour
of his first advance had so proudly proclaimed,
"This army must not retreat," turned to fly. But
everywhere he was too late. The American sharpshooters hovered around him, cutting off supplies,
and preventing him from laying roads. Deserted
by his allies, his army half gone, with less than five
days' food, with no chance of escape, Burgoyne
prepared honorably to surrender.

At nine o'clock on the morning of this day, a

hundred years ago, he signed the convention. At eleven o'clock his troops marched to this meadow, the site of old Fort Hardy, and, with tears coursing down bearded cheeks, with passionate sobs, and oaths of rage and defiance, the soldiers kissing their guns with the tenderness of lovers, or with sudden frenzy knocking off the butts of their muskets, and the drummers stamping on their drums, the king's army laid down their arms.

ASPIRATIONS OF THE AMERICAN PEOPLE

R. M. T. HUNTER

THE sense of national honor beats high in the American heart, and its every pulse vibrates at the mere suspicion of a stain upon its reputation. But that same heart is warmed with generous impulses and noble emotions. If you would moderate its lust of empire and its spirit of acquisition, appeal to its magnanimity towards a feeble and prostrate foe — appeal to it in the name of the highest aspirations which can animate the human heart, the desire for moral excellence, the love of liberty, and the noble ambition to take the post of honor among nations, and lead the advance of civilization. If our people are once awakened to a true conception of the real nature and grandeur of their destiny, the first and greatest step, in my opinion, is taken for its accomplishment. If my imagination were tasked to select the highest blessing for my countrymen, I should say, may they be true to themselves and faithful to their mission. I can conceive of nothing of which it is possible for human effort to obtain, greater than the destiny which we may reasonably hope to fulfill. If war has its dreams, dazzling in splendid pageantry, peace also has its visions of a more enduring form, of a higher and purer beauty. To solve by practical demonstration the grand problem of increasing social power consistent with personal freedom — to increase the efficiency of the human agent by enlarging individual liberty — to triumph over, not only the physical, but more difficult still, the moral difficulties which lie in the path of a man's progress, and to adorn that path with all that is rare and useful in art, and whatever is highest in civilization, are, in my opinion, the noblest achievements of which a nation is capable. These are the ends to which our ambition should be directed. If we reverse the old idea of the deity who presides over our boundaries, let us see, so far as we are concerned, that his movements are consistent with the peace of the world. The sword may be the occasional but it is not the familiar weapon of our god Terminus. The axe and the hoe are his more appropriate emblems. Let him turn aside from the habitations of civilized man; his path is toward the wilderness, through whose silent solitudes, for more than two centuries, he has been rapidly and triumphantly advancing. Let him plunge still deeper into the forest, as the natural gravitation of the tide of population impels him onward. His progress in that direction is one of unmixed beneficence to the human race. The earth smiles beneath his feet, and a new creation arises as if by enchantment at his touch. Household fires illuminate his line of march, and new-born lights, strange visitants to the night of primeval solitude, kindle on domestic altars erected to all the peaceful virtues and kindly affections which consecrate a hearth and endear a home. Victorious industry sacks the forest and mines the quarry for materials for its stately cities, or spans the stream and saps the mountain to open the way for the advance of civilization still deeper into the pathless forest and neglected wild. The light of human thought pours in winged streams from sea to sea, and the lingering nomad may have but a moment's pause, to behold the flying car which comes to invade the haunts so long secured to savage life. These are the aspirations worthy of our name and race, and it is for the American people to decide whether a taste for peace or the habits of war are most consistent with such hopes.

NATHAN HALE, THE MARTYR SPY

I. H. Brown

After the Americans were defeated on Long Island, Captain Nathan Hale, but twenty-one years old, volunteered to procure information respecting the British position and movements. He was captured September 22, 1776, and hanged as a spy the following day.

'Twas in the year that gave the nation birth —
A time when men esteemed the common good
As greater weal than private gain. A battle fierce
And obstinate had laid a thousand patriots low,
And filled the people's hearts with gloom.

Pursued like hunted deer,
The crippled army fled; and, yet, amid
Disaster and defeat, the Nation's chosen chief
Resolved his losses to retrieve. But not
With armies disciplined and trained by years
Of martial service, could he, this Fabian chief,
Now hope to check the hosts of Howe's victorious
        legions —
These had he not.

In stratagem the shrewder general
Ofttimes o'ercomes his strong antagonist.
To Washington a knowledge of the plans,
Position, strength of England's force
Must compensate for lack of numbers.

He casts about for one who'd take his life
In hand.   Lo! he stands before the chief.   In
       face,
A boy — in form, a man on whom the eye could
       rest
In search of God's perfected handiwork.
In culture, grace, and speech, reflecting all
A mother's love could lavish on an only son.

The chieftain's keen, discerning eye
Appraised the youth at his full worth, and saw
In him those blending qualities that make
The hero and the sage.   He fain would save
For nobler deeds a man whose presence marked
A spirit born to lead.
"Young man," he said, with kindly air,
"Your country and commander feel grateful that
Such talents are offered in this darkening hour.
Have you in reaching this resolve considered well
Your fitness, courage, strength, — the act, the risk,
You undertake?   Have you, in that fine balance,
       which
Detects an atom on either beam, weighed well
Your chances of escape 'gainst certain fate,
Should capture follow in the British camp?"

In tones of fitting modesty that well
Became his years, the patriot answered thus:
"My country's honor, safety, life, it ever was

My highest purpose to defend; that country's foes
Exultant sweep through ruined land and home
And field.   A thousand stricken hearts bewail
The loss of those who late our standards bore,
Appeal to us through weeping eyes whose tears
We cannot brush away with words.   The ranks
Of those now cold in death are not replaced
By living men.   The hour demands a duty rare —
Perhaps a sacrifice.   If God and training in
The schools have given me capacities
This duty to perform, the danger of the enterprise
Should not deter me from the act
Whose issue makes our country free.   In times
Like these a Nation's life sometimes upon
A single life depends.   If mine be deemed
A fitting sacrifice, God grant a quick
Deliverance."

"Enough; go then, at once," the great
Commander said.   "May Heaven's guardian angels
          give
You safe return.   Adieu."

Disguised with care, the hopeful captain crossed
The bay, and moved through British camp
Without discovery by troops or refugees.
The enemy's full strength, in men, in stores,
Munitions, guns — all military accoutrements
Were noted with exact precision; while

With graphic sketch, each trench and parapet,
Casemated battery, magazine, and every point
Strategic, was drawn with artist's skill.

The task complete, the spy, with heart
Elate, now sought an exit through the lines.
Well might he feel a soldier's pride.   An hour
        hence
A waiting steed would bear him to his friends.
His plans he'd lay before his honored chief;
His single hand might turn the tide of war,
His country yet be free.

"Halt!" a British musket leveled at
His head dimmed all the visions of his soul.
A dash — an aimless shot; the spy bore down
Upon the picket with a blow that else
Had freed him from his clutch, but for a score
Of troopers stationed near.   In vain the struggle
        fierce
And desperate — in vain demands to be released.
A tory relative, for safety quartered in
The British camp, would prove his truckling
        loyalty
With kinsman's blood.   A word — a look —
A motion of the head, and he who'd dared
So much in freedom's name was free no more.

O, Judas, self-condemned! thou art
But the type of many a trait'rous friend,

Who ere and since thy time, betrayed to death
A noble heart.   Henceforth be doubly doomed —
A base example to earth's weaker souls.

Before Lord Howe the captive youth
Was led.   "Base dog!" the haughty general said,
"Ignoble son of loyal sires! you've played the spy
Quite well I ween.   The cunning skill wherewith
You wrought these plans and charts might well
      adorn
An honest man; but in rebel's hands they're vile
And mischievous.   If aught may palliate
A traitor's act, attempted in his sovereign's camp,
I bid you speak ere I pronounce your sentence."

With tone and mien that hushed
The buzzing noise of idle lackeys in the hall,
The patriot thus replied: "You know my name —
My rank, — my treach'rous kinsman made
My purpose plain.   I've nothing further of myself
To tell beyond the charge of traitor to deny.
The brand of spy I do accept without reproach;
But never since I've known the base ingratitude
Of king to loyal subjects of his realm
Has British rule been aught to me than barbarous
Despotism which God and man abhor, and none
But dastards fear to overthrow.
For tyrant loyalty your lordship represents
I never breathed a loyal breath; and he

Who calls me traitor seeks a pretext for a crime
His trembling soul might well condemn."

" I'll hear no more such prating cant,"
Said Howe; "your crime's enough to hang a dozen
        men.
Before to-morrow's sun goes down you'll swing
'Twixt earth and heaven, that your countrymen
May know a British camp is dangerous ground
For prowling spies.   Away!"

                *   *   *   *   *   *   *

Securely bound upon a cart, amid
A speechless crowd, he stands beneath a strong
Projecting limb to which a rope, with noose
        attached,
Portends a tragic scene.   He casts his eyes
Upon the surging multitude.   Clearly now
His tones ring out as victors shout in triumph:

"Men, I do not die in vain;
My humble death upon this tree will light anew
The Torch of Liberty.   A hundred hands to one
Before will strike for country, home, and God,
And fill our ranks with men of faith in His
Eternal plan to make this people free.
A million prayers go up this day to free
The land from blighting curse of tyrant's rule.
Oppression's wrongs have reached Jehovah's
        throne:

The God of vengeance smites the foe! This land —
This glorious land, — is free — is free!
My friends, farewell! In dying thus
I feel but one regret; it is the one poor life
I have to give in Freedom's cause."

ABRAHAM LINCOLN

BISHOP JOHN P. NEWMAN

HUMAN glory is often fickle as the winds, and
transient as a summer day; but Abraham Lincoln's place in history is assured. All the symbols
of this world's admiration are his. He is embalmed
in song, recorded in history, eulogized in pane-
gyric, cast in bronze, sculptured in marble, painted
on canvas, enshrined in the hearts of his countrymen, and lives in the memories of mankind. Some
men are brilliant in their times, but their words
and deeds are of little worth to history; but his
mission was as large as his country, vast as
humanity, enduring as time. No greater thought
can ever enter the human mind than obedience to law
and freedom for all. Some men are not honored
by their contemporaries, and die neglected. Here
is one more honored than any other man while
living, more revered when dying, and destined to
be loved to the last syllable of recorded time. He
has this threefold greatness — great in life, great

in death, great in the history of the world. Lincoln will grow upon the attention and affections of posterity, because he saved the life of the greatest nation, whose ever widening influence is to bless humanity. Measured by this standard, Lincoln shall live in history from age to age.

Great men appear in groups, and in groups they disappear from the vision of the world; but we do not love or hate men in groups. We speak of Gutenberg and his coadjutors, of Washington and his generals, of Lincoln and his cabinet; but when the day of judgment comes, we crown the inventor of printing; we place the laurel on the brow of the father of his country, and the chaplet of renown upon the head of the saviour of the republic.

Some men are great from the littleness of their surroundings; but he only is great who is great amid greatness. Lincoln had great associates — Seward, the sagacious diplomatist; Chase, the eminent financier; Stanton, the incomparable Secretary of War, with illustrious senators and soldiers. Neither could take his part nor fill his position. And the same law of the coming and going of great men is true of our own day. In piping times of peace genius is not aflame, and true greatness is not apparent; but when the crisis comes, then God lifts the curtain from obscurity and reveals the man for the hour.

Lincoln stands forth on the page of history,

unique in his character, and majestic in his individuality. Like Milton's angel, he was an original conception. He was raised up for his times. He was a leader of leaders. By instinct the common heart trusted in him. He was of the people and for the people. He had been poor and laborious; but greatness did not change the tone of his spirit or lessen the sympathies of his nature. His character was strangely symmetrical. He was temperate, without austerity; brave, without rashness; constant, without obstinacy. He put caution against hope, that it might not be premature; and hope against caution, that it might not yield to dread or danger. His marvelous hopefulness never betrayed him into impracticable measures. His love of justice was only equaled by his delight in compassion. His regard for personal honor was only excelled by love of country. His self-abnegation found its highest expression in the public good. His integrity was never questioned. His honesty was above suspicion. He was more solid than brilliant; his judgment dominated his imagination; his ambition was subject to his modesty; and his love of justice held the mastery over all personal considerations. Not excepting Washington, who inherited wealth and high social position, Lincoln is the fullest representative American in our national annals. He had touched every round in the human ladder. He illustrated the possibilities of our citizenship. We are not ashamed of his humble origin. We are proud of his greatness.

We are to judge men by their surroundings, and measure their greatness by the difficulties which they surmounted. Every age has its heroes, every crisis its master. Lincoln came into power in the largest and most violent political convulsion known to history. In nothing is the sagacity and might of Lincoln's statesmanship more apparent than in his determination to save the Union of these States. This was the objective point of his administration. He denied state sovereignty as paramount to national sovereignty. States have their rights and their obligations; and their chief obligation is to remain in the Union. Some political philanthropists clamored for the overthrow of slavery, and advocated the dissolution of the Union rather than live in a country under whose government slavery was tolerated. But Lincoln was a wiser and a better philanthropist than they. He would have the Union, with or without slavery. He preferred it without, and his preference prevailed. How incomparably worse would have been the condition of the slave in a Confederacy with a living slave for its corner stone than in the Union of the States! Time has vindicated the character of his statesmanship, that to preserve the Union was to save this great nation for human liberty, and thereby advance the emancipated slave to education, thrift, and political equality.

———

AMERICANISM

HENRY CABOT LODGE

"AMERICANISM" of the right sort we cannot have too much. By Americanism I do not mean that which had a brief political existence more than thirty years ago. That movement was based on race and sect, and was, therefore, thoroughly un-American, and failed, as all un-American movements have failed in this country. True Americanism is opposed utterly to any political divisions resting on race and religion. To the race or to the sect which as such attempts to take possession of the politics or the public education of the country true Americanism says, "Hands off!"

The American idea is a free church in a free state, and a free and unsectarian public school in every ward and in every village, with its doors wide open to the children of all races and of every creed. It goes still further and frowns upon the constant attempt to divide our people according to origin or extraction. Let every man honor and love the land of his birth and the race from which he springs and keep their memory green. It is a pious and

honorable duty.   But let us have done with British-
Americans and Irish-Americans and German-
Americans, and all be Americans — nothing more
and nothing less.   If a man is going to be an
American at all, let him be so without any qualify-
ing adjectives, and if he is going to be something
else, let him drop the word American from his
personal description.

Mere vaporing and boasting become a nation as
little as a man.   But honest, outspoken pride and
faith in our country are infinitely better and more
to be respected than the cultivated reserve which
sets it down as ill-bred and in bad taste ever to
refer to our country except by way of depreciation,
criticism, or general negation.   We have a right to
be proud of our vast material success, our national
power and dignity, our advancing civilization, carrying freedom and education in its train.   But to
count our wealth and tell our numbers and rehearse
our great deeds simply to boast of them is useless
enough.   We have a right to do it only when we
listen to the solemn undertone which brings the
message of great responsibilities — responsibilities
far greater than the ordinary political and financial
issues, which are sure to find, sooner or later, a
right settlement.

Social questions are the questions of the present
and the future of the American people.   The race
for wealth has opened a broad gap between rich

and poor. There are thousands at your gates toiling from sunrise to sunset to keep body and soul together, and the struggle is a hard and bitter one. The idle, the worthless, and the criminal form but a small element of the community; but there is a vast body of honest, God-fearing workingmen and women whose yoke is not easy and whose burden is far from light. We cannot push their troubles and cares into the background, and trust that all will come right in the end. Let us look to it that differences and inequalities of condition do not widen into ruin. It is most true that these differences cannot be rooted out; but they can be modified. Legislation cannot change humanity nor alter the decrees of nature; but it can help the solution of these grave problems.

Practical measures are plentiful enough. They have to do with the hours of labor, with emigration from our overcrowded cities to the lands of the West, with wise regulation of the railroads and other great corporations. Here are matters of great pith and moment, more important, more essential, more pressing than others. They must be met; they cannot be shirked or evaded.

The past is across the water; the future is here in our keeping. We can do all that can be done to solve the social problems and fulfill the hopes of mankind. Failure would be a disaster unequaled in history. The first step to success is pride of country, simple, honest, frank, and ever present, and this is the Americanism that I would have. If we have this pride and faith, we shall appreciate our mighty responsibilities. Then, if we live up to them, we shall keep the words "an American citizen" what they now are — the noblest title any man can bear.

_____

AS THE PIGEON FLIES

C. B. Lewis

A MONSTER of iron, steel and brass stands on the slim iron rails which shoot away from the station for half a mile and then lose themselves in a green forest.

Puff-puff! The driving wheels slowly turn, the monster breathes great clouds of steam and seems anxious for the race.

A grizzly-haired engineer looks down from the cab window, while his fireman pulls back the iron door and heaves in more wood — more breath and muscle for the grim giant of the track.

The fire roars and crackles — the steam hisses and growls; every breath is drawn as fiercely as if the giant was burning to avenge an insult.

Up — up — up! The pointer on the steam-gauge moves faster than a minute-hand on a clock. The breathing becomes louder — the hiss raises to a scream — the iron rails tremble and quiver.

"Climb up!"

It is going to be a race against time and the telegraph.

S-s-s-sh!

The engineer rose up, looked ahead, glanced at the dial, and as his fingers clasped the throttle he asked the station agent :

"Are you sure that the track is clear?"

"All clear!" was the answer.

The throttle feels the pull, the giant utters a fierce scream and we are off, I on the fireman's seat, the fireman on the wood. The rails slid under us slowly — faster, and the giant screams again and dashes into the forest.

This isn't fast. The telegraph poles dance past as if not over thirty feet apart, and the board fence seems to rise from the ground, but it's only thirty-five miles an hour.

"Wood!"

The engineer takes his eyes off the track and turns just long enough to speak the word to his fireman. The iron doors swing back, and there is an awful rush and roar of flame. The fire-box appears full, but stick after stick is dropped into the roaring pit until a quarter of a cord has disappeared.

"This is forty miles an hour!" shouts the fireman in my ear, as he rubs the moisture from his heated face.

Yes, this is faster. The fence posts seem to leap from the ground as we dash along, and the telegraph poles bend and nod to us. A house—a field—a farm—we get but one glance. A dozen houses—a hundred faces—that was a station. We heard a yell from the crowd, but it had scarcely reached us before it was drowned in the great roar.

Nine miles in fourteen minutes—we've lost time. The engineer takes his eyes from the rail, makes a motion to his fireman, and the sticks drop into the roaring flames again, to make new flames.

Seven miles of clear track now, and the engineer smiles a grim smile as he lets more steam into the giant's lungs.

Ah! Not a mile a minute yet, but how we shake from side to side, how the tender leaps and bounds! Is there a fence skirting the track? There is a dark line keeping pace with us; it may be a fence. Where are the telegraph poles? Where are all those trees falling toward the track as we dashed through the bit of forest?

A yell—houses—faces—that was another station. Word has gone down the line that a "wild" locomotive is rushing a journalist across the country to catch the lightning express on another road, and the people gather to see us dash past. Seven miles in eight and a half minutes—that's better, but we must run faster!

The finger on the dial creeps slowly up — we want a reserve of steam for the last twelve miles of road — the best track of all.

The noise is deafening, the swaying and bumping is terrible. I hang fast to the seat — clutch, cling, and yet it seems as if I must be shaken to the floor.

Every moment there is a scream from the whistle; every two or three minutes the engineer makes a gesture which calls for the iron doors to be opened and the roaring, leaping flames to be fed anew.

Houses — faces — a yell! That was another station. We made the last five miles in six minutes. Did you ever ride a mile in one minute and twelve seconds? But we are to beat it.

Like a bird — like an arrow — like a bullet almost, we sped forward. Half a dozen men beside the track — section men with their handcar. They lift their hats and yell, but their voices did not reach us. We pass them as lightning flashes through the heavens. That was a farmhouse. We saw nothing but a white object — a green spot — two or three apple trees where there was a large orchard.

Scream!

Hiss!

Roar!

Shake — quiver — bound!

We are going to stop — going to halt for an instant at a station to see if the track is clear for the rush, for a mile a minute, and faster!

Scream! Scream!

The station is a mile ahead — it is beside us! The fireman leaps down with his oil-can, the engineer enters the telegraph office. Both are back in fifteen seconds.

Twelve and a half miles to go, twelve minutes in which to make it.

"We can do it!" said the engineer. "Hold fast now! We have been running — we are going to fly!"

Scream!

"Good-bye!"

As a mad horse runs, as an arrow is sent, as a carrier pigeon flies! Yes, this is a mile a minute! Fences? No — only a black line, hardly larger than my pencil. Trees? No — only one tree, all merged into one single tree, which was out of sight in a flash. Fields? Yes — one broad field, broken for an instant by a highway — a gray thread lying on the ground!

It is terrible! If we should leave the rails! If — but don't think of it! Hold fast!

Eight miles in eight minutes, not a second more or less! The lightning travels faster — so does a locomotive! Four and a half miles to go, four minutes to make it! We must run a mile every fifty-three seconds.

Scream!

Sway!

Tremble!

We are making time, but Great Heavens! it is awful, this roar, this oscillation!

One mile!

Two miles!

I dare not open my eyes! I would not look ahead on the track for all the gold ever mined!

Three miles!

Can I ever hear again? Will I ever get this deafening roar out of my ears? Will the seconds ever go by?

Scream!

The engineer shuts off steam, the fireman hurrahs. I open my eyes — we are at the station!

"I told you!" says the engineer, "and didn't I do it?"

He did, but he carried three lives in the palm of the hand that grasped the throttle.

THE SPANISH MOTHER

Sir Francis Hastings Doyle

Yes, I have served that noble chief throughout
    his proud career,
And heard the bullets whistle past in lands both
    far and near —

Amidst Italian Flowers, below the dark pines of
      the north,
Where'er the Emperor willed to pour his clouds of
      battle forth.

'Twas *then* a splendid sight to see, though terrible,
      I ween,
How his vast spirit filled and moved the wheels of
      the machine ;
Wide sounding leagues of sentient steel, and fires
      that lived to kill,
Were but the echo of his voice, the body of his
      will.

But *now* my heart is darkened with the shadows
      that rise and fall
Between the sunlight and the ground to sadden
      and appall ;
The woeful things both seen and done we heeded
      little then,
But they return, like ghosts, to shake the sleep of
      aged men.

I saw a village in the hills, as silent as a dream.
Naught stirring but the summer sound of a
      merry mountain stream ;
The evening star just smiled from heaven with
      its quiet silver eye,
And the chestnut woods were still and calm
      beneath the deepening sky.

But in that place, self-sacrificed, nor man, nor beast
    we found,
Nor fig-tree on the sun-touched slope, nor corn
    upon the ground ;
Each roofless hut was black with smoke, wrenched
    up each trailing vine,
Each path was foul with mangled meat and floods
    of wasted wine.

We had been marching, travel-worn, a long and
    burning way,
And when such welcoming we met, after that toil-
    some day,
The pulses in our maddened breasts were human
    hearts no more,
But, like the spirit of a wolf, hot on the scent of
    gore.

We lighted on one dying man, they slew him where
    he lay ;
His wife, close-clinging, from the corpse they
    tore and wrenched away ;
They thundered in her widowed ears, with frowns
    and curses grim,
" Food, woman — food and wine, or else we tear
    thee limb from limb !"

The woman, shaking off *his* blood, rose, raven-
    haired and tall,

And our stern glances quailed before one sterner
    far than all :
"Both food and wine," she said, "I have; I
    meant them for the dead,
But ye are living still, and so let them be yours
    instead."

The food was brought, the wine was brought out
    of a secret place,
But each one paused, aghast, and looked into his
    neighbor's face ;
Her haughty step and settled brow, and chill,
    indifferent mien,
Suited so strangely with the gloom and grimness
    of the scene.

She glided here, she glided there, before our
    wondering eyes,
Nor anger showed, nor shame, nor fear, nor sorrow,
    nor surprise;
At every step, from soul to soul a nameless horror
    ran,
And made us pale and silent as that silent, mur-
    dered man.

She sat, and calmly soothed her child into a slum-
    ber sweet ;
Calmly the bright blood on the floor crawled red
    around our feet.

On placid fruits and bread lay soft the shadows of
    the wine,
And we, like marble statues, glared — a chill,
    unmoving line.

The woman's voice was heard at length; it broke
    the solemn spell,
And human fear, displacing awe, upon our spirits
    fell —
"Ho! slayers of the sinewless!   Ho! tramplers
    of the weak!
What! shrink ye from the ghastly meats and life-
    bought wine ye seek?

" Feed and begone!   I wish to weep -— I bring
    you out my store —
Devour it — waste it all — and then — pass and
    be seen no more.
Poison!   Is that your craven fear?"   She snatched
    the goblet up,
And raised it to her queen-like head, as if to drain
    the cup.

But our fierce leader grasped her wrist — " No,
    woman! No!" he said;
" A mother's heart of love is deep — give it your
    child instead."
She only smiled a bitter smile — " Frenchman, I
    do not shrink —
As pledge of my fidelity, behold the infant drink!"

He fixed on hers his broad, black eye, scanning her
    inmost soul ;
But her chill fingers trembled not as she returned
    the bowl.
And we, with lightsome hardihood, dismissing idle
    care,
Sat down to eat and drink and laugh over our
    dainty fare.

The laugh was loud around the board, the jesting
    wild and light ;
But *I* was fevered with the march, and drank no
    wine that night ;
I just had filled a single cup, when through my
    very brain
Stung, sharper than a serpent's tooth, an infant's
    cry of pain.

Through all that heat of revelry, through all that
    boisterous cheer,
To every heart its feeble moan pierced like a
    frozen spear.
"Aye!" shrieked the woman, darting up, " I pray
    you trust again
A widow's hospitality in our unyielding Spain.

" Helpless and hopeless, by the light of God
    Himself I swore
To treat you as you treated *him* — that body
    on the floor.

Yon secret place I filled, to feel that, if ye did
    not spare,
The treasure of a dread revenge was ready hidden
    there.

"A mother's love is deep, no doubt; ye did not
    phrase it ill,
But in your hunger ye forgot that hate is deeper
    still.
The Spanish woman speaks for Spain; for her
    butchered love, the wife,
To tell you that an hour is all *my* vintage leaves of
    life."

I cannot paint the many forms of wild despair
    put on,
Nor count the crowded brave who sleep beneath
    a single stone ;
I can but tell you how, before that horrid hour
    went by,
I saw the murderess beneath the self-avengers die.

But though upon her wrenched limbs they leaped
    like beasts of prey,
And with fierce hands, like madmen, tore the
    quivering life away —
Triumphant hate and joyous scorn, without a trace
    of pain,
Burned to the last, like sullen stars, in that
    haughty eye of Spain.

And often now it breaks my rest, the tumult vague
    and wild,
Drifting, like storm-tossed clouds, around the
    mother and her child —
While she, distinct in raiment white, stands
    silently the while,
And sheds through torn and bleeding hair the
    same unchanging smile.

LOVE OF COUNTRY

I. H. Brown

In these days of rapid national growth, when
the citizen of to-day is supplanted by the youth
and franchised emigrant to-morrow; when a million
voters cast their ballots with no higher motive than
compliance with a custom or the dictate of a party
henchman; when one-fourth our population have
no stronger ties of residence than avarice, whose
strength varies with the financial fluctuations of the
business world; when, year by year, our shores
receive the restless spirits of other lands who
acknowledge no higher authority than their own
caprice; when so many of our youth are growing
into manhood ignorant of everything save the
means of licensed indulgence and frivolity our
liberty affords; when, as partakers of the grandest
political inheritance ever transmitted from one

generation to another, we are all about to forget the responsibilities thrust upon us in our acceptance of the blessings we enjoy, it is time to halt.

Let us teach the coming citizen that next to love of God, implanted at the mother's knee, and cultivated by daily acts of piety and benevolence, is the love of country and devotion to its happiness and perpetuity. Let the examples of patriots, in deeds of heroism and self-sacrifice, be our theme of meditation and discussion. Let our literature gleam with the noble efforts, the grand achievements of those who gave their all that we might taste the sweets of freedom undisturbed.

Let us realize that this grandest heritage of earth's martyrs came to us, not alone through the business tact and prudent foresight of our sires, but by years of toil and suffering, and by the sacrifice of precious blood; and that, though it be vouchsafed to us through blessings of a noble ancestry, its possession implies no permanence to an unworthy race.

It is ours not alone to enjoy, but to foster and protect; ours to guard from schism, vice, and crime; ours to purify, exalt, ennoble; ours to prepare a dwelling place for the purest, fairest, best of earth's humanity.

THE STORMING OF MISSION RIDGE

Benjamin F. Taylor

Imagine a chain of Federal forts, built in between with walls of living men, the line flung northward out of sight and southward beyond Lookout. Imagine a chain of mountains crowned with batteries and manned with hostile troops through a six-mile sweep, set over against us in plain sight, and you have the two fronts — the blue, the gray. Imagine the center of our line pushed out a mile and a half towards Mission Ridge, and you have the situation as it was on the morning before Thanksgiving. And what a work was to be done! One and a half miles to traverse, with narrow fringes of woods, rough valleys, sweeps of open fields, rocky acclivities, to the base of the Ridge, and no foot in all the breadth withdrawn from rebel sight. The base attained, what then? A hill struggling up out of the valley four hundred feet, rained on by bullets, swept by shot and shell; another line of works, and then, up like a Gothic roof, rough with rocks, a-wreck with fallen trees, four hundred more; another ring of fire and iron, and then the crest, and then the enemy.

To dream of such a journey would be madness; to devise it, a thing incredible; to do it, a deed impossible. But Grant was guilty of them all, and was equal to the work.

The bugle swung idly at the bugler's side. The warbling fife and rumbling drum were unheard. There was to be louder talk. Six guns at intervals of two seconds, the signal to advance. Strong and steady a voice rang out: "Number one, fire! Number two, fire! Number three, fire!" It seemed to me the tolling of the clock of destiny. And when at "Number six, fire!" the roar throbbed out with the flash, you should have seen the dead line that had been lying behind the works all day, all night, all day again, come to resurrection in the twinkling of an eye, leap like a blade from its scabbard, and sweep with a two-mile stroke toward the Ridge. From divisions to brigades, from brigades to regiments, the order ran. A minute, and the skirmishers deploy. A minute, and the first great drops begin to patter along the line. A minute, and the musketry is in full play, like the crackling whips of a hemlock fire. Men go down here and there before your eyes.

But I may tell you they did not storm that mountain as you would think. They dash out a little way, and then slacken; they creep up, hand over hand, loading and firing, and wavering and halting, from the first line of works toward the second; they burst into a charge with a cheer and go over it. Sheets of flame baptize them; plunging

shot tear away comrades on left and right.   It is
no longer shoulder to shoulder; it is God for us
all.   Ten — fifteen — twenty minutes go by like a
reluctant century.   The batteries roll like a drum.
The hill sways up like a wall before them at an
angle of forty-five degrees; but our brave mountaineers are clamboring steadily on — up — upward
still!   And what do these men follow?   Your
heart gives a great bound when you think what it
is — the regimental flag — and, glancing along the
front, count fifteen of those colors that were borne
at Pea Ridge, waved at Shiloh, glorified at Stone
River, riddled at Chickamauga.   Three times the
flag of the 27th Illinois goes down.   And you
know why.   Three dead color sergeants lie just
there; but the flag is immortal — thank God! —
and up it comes again, and the men in a row of
inverted V's move on.

I give a look at the sun behind me; it is not
more than a handbreadth from the edge of the
mountain.   Oh, for the voice that could bid that
sun stand still!   I turn to the battle again.   Those
three flags have taken flight.   They are upward
bound!   The race of the flags is growing every
moment more terrible.   The iron sledge beats on.
Hearts, loyal and brave, are on the anvil all the
way from base to summit of Mission Ridge, but
those dreadful hammers never intermit.   Things
are growing desperate up aloft; the enemy tumble

rocks upon the rising line; they light the fuses and roll shells down the steep; they load the guns with handfuls of cartridges in their haste; and, as if there were powder in the word, they shout "Chickamauga!" down upon the mountaineers.

But all would not do; and just as the sun, weary of the scene, was sinking out of sight, with magnificent bursts all along the line, exactly as you have seen the crested seas leap up at the breakwater, the advance surged over the crest, and in a minute those flags fluttered all along the fringe where fifty guns were kenneled. The scene on that narrow plateau can never be painted. As the bluecoats surged over its edge, cheer on cheer rang like bells through the valley of the Chickamauga. Men flung themselves exhausted upon the ground. They laughed and wept, shook hands, embraced, turned round, and did all four over again. It was wild as a carnival. The general was received with a shout. "Soldiers," he said, "you ought to be court-martialed, every man of you. I ordered you to take the rifle-pits, and you scaled the mountain!"

VESUVIUS AND THE EGYPTIAN

From "The Last Days of Pompeii"

EDWARD BULWER LYTTON

"GLAUCUS, the Athenian, thy time has come," said a loud and clear voice; "the lion awaits thee."

The keeper, who was behind the den, cautiously removed the grating; the lion leaped forth with a mighty and a glad roar of release. Glaucus had bent his limbs so as to give himself the firmest posture at the expected rush of the lion, with his small and shining weapon raised on high, in the faint hope that *one* well-directed thrust might penetrate through the eye to the brain of his grim foe. But, to the unutterable astonishment of all, the beast halted abruptly in the arena; then suddenly it sprang forward, but not on the Athenian. At half speed it circled round and round the space, turning its vast head from side to side with an anxious and perturbed gaze, as if seeking only some avenue of escape. Once or twice it endeavored to leap up the parapet that divided it from the audience, and, on failing, uttered rather a baffled howl than its deep-toned and kingly roar. The first surprise of the assembly at the apathy of the lion soon grew converted into resentment at its cowardice; and the populace already merged their pity for the fate of Glaucus into angry compassion for their own disappointment.

Then there was a confusion, a bustle — voices of remonstrance suddenly breaking forth and suddenly silenced at the reply. All eyes turned, in wonder at the interruption, towards the quarter of the disturbance. The crowd gave way, and suddenly Sallust appeared on the senatorial benches, his hair dishevelled — breathless — heated — half-exhausted. He cast his eyes hastily around the ring. "Remove the Athenian!" he cried. "Haste — he is innocent! Arrest Arbaces, the Egyptian; *he* is the murderer of Apaecides!"

"Art thou mad, O Sallust?" said the praetor, rising from his seat. "What means this raving?"

"Remove the Athenian! Quick! or his blood be on your head. Praetor, delay, and you answer with your own life to the emperor! I bring with me the eyewitness to the death of the priest Apaecides. Room there! stand back! give way! People of Pompeii, fix every eye upon Arbaces — there he sits! Room there for the priest Calenus!" "The priest Calenus! Calenus!" cried the mob. "*Is* it he? No — it is a dead man." "It *is* the priest Calenus," said the praetor. "What hast thou to say?" "Arbaces of Egypt is the murderer of Apaecides, the priest of Isis; these eyes saw him deal the blow. Release the Athenian; *he* is innocent!"

"It is for this, then, that the lion spared him. A miracle! a miracle!" cried Pansa.

"A miracle! a miracle!" shouted the people. "Remove the Athenian! *Arbaces to the lion!*"

And that shout echoed from hill to vale, from coast to sea: "*Arbaces to the lion!*"

"Hear me," answered Arbaces, rising calmly, but with agitation visible in his face. "This man came to threaten that he would make against me the charge he has now made, unless I would purchase his silence with half my fortune. Were I guilty, why was the witness of this priest silent at the trial? *Then* I had not detained or concealed him. Why did he not proclaim my guilt when I proclaimed that of Glaucus?"

"What!" cried Calenus, turning around to the people. "Shall Isis be thus contemned! Shall the blood of Apaecides yet cry for vengeance? Shall the lion be cheated of his lawful prey? A god! a god! I feel the god rush to my lips! *To the lion — to the lion with Arbaces!*" Sinking on the ground in strong convulsions — the foam gathered to his mouth — he was as a man, indeed, whom a supernatural power had entered! The people saw and shuddered. "It is a god that inspires the holy man! *To the lion with the Egyptian!*"

With that cry up sprang — on moved — thousands upon thousands! They rushed from the heights — they poured down in the direction of the Egyptian. The power of the praetor was as a reed beneath the whirlwind. The guards made but a feeble barrier — the waves of the human sea halted for a moment, to enable Arbaces to count the exact moment of his doom! In despair, and in a terror which beat down even pride, he glanced his eyes over the rolling and rushing crowd — when, right above them, through the wide chasm which had been left in the velaria, he beheld a strange and awful apparition — he beheld — and his craft restored his courage!

"Behold!" he shouted with a voice of thunder, which stilled the roar of the crowd; "behold how the gods protect the guiltless! The fires of the avenging Orcus burst forth against the false witness of my accusers!" The eyes of the crowd followed the gesture of the Egyptian, and beheld, with ineffable dismay, a vast vapor shooting from the summit of Vesuvius in the form of a gigantic pine tree — the trunk, blackness; the branches, fire.

Then there arose on high the universal shrieks of women; the men stared at each other, but were dumb. At that moment they felt the earth shake beneath their feet; the walls of the theater trembled; and beyond, in the distance, they heard the crash of falling roofs. An instant more and the mountain cloud seemed to roll towards them, dark and rapid, like a torrent. At the same time it cast forth from its bosom a shower of ashes mixed with vast fragments of burning stone! Over the crushing

vines, over the desolate streets, over the amphitheater itself, far and wide, with many a mighty
splash in the agitated sea, fell that awful shower!
No longer thought the crowd of justice or of Arbaces; safety for themselves was their sole thought.
Each turned to fly — each dashing, pressing, crushing against the other.   Trampling recklessly over
the fallen — amidst groans and oaths and prayers
and sudden shrieks — the enormous crowd vomited
itself forth through the numerous passages. Whither
should they fly for protection from the terrors of
the open air?

And then darker and larger and mightier spread
the cloud above them.   It was a sudden and more
ghastly Night rushing upon the realm of Noon!

A TALE OF SWEETHEARTS

George R. Sims

So you've gotten an offer of marriage?
    There's a braw and comely lad
With a home o' his own a'ready,
    An' sighing away like mad.
An' he canna tell if you love him,
    For your cheeks give ne'er a sign;
And he's frettin' his honest heart out
    Just for a word o' thine.

He told me the tale hissen, lass,
    He left me awhile ago;
You're makin' his heart a plaything,
    And winna say yes or no.
Look in your mother's eyes, lass,
    Nay, dinna droop your head;
There's naught as you need to blush for,
    For a woman was born to wed.

He's rough in his ways and a miner,
    He's grimed wi' the grime o' coal;
Better ha' grime on his hands, lass,
    Than grime on his heart and soul.
Maybe your heart's another's —
    That finnikin Lunnon chap,
As came to the town last winter,
    As'll leave again this, mayhap.

Have I guessed your secret, Jenny?
    Is that why you won't have Joe,
You've gotten a finer sweetheart,
    An' the collier chap must go?
Shall I help you to make your mind up,
    And to choose between two men?
I'll tell you a tale of sweethearts,
    An' the lass of the tale's mysen.

I was summat about your age, lass,
    An' good-lookin', too, folks said,

When a chap as came to our village
  One summer, turned my head.
He came with the player people,
  He came and he stayed awhile;
An' somehow he won my heart, lass,
  Wi' his fine play-actin' style.

But I was a promised wife then,
  My sweetheart was like thy Joe;
A Lancaster lad, a miner,
  Who worked in the mines below.
He saw what was up, did Dan'l;
  An' he came to my father's place
Wi' a look o' shame and o' sorrow
  Deep-lined in his honest face.

An' he took my hand and pressed it,
  An' he said in a chokey voice:
"My lass, they say in the village
  That you've gotten doubts o' your choice;
That another has come betwixt us —
  That your love for mysen be dead;
So it's reet I stan' aside, lass —
  Ye can marry this man instead."

An' he said to me softly: "Jenny,
  We canna be man and wife;
But if ever you need a friend, lass,
  Why, I'm your friend for life."

I went wi' my player-lover —
   We were married in Lunnon town;
For a month I was up i' the heavens,
   An' then I came crashing down.

In a year he had gone and left me,
   Wi' never a friend anigh;
Wi' a fever wearin' my brain out,
   An' a bairn as I prayed might die.
"Kill it!" the devil whispered,
   As I heard its feeble cry;
God forgive! the devil conquered,
   An' I left the bairn to die.

I fled wi' the feet o' terror;
   An' ever behind me came
A phantom that tracked my footsteps
   And shouted and called my name,
So loud that the heavens heard it,
   And I thought in my mad despair
That a hundred eyes were watching —
   I could see them everywhere.

Eight years from that day of horror —
   Eight years to the very night,
I came to my native village;
   Came in the waning light.
There was never a soul that knew me
   As I passed through the quiet street;

An' I saw through an open doorway
  One, whom I dared not meet.

A child looked out of the window,
  And seeing my wan, white face,
She uttered a cry, and her father
  In a moment was out of the place.
"Ma lass! ma lass! tha art coom,
  Coom whoam to us here at last.
I ha' waited for thee, ma Jenny,
  This mony a long year past.

"I knew as tha mon had left thee,
  I knew as tha mon were dead;
An' I thought you'd ha' coom before, lass."
  I shivered an' hung my head.
"Will you be ma wife?" he whispered,
  "I ha' waited, ma lass, for thee;
I've a bairn as wants a mither,
  The lassie, as you can see.

"Will yo' make me happy, Jenny?"
  Then I tore mysen away;
"It canna be, Dan'l!" I answered,
  "For I go to my doom to day.
I've come to my native village,
  Here, where the deed was done,
To cry out a dark night's secret
  I' the light of noonday sun.

"A murderer has come to justice,
   To forfeit her wretched life!"
He heard me without a shudder,
   An' he answered: "Be ma wife!
Be ma wife, an' forget the past, love,
   An' howld up thy bonny head,
For the bairn as yo' see in the cottage
   Is the one as yo' thought war dead."

The bairn that he saved was yo', dear,
   The man I had cast away
Had been to yo' as a feyther;
   Yo' call him your dad to-day.
And now you're a woman grown, dear,
   Mine's a story you ought to know;
It may help you to make your mind up,
   'Twixt the Lunnon chap an' Joe.

What's that? A knock at the door, lass!
   Why, your cheeks are like the rose;
You know the knock for a penny;
   You've heard afore — it's Joe's?
What do yo' whisper, Jenny?
   You've always loved him! Then —
I'll bide i' the ither room, lass,
   You can tell him his fate yo'sen.

BATTLE OF ZARAILA

OUIDA

THE African day was at its noon.

From the first break of dawn the battle had raged; now, at midday, it was at its height. Far in the interior, almost at the edge of the great desert, in that terrible season when the air that is flame by day is ice by night, and when the scorch of a blazing sun may be followed in an hour by the blinding fury of a snow-storm, the slaughter had gone on hour through hour under a shadowless sky, blue as steel, hard as a sheet of brass. The Arabs had surprised the French encampment where it lay in the center of an arid plain that was called Zaraila.

The outlying videttes, the advanced sentinels, had scrutinized so long through the night every wavering shade of cloud and moving form of buffalo in the dim distance, that their sleepless eyes, strained and aching, failed to distinguish this moving mass that was so like the brown plains and starless sky that it could scarce be told from them. The night, too, was bitter; northern cold cut hardly chillier than this that parted the blaze of one hot day from the blaze of another. The sea-winds were blowing cruelly keen, and men who at noon gladly stripped to their shirts, shivered now where they lay under canvas.

Awake while his comrades slept around him, Cecil was stretched half unharnessed. The foraging duty of the past twenty-four hours had been work harassing and heavy, inglorious and full of fatigue.

Flick-Flack, coiled asleep in his bosom, thrilled, stirred, and growled. He rose, and with the little dog under his arm, looked out from the canvas. He knew that the most vigilant sentry in the service had not the instinct for a foe afar off that Flick-Flack possessed. He gazed keenly southward, the poodle growling on; that cloud so dim, so distant, caught his sight. Was it a moving herd, a shifting mist, a shadowy play between the night and dawn?

For a moment longer he watched it; then what it was he knew, or felt by such strong instinct as makes knowledge; and like the blast of a clarion his alarm rang over the unarmed and slumbering camp.

An instant, and the hive of men, so still, so motionless, broke into violent movement, and from the tents half-clothed sleepers poured, wakened, and fresh in wakening as hounds. Perfect discipline did the rest. With marvelous, with matchless swiftness and precision they harnessed and got under arms. They were but fifteen hundred or so

in all — a single squadron of Chasseurs, two bat.
talions of Zouaves, half a corps of Tirailleurs, and
some Turcos, only a branch of the main body and
without artillery. But they were some of the
flower of the army of Algiers, and they roused in
a second. Yet, rapid in its wondrous celerity as
their united action was, it was not so rapid as the
downward sweep of the war-cloud that came so
near, now growing clearer and clearer out of the
darkness, till the Arabs whirled down upon them,
met a few yards in advance by the answering
charge of the Light Cavalry.

There was a crash as if rock were hurled upon
rock, as the Chasseurs, scarce seated in saddle,
rushed forward to save the pickets, to encounter
the first blind force of the attack, and to give the
infantry, further in, more time for harness and defense. Out of the caverns of the night an armed
multitude seemed to have suddenly poured. A
moment ago they had slept in security; now thousands on thousands whom they could not number,
whom they could but dimly even preceive, were
thrown on them in immeasurable hosts, which the
encircling cloud of dust served but to render
vaster, ghastlier, and more majestic.

The Chasseurs could not charge; they were
hemmed in, packed between bodies of horsemen
that pressed them together as between iron plates;
now and then they could cut their way through,

ciear enough to reach their comrades of the demie cavalerie, but as often as they did so, so often the overwhelming numbers of the Arabs surged in on them afresh like a flood, and closed upon them and drove them back.

Every soldier in the squadron that lived kept his life by sheer breathless, ceaseless, hand-to-hand sword-play, hewing right and left, front and rear, without pause, as, in the great tangled forests of the West, men hew aside branch and brushwood ere they can force one step forward.

The Chef d'Escadron had been shot dead as they had first swept out to encounter the advance of the desert horsemen; one by one the officers had been cut down, singled out by the keen eyes of their enemies. At last there remained but a mere handful out of all the brilliant squadron that had galloped down in the gray of the dawn to meet the whirlwind of Arab fury. At their head was Cecil.

Two horses had been killed under him, and he had thrown himself afresh across unwounded chargers, whose riders had fallen in the mêlée, and at whose bridles he had caught as he shook himself free of the dead animal's stirrups. His head was uncovered; his uniform, hurriedly thrown on, had been torn aside, and his chest was bare to the red folds of his sash; he was drenched with blood, not his own, that had rained on him as he fought, and his face and his hands were black with smoke and

with powder. He could not see a yard in front of
him; he could not tell how the day went anywhere,
save in that corner where his own troop was hemmed in. All he could see was that every officer of
Chasseurs was down, and that unless he took the
vacant place and rallied them together, the few
score troopers that were still left would scatter,
confused and demoralized, as the best soldiers w⁺l
at times when they can see no chief to follow.

He spurred the horse he had just mounted
against the dense crowd opposing him, against the
hard, black wall of dust, and smoke, and steel, and
savage faces, and lean, swarthy arms, which were
all that his eyes could see, and that seemed impenetrable as granite, moving and changing though
it was. He thrust the gray against it, while he
waved his sword above his head:

"En avant, mes frères! France! France!
France!"

His voice, well-known, well-loved, thrilled the
hearts of his comrades, and brought them together
like a trumpet-call. They had gone with him
many a time into the hell of battle, into the jaws
of death. They surged about him now, striking,
thrusting, forcing with blows of their sabers or
their lances and blows of their beasts' forefeet a
passage one to another, until they were reunited
once more as one troop, while their shrill shouts,
like an oath of vengeance, echoed after him in the

butchery that has pealed victorious over so many fields from the soldiery of France. They loved him; he had called them his brethren. They were like lambs for him to lead, like tigers for him to incite.

"Suivez moi!" he shouted.

Then, like arrows launched at once from a hundred bows, they charged, he still slightly in advance of them, the bridle flung upon his horse's neck, his head and breast bare, one hand striking aside with his blade the steel shafts as they poured on him, the other holding high above the press the Eagle of the Bonapartes.

For the moment the Arabs recoiled under the shock of that fiery onslaught; for the moment they parted and wavered and oscillated beneath the impetus with which he hurled his hundred Chasseurs on them, with that light, swift, indescribable rapidity and resistlessness of attack characteristic of the African Cavalry.

But in another minute the Arabs closed in on every side; wheeling their swift coursers hither and thither; striking with lance and blade; hemming in, beyond escape, the doomed fragment of the Frankish squadron till there remained of them but one small nucleus, driven close together, rather as infantry will form than as cavalry usually does — a ring of horsemen, of which every one had his face to the foe; a solid circle curiously wedged one against the other, with the bodies of chargers and of men deep around them, and with the ground soaked with blood till the sand was one red morass.

Cecil held the Eagle still, and looked round on the few left to him.

"You are the sons of the Old Guard; die like them."

They answered with a pealing cry, terrible as the cry of the lion in the hush of night, but a shout that had in it assent, triumph, fealty, victory, even as they obeyed him and drew up to die.

There was a pause. The Arabs honored these men, who, alone and in the midst of the hostile force, held their ground and prepared thus to be slaughtered one by one, till, of all the squadron that had ridden out in the darkness of the dawn, there should be only a black, huddled, stiffened heap of dead men and dead beasts. The chief who led them pressed them back, withholding them from the end that was so near to their hands when they should stretch that single ring of horsemen all lifeless in the dust.

"You are great warriors," he cried, in the Sabir tongue; "surrender, we will spare!"

Cecil looked back once more on the fragment of his troop, and raised the Eagle higher aloft where the wings should glisten in the fuller day. Half naked, scorched, blinded, with an open gash in his shoulder where a lance had struck, and with his brow wet with the great dews of the noon heat and the breathless toil, his eyes were clear as they flashed with the light of the sun in them; his mouth smiled as he answered:

"Have we shown ourselves cowards, that you think we shall yield?"

A hurrah of wild delight from the Chasseurs he led greeted and ratified the choice: "On meurt — on ne se rend pas!" they shouted in the words, which, even if they be legendary, are too true to the spirit of the soldiers of France not to be as truth in their sight. Then, with their swords above their heads, they waited for the collision of the terrible attack which would fall on them upon every side, and strike all the sentient life out of them before the sun should be one point higher in the heavens. It came. With a yell as of wild beasts in their famine, the Arabs threw themselves forward, the chief himself singling out the "fair Frank" with a violence of a lion flinging himself on a leopard. One instant longer, one flash of time, and the tribes pressing on them would have massacred them like cattle driven into the pens of slaughter. Ere it could be done, a voice like the ring of a silver trumpet echoed over the field:

"En avant! En avant! Tue, tue, tue!"

Above the din, the shouts, the tumult, the echoing of the distant musketry, that silvery cadence rang; down into the midst, with the tricolor waving above her head, the bridle of her fiery mare between her teeth and her pistol leveled in deadly aim, rode La Cigarette.

The lightning fire of the crossing swords played round her, the glitter of lances dazzled her eyes, the reek of smoke and of carnage was round her; but she dashed down into the heart of the conflict as gayly as though she rode at a review, laughing, shouting, waving her torn colors that she grasped, with her curls blowing back in the breeze, and her bright young face set in the warrior's lust. Behind her, by scarcely a length, galloped three squadrons of Chasseurs and Spahis, trampling headlong over the corpse-strewn field, and breaking through the masses of the Arabs as though they were seas of corn.

She wheeled her mare round by Cecil's side at the moment when, with six swift passes of his blade, he had warded off the chief's blows and sent his own sword down through the chest-bones of the Bedouin's mighty form.

"Well struck!   The day is turned!   Charge!"

She gave the order as though she were a marshal of the Empire; the sun-blaze fell on her where she sat on the rearing, fretting, half-bred gray, with the tricolor folds above her head and her teeth tight gripped on the chain-bridle, and her face all glowing and warm and full of the fierce fire of war — a little Amazon in scarlet and blue and gold.

Cigarette had saved the day.

OPPORTUNITIES OF THE SCHOLAR

WE are standing in the daybreak of the second century of this Republic. The fixed stars are fading from the sky, and we grope in uncertain light. Strange shapes have come with the night. Established ways are lost — new roads perplex, and widening fields stretch beyond the sight. The unrest of dawn impels us to and fro — but Doubt stalks amid the confusion, and even on the beaten paths the shifting crowds are halted, and from the shadows the sentries cry: "Who comes there?" In the obscurity of the morning tremendous forces are at work. Nothing is steadfast or approved. The miracles of the present belie the simple truths of the past. The Church is besieged from without and betrayed from within. Behind the courts smolders the rioter's torch and looms the gibbet of the anarchists. Government is the contention of partisans and the prey of spoilsmen. Trade is restless in the grasp of monopoly, and commerce shackled with limitation. The cities are swollen and the fields are stripped. Splendor streams from the castle, and squalor crouches in the home. The universal brotherhood is dissolving, and the people are huddling into classes. The hiss of the

Nihilist disturbs the covert, and the roar of the mob murmurs along the highway. Amid it all beats the great American heart undismayed, and standing fast by the challenge of his conscience, the citizen of the Republic, tranquil and resolute, notes the drifting of the spectral currents, and calmly awaits the full disclosures of the day.

Who shall be the heralds of this coming day? Who shall thread the way of honor and safety through these besetting problems? Who shall rally the people to the defense of their liberties, and stir them until they shall cry aloud to be led against the enemies of the Republic? You, my countrymen, you! The university is the training camp of the future; the scholar the champion of the coming years. Napoleon overran Europe with drum-tap and bivouac — the next Napoleon shall form his battalions at the tap of the school-house bell, and his captains shall come with cap and gown. Waterloo was won at Oxford — Sedan at Berlin. So Germany plants her colleges in the shadow of the French forts, and the professor smiles amid his students as he notes the sentinel stalking against the sky. The farmer has learned that brains mix better with his soil than the waste of sea-birds, and the professor walks by his side as he spreads the showers in the verdure of his field, and locks the sunshine in the glory of his harvest. A button is pressed by a child's finger and the

work of a million men is done. The hard is nothing — the brain everything. Physical prowess has
had its day, and the age of reason has come. The
lion-hearted Richard challenging Saladin to single
combat is absurd, for even Gog and Magog shall
wage the Armageddon from their closets and look
not upon the blood that runs to the bridle-bit.
Science is everything! She butchers a hog in
Chicago, draws Boston within three hours of New
York, renews the famished soil, routs her viewless
bondsmen from the electric center of the earth,
and then turns to watch the new Icarus, as mounting in his flight to the sun, he darkens the bur-
nished ceiling of the sky with the shadow of his
wing.

Learning is supreme, and you are its prophets.
Here the Olympic games of the Republic — and you
its chosen athletes. It is yours, then, to grapple
with these problems, to confront and master these
dangers. Yours to decide whether the tremendous
forces of this Republic shall be kept in balance,
or, whether unbalanced they shall bring chaos;
whether 60,000,000 men are capable of self-government, or whether liberty shall be lost to them
who would give their lives to maintain it. Your
responsibility is appalling. You stand in the pass
behind which the world's liberties are guarded.
This government carries the hopes of the human
race. Blot out the beacon that lights the portals

of this Republic and the world is adrift again. But save the Republic; establish the light of its beacon over the troubled waters, and one by one the nations of the earth shall drop anchor and be at rest in the harbor of universal liberty.

A MURDERER'S CONFESSION

Edgar Allan Poe

TRUE!—nervous—very, very, dreadfully nervous I had been and am; but why will you say that I am mad? Hearken! and observe how healthily—how calmly I can tell you the whole story.

It is impossible to say how first the idea entered my brain; but once conceived, it haunted me day and night. Object, there was none. Passion, there was none. I loved the old man. He had never wronged me. He had never given me insult. For his gold I had no desire. I think it was his eye! Yes, it was this! One of his eyes resembled that of a vulture—a pale blue eye, with a film over it. Whenever it fell upon me, my blood ran cold; and so by degrees—very gradually—I made up my mind to take the life of the old man, and thus rid myself of the eye forever.

You fancy me mad. Madmen know nothing. But you should have seen me. You should have

seen how wisely I proceeded — with what caution
— with what foresight — with what dissimulation
I went to work! I was never kinder to the old
man than during the whole week before I killed
him. And every night, about midnight, I turned
the latch of his door and opened it — oh, so gently! and then, when I had made an opening sufficient for my head, I put in a dark lantern, all
closed, closed so that no light shone out, and then
I thrust in my head. Oh, you would have laughed
to see how cunningly I thrust it in! I moved it
slowly — very, very slowly, so that I might not
disturb the old man's sleep. It took me an hour
to place my whole head within the opening so far
that I could see him as he lay upon the bed.
Ha! — would a madman have been so wise as
this? And then, when my head was well in the
room, I undid the lantern cautiously — oh, so
cautiously — (for the hinges creaked). I undid it
just so much that a single thin ray fell upon the
vulture eye. And this I did for seven long
nights — every night just at midnight — but I
found the eye always closed ; and so it was impossible to do the work ; for it was not the old man
who vexed me, but his Evil Eye.

Upon the eighth night I was more than usually
cautious in opening the door. To think that
there I was, opening the door, little by little, and
he not even to dream of my secret deeds or

thoughts. I fairly chuckled at the idea ; and per·haps he heard me ; for he moved on the bed sud-denly, as if startled. Now you may think that I drew back — but no. His room was as black as pitch with the thick darkness (for the shutters were close fastened, through fear of robbers), and so I knew that he could not see the opening of the door, and I kept pushing it on steadily, steadily.

I had my head in, and was about to open the lantern, when my thumb slipped upon the tin fastening, and the old man sprang up in the bed, crying out : " Who's there?"

I kept quite still and said nothing. For a whole hour I did not move a muscle, and in the meantime I did not hear him lie down.

Presently I heard a slight groan, and I knew it was the groan of mortal terror. It was not a groan of pain or of grief — oh, no! — it was the low, stifled sound that arises from the bottom of the soul when overcharged with awe. I knew the sound well. I knew that he had been lying awake ever since the first slight noise, when he had turned in the bed. His fears had been ever since growing upon him. He had been trying to fancy them causeless, but could not.

When I had waited a long time, very patiently, without hearing him lie down, I resolved to open a little — a very, very little crevice in the lantern. So I opened it — you cannot imagine how stealthily,

stealthily — until at length a single dim ray, like the thread of the spider, shot from out the crevice and fell upon the vulture eye.

It was open — wide, wide open — and I grew furious as I gazed upon it. I saw it with perfect distinctness — all a dull blue, with a hideous veil over it that chilled the very marrow in my bones; but I could see nothing else of the old man's face or person; for I had directed the ray, as if by instinct, precisely upon the spot.

Now, there came to my ears a low, dull, quick sound, such as a watch makes when enveloped in cotton. I knew that sound well, too. It was the beating of the old man's heart. It increased my fury, as the beating of a drum stimulates the soldier into courage.

But even yet I refrained and kept still. I scarcely breathed; I held the lantern motionless. I tried how steadily I could maintain the ray upon the eye. Meantime the hellish tattoo of the heart increased. It grew quicker and quicker, and louder and louder every instant. The old man's terror must have been extreme! It grew louder, I say, louder every moment; do you mark me well? I have told you that I am nervous; so I am. And now at the dead hour of night, amid the dreadful silence of that old house, so strange a noise as this excited me to uncontrollable terror. Yet for some minutes longer I refrained and stood still.

But the beating grew louder, louder ! I thought the heart must burst.

And now a new anxiety seized me — the sound could be heard by a neighbor! The old man's hour had come! With a loud yell I threw open the lantern and leaped into the room. He shrieked once — once only. In an instant I dragged him to the floor, and pulled the heavy bed over him. I then smiled gayly to find the deed so far done. But for many minutes the heart beat on with a muffled sound. This, however did not vex me ; it would not be heard through the wall. At length it ceased. The old man was dead. I removed the bed and examined the corpse. I placed my hand upon the heart and held it there many minutes. There was no pulsation. He was stone dead. His eye would trouble me no more.

If still you think me mad, you will think so no longer when I describe the wise precautions I took for the concealment of the body. First of all I dismembered the corpse. I then took up three planks from the flooring of the chamber and deposited all between the scantlings. I then replaced the boards so cleverly, so cunningly, that no human eye — not even his — could have detected anything wrong.

When I had made an end of these labors it was four o'clock — still dark as midnight. As the bell sounded the hour, there came a knocking at the street door. I went down to open it with a light heart — for what had I now to fear? Then entered three men, who introduced themselves, with perfect suavity, as officers of the police. A shriek had been heard by a neighbor during the night ; suspicion of foul play had been aroused ; information had been lodged at the police office, and they (the officers) had been deputed to search the premises.

I smiled — for what had I to fear? I bade the gentlemen welcome. The shriek, I said, was my own in a dream. The old man, I mentioned, was absent in the country. I took my visitors all over the house. I bade them search — search well. I led them at length to his chamber. I showed them his treasures, secure, undisturbed. In the enthusiasm of my confidence I brought chairs into the room, and desired them here to rest from their fatigues, while I myself, in the wild audacity of my perfect triumph, placed my own seat upon the very spot beneath which reposed the corpse of the victim.

The officers were satisfied. My manner had convinced them. I was singularly at ease. But ere long I felt myself getting pale and wished them gone. My head ached, and I fancied a ringing in my ears ; but still they sat and still they chatted. The ringing became more distinct ; it continued and gained definitiveness — until at length I found that the noise was not within my ears.

No doubt I now grew very pale; but I talked more fluently and with a heightened voice. Yet the sound increased — and what could I do? It was a low, dull, quick sound — much such a sound as a watch makes when enveloped in cotton. I gasped for breath — and yet the officers heard it not. I talked more quickly — more vehemently; but the noise steadily increased. I arose and argued about trifles, in a high key and with violent gesticulations; but the noise steadily increased. Why would they not be gone? I paced the floor to and fro with heavy strides, as if excited to fury by the observations of the men — but the noise steadily increased. O God! what could I do? I foamed — I raved — I swore! I swung the chair upon which I had been sitting, and grated it upon the boards, but the noise arose over all and continually increased. It grew louder — louder — louder. And still the men chatted pleasantly and smiled. Was it possible they heard not?

They heard! — they suspected! — they knew! — they were making a mockery of my horror! This I thought, and this I think. But anything was better than this agony! Anything was more tolerable than this derision! I can bear those hypocritical smiles no longer! I felt that I must scream or die! — and now — again! — hark! louder! louder! louder! louder!

"Villains!" I shrieked, "dissemble no more!
I admit the deed — tear up the planks! here!
here! It is the beating of his hideous heart!"

———

THE VOLUNTEER ORGANIST

S. W. Foss

THE gret big church wuz crowded full uv broad-
　　　cloth an' uv silk,
An' satins rich as cream thet grows on our ol'
　　　brindle's milk;
Shined boots, biled shirts, stiff dickeys, an' stove-
　　　pipe hats were there,
An' dudes 'ith trouserloons so tight they couldn't
　　　kneel down in prayer.

The elder in his poolpit high, said, as he slowly riz:
"Our organist is kep' to hum, laid up 'ith roomatiz,
An' as we hev no substitoot, as Brother Moore
　　　ain't here,
Will some 'un in the congregation be so kind 's to
　　　volunteer?"

An' then a red-nosed, blear-eyed tramp, of low-
　　　toned, rowdy style,
Give an interductory hiccup, an' then swaggered
　　　up the aisle.
Then thro' that holy atmosphere there crep' a
　　　sense er sin,
An' thro' thet air of sanctity the odor uv ol' gin.

Then Deacon Purington he yelled, his teeth all set
     on edge:
"This man perfanes the house of God! W'y,
     this is sacrilege!"
The tramp didn' hear a word he said, but slouched
     'ith stumblin' feet,
An' stalked an' swaggered up the steps, an' gained
     the organ seat.

He then went pawin' thro' the keys, an' soon there
     rose a strain
Thet seemed to jest bulge out the heart, an'
     'lectrify the brain;
An' then he slapped down on the thing 'ith hands
     an' head an' knees,
He slam-dashed his hull body down kerflop upon
     the keys.

The organ roared, the music flood went sweepin'
     high an' dry,
It swelled into the rafters, an' bulged out into
     the sky;
The ol' church shook and staggered, an' seemed to
     reel an' sway,
An' the elder shouted "Glory!" an' I yelled out
     "Hooray!"

An' then he tried a tender strain thet melted in
     our ears,

Thet brought up blessed memories and drenched
      'em down 'ith tears;
An' we dreamed uv ol' time kitchens, 'ith Tabby
      on the mat,
Uv home an' luv an' baby days, an' mother, an'
      all that!

An' then he struck a streak uv hope — a song from
      souls forgiven —
Thet burst from prison bars uv sin, an' stormed
      the gates uv heaven;
The morning stars together sung — no soul was
      left alone —
We felt the universe wuz safe, an' God was on His
      throne!

An' then a wail of deep despair an' darkness come
      again,
An' long, black crape hung on the doors uv all the
      homes uv men;
No luv, no light, no joy, no hope, no songs of glad
      delight,
An' then — the tramp, he swaggered down an'
      reeled out into the night!

But we knew he'd tol' his story, tho' he nevei
      spoke a word,
An' it was the saddest story thet our ears had ever
      heard;

He hed tol' his own life history, an' no eye was
    dry thet day,
W'en the elder rose an' simply said: "My brethren,
    !et us pray."

A BATTERY IN HOT ACTION

CHICAGO TRIBUNE

Did you ever see a battery take position?

It hasn't the thrill of a cavalry charge, nor the
grimness of a line of bayonets moving slowly and
determinedly on, but there is a peculiar excitement
about it that makes old veterans rise in their sad-
dles and cheer.

We have been fighting at the edge of the woods.
Every cartridge-box has been emptied once or
more, and one-fourth of the brigade has melted
away in dead and wounded and missing. Not a
cheer is heard in the whole brigade. We know
that we are being driven foot by foot, and that
when we break once more the line will go to
pieces and the enemy will pour through the gap.

Here comes help!

Down the crowded highway gallops a battery,
withdrawn from some other position to save ours.
The field fence is scattered while you could count
thirty, and the guns rush from the hills behind us.
Six horses to a piece — three riders to each gun.

Over dry ditches where a farmer would not drive a wagon, through clumps of bushes, over logs a foot thick, every horse on the gallop, every rider lashing his team and yelling — the sight behind us making us forget the sight in front. The guns jump two feet high as the heavy wheels strike a rock or log, but not a horse slackens his pace, not a cannoneer loses his seat. Six guns, six caissons, sixty horses, eighty men, race for the brow of the hill as if he who should reach it first would be knighted.

A moment ago the battery was a confused mob. We look again, and six guns are in position, the detached horses hurrying away, the ammunition chests open, and along our line runs the command :

"Give them one more volley and fall back to support the guns." We have scarcely obeyed when boom! boom! opens the battery, and jets of fire jump down and scorch the green trees under which we fought and despaired.

The shattered old brigade has a chance to breathe for the first time in three hours, as we form a line and lie down. What grim, cool, fellows those cannoneers are! Every man is a perfect machine. Bullets splash dust in their faces, but they do not wince. Bullets sing over and around ; they do not dodge. There goes one to the earth, shot through the head as he sponged his gun. That machinery loses just one beat, misses just one cog in the wheels, and then works away again as before.

Every gun is using short-fuse shell. The ground shakes and trembles, the roar shuts out all sound from a line three miles long, and the shells go shrieking into the swamp to cut trees short off, to mow great gaps in the bushes, hunt out and shatter and mangle men until their corpses cannot be recognized as human. You would think a tornado was howling through the forest followed by billows of fire, and yet men live through it — aye! press forward to capture the battery. We can hear their shouts as they form the rush.

Now the shells are changed for grape and canister, and guns are fired so fast that all reports blend into one mighty roar. The shriek of a shell is the wickedest sound in war, but nothing makes the flesh crawl like the demoniacal singing, purring, whistling grape shot, and the serpent-like hiss of canister.

Men's legs and heads are torn from bodies and bodies cut in twain. A round shot or shell takes two men out of the ranks as it crashes through. Grape and canister mow a swath and pile the dead on top of each other.

Through the smoke we see a swarm of men. It is not a battle line, but a mob of men desperate enough to bathe their bayonets in the flame of the guns. The guns leap from the ground, almost, as they are depressed on the foe, and shrieks and screams and shouts blend into one awful and steady cry. Twenty men out of the battery are down, and the firing is interrupted. The foe accept it as a sign of wavering and come rushing on. They are not ten feet away when the guns give them the last shot. That discharge picks the living men off their feet and throws them into the swamp, a blackened, bloody mass.

Up, now, as the enemy are among the guns. There is a silence of ten seconds, and then the flash and roar of more than three thousand muskets and a rush forward with bayonets. For what? Neither on the right nor the left nor in front is a living foe! There are corpses around us which have been struck by three, four, and even six bullets, and nowhere on this acre of ground is a wounded man. The wheels of the guns cannot move until the blockade of dead is removed. Men cannot pass from caisson to gun without passing over windrows of dead. Every gun and wheel is smeared with blood; every foot of grass has its horrible stain.

And yet historians write of the glory of war!

THE CHARIOT RACE

LEW WALLACE

When the dash for position began, Ben-Hur was on the extreme left of the six. For a moment, like the others, he was half-blinded by the light in the arena; yet he managed to catch sight of his antagonists and divine their purpose. At Messala, who was more than an antagonist to him, he gave one searching look. The Israelite thought he saw the soul of the man as through a glass, darkly: cruel, cunning, desperate; not so excited as determined — a soul in a tension of watchfulness and fierce resolve. At whatever costs, at all hazards, he would humble this enemy! Regard for life even should not hold him back.

When not half-way across the arena, he saw that Messala's rush would, if there was no collision, and the rope fell, give him the wall.

The rope fell and all the fours but his sprang into the course under urgency of voice and lash. He drew head to the right, and, with all the speed of his Arabs, darted across the trails of his opponents. So while the spectators were shivering at the Athenian's mishap, and the Sidonian, Byzantine, and Corinthian were striving, with such skill as they possessed, to avoid involvement in the ruin, Ben-Hur swept around and took the course neck and neck with Messala, though on the outside. The marvelous skill shown in making the change thus from the extreme left across to the right without appreciable loss did not fail the sharp eyes upon the benches: the Circus seemed to rock and rock again with prolonged applause.

And now, racing together side by side, a narrow interval between them, the two neared the second goal.

A hush fell over all the Circus, so that for the first time in the race the rattle and clang of the cars plunging after the tugging steeds were distinctly heard. Then, it would seem, Messala observed Ben-Hur and recognized him, and at once the audacity of the man flamed out.

"Down, Eros! Up Mars!" he shouted, whirling his lash. "Down, Eros! Up Mars!" he repeated, and gave the Arab steeds of Ben-Hur a cut, the like of which they had never known.

The blow was seen in every quarter. The silence deepened and the boldest held his breath, waiting for the outcome. Only a moment thus: then involuntarily, down from the balcony as thunder falls, burst the indignant cry of the people.

The four sprang forward affrighted. No hand had ever been laid upon them except in love. Forward they sprang as with one impulse, and forward leaped the car. Where got Ben-Hur the large hand and mighty grip? Where but from the oar with which so long he fought the sea? So he gave the four free rein, and called to them in soothing voice, trying merely to guide them round the dangerous turn; and before the fever of the people began to abate, he had back the mastery. Nor that only: on approaching the first goal he was again side by side with Messala, bearing with him the sympathy and admiration of every one not a Roman.

The sixth round was entered upon without change of relative position.

Gradually the speed had been quickened — gradually the blood of the competitors warmed with the work. Men and beasts seemed to know alike that the final crisis was near, bringing the time for the winner to assist himself.

Messala's horses were running with their heads low down; from the balcony their bodies appeared actually to skim the earth; their nostrils showed blood-red in expansion; their eyes seemed straining in their sockets. On they dashed. As they neared the second goal, Ben-Hur turned in behind the Roman's car.

The joy of the Messala faction reached its bound; they screamed and howled, and tossed their colors; and Sanballat filled his tablets with wagers of their tendering.

Thus to the first goal and around it, Messala, fearful of losing his place, hugged the stony wall with perilous clasp; a foot to the left and he had been dashed to pieces; yet when the turn was finished, no man, looking at the wheel-tracks of the two cars, would have said, "Here went Messala, there the Jew." They left but one trace behind them. Half-way round the course and he was still following; at the second goal, even still no change.

And now, to make the turn, Messala began to draw in his left hand steeds. His spirit was high. The Roman genius was still president. On the pillars, only six hundred feet away, were fame, fortune, promotion, and a triumph ineffably sweetened by hate, all in store for him! That moment Ben-Hur leaned forward over his Arabs and gave them the reins. Out flew the many-folded lash in his hands; over the backs of the startled steeds it writhed and hissed, and hissed and writhed again and again; and, though it fell not, there were both sting and menace in its quick report. Instantly, not one, but the four as one, answered with a leap that landed them alongside the Roman's car. Messala, on the perilous edge of the goal, heard but dared not look to see what the awakening portended. From the people he received no sign. Above the noises of the race there was but one voice, and that was Ben-Hur's. In the old Aramaic, as the sheik himself, he called to the Arabs: "On, Atair! On, Rigel! What, Antares! dost thou linger now? Good horse — oho, Aldebaran! I hear them singing in the tents. I hear the children singing, and the women, singing of the stars, of Atair, Antares, Rigel, Aldebaran, victory — and the song will never end. Well done! Home to-morrow, under the black tent — home! On, Antares! The tribe is waiting for us, and the master is waiting! 'Tis done! 'Tis done! Ha! ha! We have over-thrown the proud! The hand that smote us is in the dust! Ours the glory! Ha! ha! Steady! The work is done — soho! Rest!"

The thousands on the benches understood it all; they saw the signal given — the magnificent response; the four close outside Messala's outer wheel; Ben-Hur's inner wheel behind the other's car — all this they saw. Then they heard a crash loud enough to send a thrill through the Circus, and out over the course a spray of shining white and yellow flinders flew. Down on its right side toppled the bed of the Roman's chariot. There was a rebound, as of the axle hitting the hard earth; another and another; then the car went to pieces; and Messala, entangled in the reins, pitched forward headlong.

The Sidonian, who had the wall next behind, could not stop or turn out. Into the wreck full speed he drove; then over the Roman, and into the latter's four, all mad with fear. Presently, out of the turmoil, the fighting of horses, the resound of blows, the murky cloud of dust and sand, he crawled, in time to see the Corinthian and Byzantine go on down the course after Ben-Hur, who had not been an instant delayed.

The people arose, and leaped upon the benches, and shouted and screamed. Those that looked that way caught glimpses of Messala, now under the trampling of the fours, now under the abandoned cars. He was still; they thought him dead; but far the greater number followed Ben-Hur in his career. They had seen the transformation of the man, and themselves felt the heat and glow of his spirit, the heroic resolution, the maddening energy of action with which, by look, word, and gesture, he so suddenly inspired his Arabs. And such running! It was rather the long leaping of lions in harness; but for the lumbering chariot, it seemed the four were flying. When the Byzantine and Corinthian were half-way down the course, Ben-Hur turned the first goal.

And the race was won!

THE BATTLE OF BANNOCKBURN

Grace Aguilar

Early on the morning of the 23d, intelligence was brought King Robert of the march of the English army from Falkirk, and, without a moment's delay, the patriot sovereign drew forth his rejoicing troops, to form them in the line of battle on which he had resolved. The drums rolled to arms; the silver clarions and deeper trumpets echoed and reëchoed from various sides, and under each, the gallant soldiery sprang up around their respective leaders. Slowly Bruce rode along the line once and again, then he paused, and a deep, breathless stillness for a brief minute prevailed. It was broken by his voice, clear, sonorous, rich, distinguished for many paces round:

"Men of Scotland, we stand here on the eve of a mighty struggle. Slavery or freedom are in the balance; misery or joy hinge on the result. I hesitate not to avow there are fearful odds against us. England hath more than treble our number; but, soldiers, your monarch fears not — the fewer men, the greater glory! We shall win, we shall give freedom to our country, fling from us her last chain, crushed to atoms, into dust; and to do this, what do we need? — bold hearts and willing hands, and those who have them not, let them now depart. Friends, subjects, fellow-soldiers, if there be any amongst ye whose hearts fail them, who waver in their determination to conquer or die with Robert Bruce, I give ye liberty, perfect liberty, to depart hence. Our hearts are not all cast in the same mold, and if there be any excuse for wavering spirits, men of Scotland, behold it in the whelming flood that England's power hath gathered to appall us. Be this proclaimed: I would not one hand should stay whose heart hath failed."

Scarce had he ceased to speak when the wild cry of confidence, of love, of fidelity to death, burst from every lip.

"To the death, to the death, we will abide with thee — thy fate is ours, whatever it may be — victory or death — we will share it! Death hath no terror when thou art by! Victory shall be ours, for 'tis the Bruce that leads; with thee we live or die!"

And then, as by magic — calmed, silenced, disciplined as before — they fell into their ranks, and waited the orders of their king.

About four hours after noon of the same day, the vanguard of the English came in sight; standard and pennon, banner and plume, of every shade and gorgeous material, gleamed in the sunshine, as moving pavilions, ere their bearers could be distinguished. Bruce, riding forward, fancied he perceived a large body of men detaching themselves from the main body of the English, and advancing cautiously through some low, marshy ground in the direction of the castle.

"Ha!" he shouted in a voice that called the attention of his leaders at once. "Randolph, Randolph! See yon cloud of dust and lances; they have passed your ward."

"But gained not the goal," answered Randolph.

the red flush of indignation mounting to his cheek; "nor shall they, my liege. Follow me, men!" And with about four score spearmen he dashed onward, halted in the spot the English must pass, and in that compact circle of three-lined pointed spears — one rank kneeling, the next stooping, the last upright — awaited the charge of eight hundred horse.

On came the English cavalry, but unable to penetrate the sharp phalanx presented to them, they fell back in complete disorder, like a repelled tide, amid whose retreating waves Randolph's men stood like a stubborn rock, and the first day's fight was ended.

There was deep silence on the plain of Bannockburn — silence, as if not a breathing soul were there; yet when the shrouding drapery of night was drawn aside, when the deep, rosy tint of the eastern skies proclaimed the swift advance of the god of day, what a glorious scene was there! Both armies were drawn forth facing each other. The vanguard of the English, composed of the archers and billmen, under command of Gloucester and Hereford, forming an impenetrable mass of above twenty thousand infantry, with a strong body of glittering men-at-arms to support them, occupied the foremost space, directly in the rear, and partly on their right. In front, and slightly in the rear of Gloucester's infantry, stood a regally attired group of about four hundred chevaliers, in the center of which, gallantly mounted and splendidly accoutred in golden armor, his charger barded in unison, bearing himself in very truth right royally and bravely, as the son of his father, the monarch of England sat, his white and crimson plumes falling from his golden helmet in thick masses to his shoulder.

Suddenly a hundred trumpets sounded from the English line, followed by a rush like thunder, and a discharge of arrows so thick, so close, the very air was darkened. Onward, in full career against Edward Bruce's left wing, the Earls of Hereford and Gloucester rushed; but one glance sufficed to prove somewhat had chanced to discompose their steady union, and that they had rushed forward to the charge with infinitely more of rivalship than order. Again and yet again they strove to penetrate the solid ranks of the Scottish spearmen; horses rolled on the earth, flung headlong back by the massive spears, leaving their masters, often unwounded, to the mercy of their foes. Fiercely and valiantly the earls struggled to retrieve their first error and restore order to their men-at-arms.

Meanwhile, taking advantage of this confusion, Douglas and Randolph, at the head of their respective divisions, attacked with skill and admirably tempered courage the mass of infantry, who stood bewildered at the unexpected discomfiture of the body they had looked to for support; the charge, however, roused them to their wonted courage, and they resisted nobly.   Again the archers raised their deadly weapons to the ear, and again the air became thick with the flight of arrows, longer, heavier, more continued than before.   Their effect was too soon perceived in the ranks of the spearmen; many places left void, which had received unmoved the charge of the men-at-arms.   Quick as the lightning flash King Robert darted along the line.   " Now, then, on for Scotland — the Bruce and liberty!" he shouted, and quick as the words were spoken, the Marshal of Scotland, at the head of four hundred men-at-arms, wheeled round full gallop, and charged the English bowmen in the flank and rear with such vigor and precision as speedily to turn them from their fatal attack upon the Scots to their own defense.   It was now the Scottish archers' turn to gall their adversaries, and the flight of arrows fell swift and true.

Then Bruce returned to his post; his eagle glance moved not for an instant from the field. Order had disappeared from the English ranks, their massive bands broken through and through, tottering, falling like gigantic columns shaken by mighty winds; while firm, cool, inflexible, the bodies of the Scotch rushed amongst them, dealing destruction at every step, proving superiority, valor, strength in the very face of numbers.

The strife was becoming more and more general, more and more deadly, despite the multitude in rapid retreat. Edward of England still kept his ground, flying from post to post, from group to group, urging, impelling, conjuring them still to stand, to recall the ancient glories of his father, and make one last effort for England's honor, and struck by this unexpected spirit in their much-abused sovereign, his warriors, rallying the drooping spirits of their men, still presented a formidable front to their determined foes. The order of battle was utterly broken; but above a score of detached troops still struggled on, falling on both sides without giving an inch of ground.

Scathless the monarch of Scotland rode that field; the distant arrow bounded harmless from his faultless armor; the weapons, close at hand, turned ere they struck one blow; the lance had no power to turn his gigantic charger from his onward way; and thus he seemed, alike in view of friends and foes, the spirit of that mighty strife, the soul of victory, on which no mortal hand had power. Again the terrible war-cry sounded; new shouts arose of triumph, the closing ranks of the English fell back, appalled by the sound, then, panic-stricken, fled; the last link of slavery was broken and Scotland was free.

A RAJPUT NURSE

Edwin Arnold

"Whose tomb have they builded, Vittoo, under
    the tamarind tree,
With its door of the rose-veined marble, and white
    dome stately to see?
Was he holy Brahman, or Gogi, or a king of the
    Rajput line,
Whose urn rests here by the river, in the shade of
    this beautiful shrine?"

"May it please you," quoth Vittoo, salaaming,
    "Protector of all the poor!
It was not for holy Brahman they carved that deli-
    cate door,
Nor for Gogi, nor Rajput Rana, did they build
    this gem of our land,
But to tell of a Rajput woman, as long as the
    stones should stand!

"Her name was Moti: the pearl name! 'Twas
    far in the ancient times,
But her moon-like face, and her teeth of pearl,
    are sung of still in our rhymes,
And because she was young and comely, and of
    good repute, and had laid
A babe in the arms of her husband — the palace
    nurse she was made.

"For the sweet chief Queen of our Rana in Jey-
    pore city had died,
Leaving a motherless infant, the heir of that
    house of pride,
The heir of the Peacock Banner, of the Shield of
    Gold, of the Throne
Which traces its record of glory to the years when
    it stood alone;

"To ages when from the sunlight the first of our
    kings came down,
And had the earth for his footstool, and wore the
    stars for his crown,
As all good Rajputs have told us, this Moti was
    proud and true
With the prince of the land on her bosom, and
    her own brown baby, too.
So leal was the blood of her body, so fast the faith
    of her heart,
It passed to her new-born infant, who took of her
    trust its part.

"It would not drink at the breast-milk till the
    prince had drunken his fill,
It would not sleep to the cradle-song till the prince
    was lulled and still;
And it lay at night with its small arms clasped
    'round the Rana's child,
As if those hands of the rose-leaf could guard from
    treason wild.

"For treason was wild in the country, and villain-
ous men had sought

The life of the heir of the Gadi ; to the palace in
secret brought,

With bribes to the base, and with knife-thrusts to
the faithful, they.found their way

Through the fence of the guards, and the gate-
ways, to the hall where the women lay.

"There Moti, the foster mother, sat singing the
children to rest,

Her baby at play on her knees, and the king's son
held to her breast;

And the dark slave-maidens round her beat low on
the cymbal-skin,

Keeping the time of her soft song — when Saheb!
there hurried in

A breathless watcher who whispered, with horror
in eyes and face,

'O, Moti! men come to murder my lord, the
prince, in this place !

They have bought the help of the gate-guards, or
slaughtered them unawares,

Hark! that is the sound of their tulwarst, that
clatter upon the stairs!'

"For one breath she caught up her baby from her
knee to her heart, and let

The king's child sink from her bosom, with lips
still clinging and wet ;

Then tore from the prince his head-cloth, and the
    putta of pearls from his waist,
And bound the belt on her infant, and the cap on
    his brows in haste.

" And laid her own dear offspring, her flesh and
    blood on the floor,
With the girdle of pearls around him, and the cap
    that the king's son wore;
While close to her heart — which was breaking —
    she folded the Raja's joy;
And — even as the murderers lifted the purdah —
    She fled with his boy!

" But there (as they deemed) in his jewels, lay the
    Chota-Rana, the heir;
' The cow witn two calves has escaped us!' one
    cried — ' it is right and fair
She shall save her own baby! no matter! the edge
    of a Katar ends
This spark of Lord Raghoba's sunlight!—stab
    thrice and four times, O friends!'

"And the Rajput women will have it — I know
    not if this can be so —
That Moti's son in the putta and golden cap crooned
    low
When the sharp blades pierced to his small heart,
    with never a moan or wince,
But died with a babe's light laughter, because he
    died for his prince!

"Thereby did that Rajput mother preserve the
    line of our kings!"
" O Vittoo!" I said, " but they gave her much
    gold and beautiful things,
And garments and land for her people, and a home
    in the palace?   Maybe
She had grown to love that princeling even more
    than the child on her knee."

" May it please the presence!" quoth Vittoo, "it
    seemeth not so ; they gave
The gold, and the garments and jewels, as much
    as the proudest should have ;
But the same night, deep in her bosom, she buried
    a knife and smiled,
Saying this : 'I have saved my Rana!   I must go
    to suckle my child!'"

MICHAEL STROGOFF

Jules Verne

This scene opens at the time when Ivan Ogareff
the Tartar spy, disguised as Michael Strogoff the
Czar's courier, having caused torrents of mineral
oil to be cast upon the surface of the river Angara,
had set fire to it with the design of betraying into
the hands of his allies the town of Irkutsk, which
stands upon its banks.   The Tartars were awaiting

the signal, when Michael Strogoff and Nadia, having swum the stream beneath the flames, succeeded in reaching the town.

They entered the palace, which was open for all. In the midst of the general confusion no one noticed them, although their clothes were dripping wet. There, in the midst of so great a crowd, they found themselves separated from each other. Nadia, distracted, ran along the lower rooms, called her companion, and asked to be led before the Grand Duke.

A door, leading into a room that was inundated with light, opened itself before her. She entered, and found herself unexpectedly face to face with him whom she had seen at Ichim, whom she had seen at Tomsk—in the presence of that man whose cursed hand an instant later would have delivered up the city.

"Ivan Ogareff!" cried she.

On hearing his name pronounced, the miserable wretch trembled. His true name being once known, all his plans would be ruined. He had only one thing to do: to kill the being, whoever it might be, who had just pronounced it.

Ivan Ogareff threw himself on Nadia; but the young girl, with a knife in her hand, placed her back to the wall, resolved to defend herself.

"Ivan Ogareff!" again cried Nadia; knowing well that detested name would bring succor to her.

"Ah! you shall be silent!" said the traitor.

"Ivan Ogareff!" cried a third time the intrepid young girl, in a voice whose hate had increased tenfold the force.

Drunk with fury, Ivan Ogareff drew a dagger from his belt, rushed upon Nadia, and forced her back into a corner of the room. It was nearly over with her, when Ivan Ogareff, suddenly knocked down by a tremendous blow, rolled to the ground.

"Michael!" cried Nadia.

It was Michael Strogoff. He had heard the appeal of Nadia. Guided by her voice, he had arrived at the room of Ivan Ogareff, and he had entered by the door which had been left open.

"Fear nothing, Nadia," he said, as he placed himself between her and Ivan Ogareff.

"Ah!" screamed the young girl, "take care, brother! The traitor is armed! He can see well."

Ivan Ogareff had risen, and, believing that he had the advantage over a blind man, he threw himself upon Michael Strogoff, who with one hand seized the arm of him who could see well, and with the other turning aside his weapon, he threw him a second time to the ground.

Ivan Ogareff, pale with fury and shame, remembered that he was carrying a sword. He drew it from the scabbard and returned to the combat.

He had only to deal with a blind man, for he recognized Michael Strogoff.

Nadia, terrified at the danger which threatened her companion in such an unequal struggle, ran to the door calling "Help!"

"Shut that door, Nadia!" said Michael Strogoff. "Do not call any one, and let me do it! The courier of the Czar has nothing to fear to-day from this wretch. Let him come at me, if he dares. I am waiting for him."

The traitor did not dream of fighting, but of assassinating him whose name he had stolen.

At length, he dealt a blow, and thrust his sword full at the breast of Michael Strogoff.

An imperceptible movement of the knife of the blind man turned the blow. Michael Strogoff had not been touched, and he coolly seemed to wait another attack without, however, challenging it.

A cold sweat ran from the face of Ivan Ogareff. He recoiled a pace, and then made another thrust. But the second blow, like the first, fell harmless. A simple parrying with the large knife had sufficed to turn aside the sword of the traitor.

The latter, mad with rage and terror before that living statue, fixed his terrified look on the large open eyes of the supposed blind man. Those eyes, that seemed to read the very bottom of his heart, those eyes seemed to have for him an awful fascination.

Suddenly, Ivan Ogareff gave a cry. An unexpected light had entered his brain.

"He can see!" cried he; "he can see!"

And like a deer trying to reënter its cave, step by step, terrified, he retreated to the lower end of the room.

Then the statue took life, the blind man walked straight to Ivan Ogareff and placed himself in front of him.

"Yes, I see!" said he. "I see the blow of the knout with which I have marked you, traitor and coward! I see the place where I am going to strike you! Defend your life! It is a duel which I condescend to offer you! My knife will suffice me against your sword!"

"He sees!" said Nadia. "God of mercy! Is it possible?"

Ivan Ogareff felt himself to be lost. But suddenly taking courage, sword in front, he rushed upon his impassable adversary. The two blades crossed, but at the first clash of the knife of Michael Strogoff, the sword flew in pieces, and the wretch, pierced to the heart, fell dead to the ground.

At that moment the door of the room, pushed from the outside, opened. The Grand Duke, accompanied by some officers, showed himself on the threshold; he advanced; he recognized on the ground the dead body of him whom he thought to be the courier of the Czar. And then, in a threatening voice, "Who has slain this man?" he asked.

"I," replied Michael Strogoff.

One of the officers placed a revolver to his head, ready to fire.

"Your name?" asked the Grand Duke, before giving the order to shoot him dead.

"Your Highness," answered Michael Strogoff, "ask me rather the name of the man stretched at your feet!"

"That man I have recognized. He is the servant of my brother! He is the Czar's courier!"

"That man, your Highness, is not a courier from the Czar. He is Ivan Ogareff."

"Ivan Ogareff!" cried the Grand Duke.

"Yes; Ivan the traitor!"

"But you! who are you?"

"Michael Strogoff!"

NYDIA'S SACRIFICE

Bulwer Lytton

Mount Vesuvius was fast burying the city of Pompeii. Glaucus, in despair, gave up the attempt to lead Ione to a place of safety, and with her sank down beneath the arch leading to the Forum. Here Nydia, the blind flower-girl, found him and said:

"Arise, follow me! Take my hand! Glaucus, thou shalt be saved!"

In wonder and sudden hope, Glaucus arose.

Half leading, half carrying Ione, he followed his guide. With admirable discretion, she avoided the path which led to the crowd she had quitted, and by another route sought the shore.

After many pauses and incredible perseverance, they gained the sea, and joined a group who, bolder than the rest, resolved to hazard any peril rather than continue in such a scene. In darkness they put forth to sea; but, as they cleared the land and caught new aspects of the mountain, its channel of molten fire threw a partial redness over the waves.

Utterly exhausted and worn out, Ione slept on the breast of Glaucus, and Nydia lay at his feet. Meanwhile the shower of dust and ashes, still borne aloft, fell into the wave, and scattered their snows over the deck.

The next day meekly, softly, beautifully, dawned at last the light over the trembling deep! — the winds were sinking into rest — the foam died from the glowing azure of that delicious sea. Around the east, thin mists caught gradually the rosy hues that heralded the morning. Light was about to resume her reign.

There was no *shout* from the mariners at the dawning light — it had come too gradually, and they were too wearied for such sudden bursts of joy — but there was a low, deep murmur of thankfulness amidst those watchers of the long night.

They looked at each other and smiled — they took heart — they felt once more that there was a world around them and a God above them! And in the feeling that the worst was passed, the over-wearied ones turned round, and fell placidly to sleep. In the growing light of the skies there came the silence which night had wanted: and the bark drifted calmly onward to its port. A few other vessels, bearing similar fugitives, might be seen in the expanse, apparently motionless, yet gliding also on. There was a sense of security, or companionship, and of hope, in the sight of their slender masts and white sails. What beloved friends, lost and missed in the gloom, might they not bear to safety and to shelter!

In the silence of the general sleep, Nydia rose gently. She bent over the face of Glaucus — she inhaled the deep breath of his heavy slumber — timidly and sadly she kissed his brow — his lips; she felt for his hand — it was locked in that of Ione; she sighed deeply, and her face darkened. Again she kissed his brow, and with her hair wiped from it the damp of night. "May the gods bless you, Athenian!" she murmured; "may you be happy with your beloved one! — may you sometimes remember Nydia! Alas! she is of no further use on earth!"

With these words she turned away. Slowly she crept along by the platforms to the farther side of the vessel, and pausing, bent low over the deep; the cool spray dashed upward on her feverish brow. "It is the kiss of death," she said — "it is welcome." The balmy air played through her waving tresses — she put them from her face, and raised those eyes — so tender, though sightless — to the sky, whose soft face she had never seen.

"No, no!" she said, half aloud and in a musing and thoughtful tone, "I cannot endure it; this jealous, exacting love — it shatters my whole soul in madness! I might harm him again — wretch that I was! I have saved him — twice saved him — happy, happy thought — why not *die* happy? — it is the last glad thought I can ever know. Oh, sacred sea! I hear thy voice invitingly — it hath a freshening and joyous call. They say that in thy embrace is dishonor — that thy victims cross not the fatal Styx — be it so! — I would not meet him in the Shades, for I should meet him still with *her?* Rest — rest — rest! — there is no other Elysium for a heart like mine!"

A sailor, half dozing on the deck, heard a slight splash on the waters. Drowsily he looked up, and behind, as the vessel merrily bounded on, he fancied he saw something white above the waves; but it vanished in an instant. He turned round again, and dreamed of his home and children.

When the lovers awoke, their first thought was of each other — their next of Nydia! She was

not to be found — none had seen her since the
night. Every crevice of the vessel was searched —
there was no trace of her. Mysterious from first
to last, the blind Thessalian had vanished forever
from the living world! They guessed her fate in
silence; and Glaucus and Ione, while they drew
nearer to each other (feeling each other the world
itself) forgot their deliverance, and wept as for a
departed sister.

BEST POLICY IN REGARD TO NATU-RALIZATION

Lewis C. Levin

EACH hour will behold this tide of foreign emigration rising higher and higher, growing stronger
and stronger, rushing bolder and bolder. The past
furnishes no test of the future, and the future
threatens to transcend all calculations of this
formidable evil. View this great subject in any
light, and it still flings back upon us the reflected
rays of reason, patriotism, and philanthropy. The
love of our native land is an innate, holy, and in-
eradicable passion. Distance only strengthens it —
time only concentrates the feeling that causes the
tear to gush from the eye of the emigrant, as old
age peoples by the vivid memory the active present
with the happy past. In what land do we behold

the foreigner who denies this passion of the heart?
It is nature's most holy decree, nor is it in human
power to repeal the law which is passed on the
mother's breast and confirmed by the father's
voice. The best policy of the wise statesman is to
model his laws on the holy ordinances of nature.
If the heart of the alien is in his native land — if
all his dearest thoughts and fondest affections
cluster around the altar of his native gods — let us
not disturb his enjoyments by placing this burden
of new affections on his bosom, through the moral
force of an oath of allegiance, and the onerous obligation of political duties that are against his sympathies, and call on him to renounce feelings that
he can never expel from his bosom. Let us secure
him the privilege at least of mourning for his
native land by withholding obligations he cannot
discharge either with fidelity, ability, or pleasure.

Give him time to wean himself from his early
love. A long list of innumerable duties will
engage all his attention during his political novi-
tiate, in addition to those comprised in reforming
the errors and prejudices of the nursery, and in
creating and forming new opinions, congenial to
the vast field which lies spread before him in
morals, politics, and life. A due reflection will
convince every alien, when his passions are not in-
flamed by the insidious appeals of senseless demagogues, that his highest position is that of a moral

agent in the full enjoyment of all the attributes
of civil freedom, preparing the minds and
hearts of his children to become faithful, intelligent, and virtuous republicans, born to a right
that vindicates itself by the holy ties of omnipotent
Nature, and which, while God sanctions and conse-
crates, no man can dispute.

———

THE LITTLE OUTCAST'S PLEA

WE laid in a cell, Mister Judge, all night long,
Jimmie and me, waitin' and wishin' for the mornin'
    to dawn,
'Cause we couldn't sleep, Mister Judge, in that
    cold, damp place,
And Jimmie was most scared to death at the wild,
    mad race
That the rats kept runnin' all through the dark
    night;
That's why we were glad, Mister Judge, to see
    the daylight.

Please, Mister Judge, we are not very bad little
    boys,
And the policeman what took us said we're some
    mother's joys.
He was wrong, Mister Judge, and should only
    have said
That we're two little outcasts, and our mother is
    dead —

And there's no one to care for us, at least here
    below,
And no roof that shelters us from the rain and the
    snow.

A preacher once told us that way up in the blue
There was a God that was watchin' all that little
    boys do,
And that He loved little children, and His love it
    was free;
But I guess, Mister Judge, He don't love Jimmie
    or me,
For I prayed, and I prayed, till I was 'most out of
    breath,
For something to eat and to keep Jimmie from
    death.

And that's why we're here, Mister Judge, for you
    know
There was no help from above — I must find it be-
    low.
'Twas no use beggin' and be told in God I must
    trust,
For I begged all the day, and got never a crust;
And there was poor Jimmie, holdin' his cold little
    feet,
And cryin' and moanin' for somethin' to eat.

So I went to a house that was not very far,
And saw, Mister Judge, that the back door was ajar,

And a table was settin' right close by the door,
Just loaded with pies, about twenty or more.
So I quickly slipped in and grabbed one to my
      breast;
The policeman then caught us, and you know the
      rest.

Discharged, did you say, Mister Judge! both
      Jimmie and I?
And—and we ain't got to be jailed 'cause I took a
      pie!
And we can eat all we want!—how funny 'twill
      seem.
Say, Jimmie, pinch me, for I think it's a dream.
And you'll give us work, summer, winter and fall?
Say, Jimmie, I think there's a God, after all!

TRUTH AND VICTORY

D. C. SCOVILLE

THE face of the world is changing. When
crazy old John Coffin went down to the Battery,
and looking eastward over New York Bay, called
out, "Attention, Europe! Nations! by the right,
wheel!" he saw what sane men see now. Nations
are discovering there is something more terrible
than armies, something more reliable than battalions and bayonets, something wiser than senates,

something greater than royalty, something sweeter than liberty. Through the gospel of Peace and through the gospel of War one name is sounding over the continents. Truth! inspires the student of history; Truth! is the watchword of science; Truth! is the victorious cry of Christianity. Graven on the intellect of the statesman, burned into the brain of the philosopher, blazoned upon the standard borne in the van of the army of progress, Truth! is the animating shout of the ages.

In these days of political corruption, while one after another of our trusted leaders falls before the righteous and relentless indignation of public sentiment, it helps him who despairs of the future to remember that company in whose veins flows the young blood of the nation, in whose eyes kindle the fires of a pure faith, and from whose hearts radiate the strong purposes that make nations and direct civilization. These shall rise up when need is, and go into life's great battle with unfaltering heroism; and under their banner shall gather the world's best and bravest youth.

In the terrible battle of Balaklava two British regiments were calmly awaiting the advance of twelve times their number of Russians. It was a fearful moment. The English and French generals and thousands of soldiers looked from the heights above upon this heroic handful of silent,

motionless men who, with sublime courage, held
the honor of Britain in that supreme hour. The
glittering lines of Russians came confidently on.
They halted in very wonderment at the heroism of
the devoted band of English. Suddenly the British trumpets sounded the charge, and the Scotch
Greys dashed at the foremost line of Russians.
It yielded and broke. Again the heroic little band
gathered its thinned and broken ranks, and flung
itself against the second line. "God save the
Queen! they are lost!" cried a thousand of their
comrades from the heights. It seemed madness,
it was madness; but it was madness which knows
nothing but success. Ten minutes of the agony of
suspense, and then a wild, spontaneous, tumultuous cheer burst from the watching thousands on
the hills, and Balaklava was won. There, on
the spot where victory rewarded valor, they
lifted tenderly up a dying Highlander. He
plucked from his breast a cross of honor, through
which the fatal bayonet had crashed. "Take this
to mother," said he, "and tell her I was struck
when we charged the first line, but I could not die
till we had carried the second."

And so, in the infinitely nobler battle of life,
remember, as you stand single and unsupported in
the conflict of Truth, that the hosts of Heaven,
whose cause is that day intrusted to your keeping,
are watching you with infinite solicitude. Heed

not the odds against you.   Ask for no allies.
Depend upon no reinforcements.   Against all.the
world, against wrong government, against corrupt
society, you alone are invincible, you alone
irresistible.

FORT WAGNER

ANNA E. DICKINSON

THROUGH the whole afternoon there had been a
tremendous cannonading of the fort from the gunboats and the land forces.   About six o'clock
there came moving up the island, over the burning
sands and under the burning sky, a stalwart,
splendid appearing set of men who looked equal
to any daring and capable of any heroism.   Weary,
travel-stained with the mire and rain of a two
days' tramp; weakened by the incessant strain
and lack of food; with gaps in their ranks made
by the death of comrades who had fallen in battle
but a little time before, it was plain to be seen of
what stuff these men were made, and for what
work they were ready.

As this regiment, the famous Fifty-fourth,
came up the island to take its place at the head of
the storming party in the assault on Wagner, it
was cheered from all sides by the white soldiers.

The day was lurid and sultry.   Great masses of
cloud, heavy and black, were piled in the western

sky, fringed here and there by an angry red, and
torn by vivid streams of lightning. Not a breath
of wind shook the leaves or stirred the high, rank
grass by the waterside; a portentous and awful
stillness filled the air. Quiet, with the like
awful and portentous calm, the black regiment,
headed by its young, fair-haired, knightly colonel,
marched to its destined place and action. A
slightly rising ground, raked by a murderous fire;
a ditch holding three feet of water; a straight lift
of parapet thirty feet high — an impregnable
position, held by a desperate and invincible foe.
Here the word of command was given:

"We are ordered and expected to take Battery
Wagner at the point of the bayonet. Are you
ready?"

"Ay, ay, sir! ready!" was the answer.

And the order went pealing down the line:
"Ready! Close ranks! Charge bayonets! Forward! Double-quick, march!" and away they
went, under a scattering fire, in one compact line
till within one hundred feet of the fort, when the
storm of death broke upon them. Every gun
belched forth its great shot and shell; every rifle
whizzed out its sharp-singing, death-freighted mes-
senger. The men wavered not for an instant;
forward — forward they went. They plunged
into the ditch; waded through the deep water, no
longer of muddy hue. but stained crimson with

their blood ; and commenced to climb the parapet. The foremost line fell, and then the next, and the next. On, over the piled-up mounds of dead and dying, of wounded and slain, to the mouth of the battery; seizing the guns; bayoneting the gunners at their posts; planting their flag and struggling around it; their leader on the walls, sword in hand, his blue eyes blazing, his fair face aflame, his clear voice calling out: " Forward, my brave boys!" — then plunging into the hell of battle before him.

As the men were clambering up the parapet their color sergeant was shot dead. A nameless hero who was just behind sprang forward, seized the staff from his dying hand, and with it mounted upward. A ball struck his right arm ; but before it could fall shattered at his side, his left hand caught the flag and carried it onward. Though faint with loss of blood and wrung with agony, he kept his place — the colors flying — up the slippery steep ; up to the walls of the fort; on the wall itself, planting the flag where the men made that brief, splendid stand, and melted away like snow before furnace heat. Here a bayonet thrust met him and brought him down, a great wound in his brave breast, but he did not yield ; dropping to his knees, pressing his unbroken arm upon the gaping wound — the colors still flew, an inspiration to the men about him, a defiance to the foe.

At last when the shattered ranks fell back, sullenly and slowly retreating, he was seen painfully working his way downward, still holding aloft the flag, bent evidently on saving it, and saving it as flag had rarely, if ever, been saved before.

Slowly, painfully he dragged himself onward — step by step down the hill, inch by inch across the ground — to the door of the hospital; and then, while dying eyes brightened, while dying men held back their souls from the eternities to cheer him, gasped out : " I did — but do — my duty, boys — and the dear — old flag — never once — touched the ground " — and then, away from the reach and sight of its foes, in the midst of its defenders who loved and were dying for it, the flag at last fell.

The next day a flag of truce went up to beg the body of the heroic young chief who had so led that marvelous assault. It came back without him. A ditch, deep and wide, had been dug; his body and those of twenty-two of his men, found dead upon and about him, flung into it in one common heap ; and the word sent back was : " We have buried him with his niggers."

It was well done. Slavery buried these men, black and white together — black and white in a common grave. Let Liberty see to it, then, that black and white be raised together in a life better than the old.

THE ELEMENTS OF NATIONAL WEALTH

James G. Blaine

The territory which we occupy is at least three million square miles in extent, within a fraction as large as the whole of Europe. The state of Texas alone is equal in area to the empire of France and the kingdom of Portugal united; and yet these two monarchies support a population of forty millions, while Texas has but six hundred thousand inhabitants. The land that is still in the hands of government, not sold or even preëmpted, amounts to a thousand million of acres — an extent of territory thirteen times as large as Great Britain, and equal in area to all the kingdoms of Europe, Russia and Turkey alone excepted.

Combined with this great expanse of territory, we have facilities for the acquisition and consolidation of wealth — varied, magnificent, immeasurable. The single state of Illinois, cultivated to its capacity, can produce as large a crop of cereals as has ever been grown within the limits of the United States, while Texas, if peopled but half as densely as Maryland even, could give an annual return of cotton larger than the largest that has ever been grown in all the Southern States combined.

Our facilities for commerce and exchange, both

domestic and foreign — who shall measure them?
Our oceans, our vast inland seas, our marvelous
flow of navigable streams, our canals, our network
of railroads more than thirty thousand miles in
extent — these give us avenues of trade and chan-
nels of communication both natural and artificial
such as no other nation has ever enjoyed.   Our
mines of gold and silver and iron and copper and
lead and coal, with their untold and unimaginable
wealth, spread over millions of acres of territory,
in the valley, on the mountain side, along rivers,
yielding already a rich harvest, are destined yet
to increase a thousandfold, until their everyday
treasures,

> . . . familiar grown,
> Shall realize Orient's fabled dream.

These are the great elements of material progress, and they comprehend the entire circle of
human enterprise — agriculture, commerce, manu-
factures, mining. They give into our hands, under
the blessing of Almighty God, the power to command our fate as a nation. They hold out to us
the grandest future reserved for any people; and
with this promise they teach us the lesson of
patience, and render confidence and fortitude a
duty.

With such amplitude and affluence of resources,
and with such a vast stake at issue, we should be
unworthy of our lineage and our inheritance if we

for one moment distrusted our ability to maintain
ourselves a united people, with "one country, one
constitution, one destiny."

THE MAIDEN MARTYR

A TROOP of soldiers waited at the door ;
A crowd of people gathered in the street,
Aloof a little from them bared sabers gleamed
And flashed into their faces.   Then the door
Was opened, and two women meekly stepped
Out of the prison.   One was weak and old,
A woman full of tears and full of woes ;
The other was a maiden in her morn ;
And they were one in name and one in faith,
Mother and daughter in the bond of Christ
That bound them closer than the ties of blood.
   The troop moved on ; and down the sunny street
The people followed, ever falling back
As in their faces flashed the naked blades.
But in the midst the women simply went
As if they two were walking side by side
Up to God's house on some still Sabbath morn ;
Only they were not clad for Sabbath day,
But as they went about their daily tasks;
They went to prison and they went to death,
Upon their Master's service.
   On the shore
The troopers halted ; all the shining sands

Lay bare and glistering; for the tide had
Drawn back to its farthest margin's weedy mark,
And each succeeding wave, with flash and curve,
Drew nearer by a hand-breadth.   " It will be
A long day's work," murmured those murderous
          men
As they slacked rein.   The leader of the troops
Dismounted, and the people passing near
Then heard the pardon proffered with the oath
Renouncing and abjuring part with all
The persecuted, covenanted folk,
But both refused the oath : " Because," they said,
" Unless with Christ's dear servants we have part,
We have no part with Him."

   On this they took
The elder Margaret, and led her out
Over the sliding sands, the weedy sludge,
The pebbly shoals, far out, and fastened her
Unto the farthest stake, already reached
By every rising wave, and left her there ;
And as the waves crept about her feet she prayed
" That He would firm uphold her in their midst,
Who holds them in the hollow of His hand."

   The tide flowed in.   And up and down the shore
There paced the Prophet and the Laird of Lag,
Grim Grierson — with Windram and with Gra·
          hame,
And the rude soldiers, jesting with coarse oaths,
As in the midst the maiden meekly stood,

Waiting her doom delayed, said, " She would
Turn before the tide, seek refuge in their arms
From the chill waves."   But ever to her lips
There came the wondrous words of life and peace ;
" If God be for us, who can be against?"
"Who shall divide us from the love of Christ?"
" Nor height, nor depth, nor any other creature."
    And still the tide was flowing in ;
They turned young Margaret's face toward the
        sea,
Where something white was floating — something
White as the sea-mew that sits upon the wave ;
But as she looked it sank ; then showed again ;
Then disappeared.   And round the shore
And stake the tide stood ankle-deep.
    Then Grierson,
With cursing, vowed that he would wait
No more, and to the stake the soldier led her
Down, and tied her hands, and round her
Slender waist too roughly cast the rope ; for
Windram came and eased it while he whispered
In her ear, " Come, take the test and you are free."
And one cried, " Margaret, say but God save
The King!"   " God save the King of His great
        grace,"
She answered, but the oath she would not take.
    And still the tide flowed in,
And drove the people back and silenced them.
The tide flowed in, and rising to her knees,

She sang the Psalm, " To Thee I lift my soul";
The tide flowed in, and rising to her waist,
" To Thee, my God, I lift my soul," she sang.
The tide flowed in, and rising to her throat,
She sang no more, but lifted up her face,
And there was glory over all the sea,
A flood of glory, and the lifted face
Swam in it till it bowed beneath the flood,
And Scotland's maiden martyr went to God.

DUTY OF LITERARY MEN TO AMERICA

Grimke

WE cannot honor our country with too deep a
reverence; we cannot love her with an affection
too pure and fervent; we cannot serve her with an
energy of purpose or a faithfulness of zeal too
steadfast and honest. And what is our country?
It is not the East, with her hills and her valleys, with
her countless sails, and the rocky ramparts of her
shores. It is not the North, with her thousand
villages, and her harvest home, with her frontiers
of the lake and the ocean. It is not the West,
with her forest-sea and her inland isles, with her
luxuriant expanses, clothed in the verdant corn,
with her beautiful Ohio, and her majestic Missouri.
Nor is it yet the South, opulent in the mimic

snow of the cotton, in the rich plantations of the
rustling cane, and in the golden robes of the rice-
field.   What are these but the sister families of
one greater, better, holier family, our country?   I
come not here to speak the dialect, or to give the
counsels of the patriot statesman ; but I come, a
patriot scholar, to vindicate the rights, and to plead
for the interests of American Literature.   And be
assured that we cannot, as patriot scholars, think
too highly of that country, or sacrifice too much
for her.   And let us never forget, let us rather
remember with a religious awe, that the union of
these States is indispensable to our Literature, as
it is to our national independence and our civil
liberties, to our prosperity, happiness, and improvement.   If, indeed, we desire to behold a Literature
like that, which has sculptured with such energy
of expression, which has painted so faithfully and
vividly, the crimes, the vices, the follies of ancient
and modern Europe ; if we desire that our land
should furnish for the orator and the novelist, for
the painter and the poet, age after age, the wild
and romantic scenery of war ; the glittering march
of armies, and the revelry of the camp, the
shrieks and blasphemies, and all the horrors of
the battlefield ; the desolation of the harvest,
and the burning cottage ; the storm, the sack,
and the ruin of cities ; if we desire to un-
chain the furious passions of jealousy and selfish-

ness, of hatred, revenge and ambition, those lions
that now sleep harmless in their den ; if we desire
that the lake, the river, the ocean, should blush
with the blood of brothers ; that the winds should
waft from the land to the sea, from the sea to the
land, the roar and the smoke of battle ; that the
very mountain tops should become the altars for the
sacrifice of brothers ; if we desire that these, and
such as these — the elements, to an incredible
extent, of the Literature of the old world — should
be the elements of our Literature, then, but then
only, let us hurl from its pedestal the majestic
statue of our Union, and scatter its fragments over
all our land.   But, if we covet for our country the
noblest, purest, loveliest Literature the world
has ever seen, such a Literature as shall honor
God, and bless mankind ; a Literature, whose
smiles might play upon an angel's face, whose
tears " would not stain an angel's cheek " ; then
let us cling to the union of these States, with a
patriot's love, with a scholar's enthusiasm, with a
Christian's hope.   On her heavenly character, as
a holocaust self-sacrificed to God ; at the height of
her glory, as the ornament of a free, educated,
peaceful, Christian people, American Literature
will find that the intellectual spirit is her very
tree of life, and that Union her garden of paradise.

NO ROOM FOR MOTHER

Lockport Express

" Going north, madam?"

" No, ma'am."

" Going south, then?".

" I don't know, ma'am."

" Why, there are only two ways to go."

" I didn't know.   I was never on the cars.   I am waiting for the train to go to John."

" John?   There is no town called John.   Where is it?"

" Oh, John's my son.   He's out in Kansas on a claim."

" I am going right to Kansas myself.   You intend to visit?"

" No, ma'am."   She said it with a sigh so heart-burdened the stranger was touched.

" John sick?"

" No."

The evasive tone, the look of pain in the fur-rowed face were noticed by the stylish lady as the gray head bowed upon the toil-marked hand.   She wanted to hear her story — to help her.

" Excuse me — John in trouble?"

" No, no — I'm in trouble.   Trouble my old heart never thought to see."

" The train does not come for some time.   Here, rest your head upon my cloak."

"You are kind. If my own were so I should not be in trouble to-night."

"What is your trouble? Maybe I can help you."

"It's hard to tell it to strangers, but my old heart is too full to keep it back. When I was left a widow with three children I thought it was more than I could bear; but it wasn't so bad as this——"

The stranger waited till she recovered her voice to go on.

"I had only the cottage and my willing hands. I toiled early and late all the years till John could help me. Then we kept the girls at school, John and me. They were married not long ago. Married rich, as the world goes. John sold the cottage, sent me to the city to live with them, and he went west to begin for himself. He said he had provided for the girls and they would provide for me now——"

Her voice chokéd with emotion. The stranger waited in silence.

"I went to them in the city. I went to Mary's first. She lived in a great house, with servants to wait on her; a house many times larger than the little cottage—but I soon found there wasn't room enough for me ——"

There tears stood in the lines on her cheeks. The ticket agent came out softly, stirred the fire and went back. After a pause she continued:

" I went to Martha's — went with a pain in my heart I never felt before.   I was willing to do anything so as not to be a burden.   But that wasn't it.   I found they were ashamed of my bent, old body and my withered face — ashamed of my rough, wrinkled hands — made so toiling for them."

The tears came thick and fast now.   The stranger's hand rested caressingly on the gray head.

" At last they told me I must live at a boarding house and they'd keep me there.   I couldn't pay anything back.   My heart was too full of pain.   I wrote to John what they were going to do.   He wrote right back a long, kind letter for me to come right to him.   I always had a home while he had a roof, he said.   To come right there and stay as long as I lived; that his mother would never go out to strangers.   So I am going to John.   He's got only his rough hands and great, warm heart, but there's room for his old mother.   God bless him."

The stranger brushed a tear from her fair cheek and awaited the conclusion.

"Some day when I am gone where I'll never trouble them again, Mary and Martha will think of it all; some day, when the hands that toiled for them are folded and still; when the eyes that watched over them through many a weary night are closed forever; when the little old body, bent with the burdens it bore for them, is put where it can never shame them."

The agent drew his hand quickly before his eyes, and went out as if to look for a train. The stranger's jewelled fingers stroked the gray locks, while the tears of sorrow and the tears of sympathy fell together. The weary heart was unburdened. Soothed by a touch of sympathy, the troubled soul yielded to the longing for rest, and she fell asleep. The agent went noiselessly about his duties that he might not wake her. As the fair stranger watched she saw a smile on the careworn face. The lips moved. She bent down to hear.

"I'm doing it for Mary and Martha. They'll care for me some time."

She was dreaming of the days in the little cottage — of the fond hopes which inspired her long before she learned, with a broken heart, that some day she would turn, homeless in the world, to go to John.

MARGUERITE

Evelyn Noble Schroeder

It was Decoration Day, some years ago — that day which means so very much and whose name suggests so very little. Marguerite knew that it was "Decoration Day," but she could not tell what it meant. She did not understand the long procession, the music, the flowers, and all; she only knew that she had been sent to sell her flowers because it was some kind of a flower day. Daisies she had in her large basket — bright gold and white daisies; and she had a little bunch in her tiny hand which she held out to passers-by as she said: "Daisies, fresh daisies, five cents a bunch?"

She stood at the foot of the beautifully-decorated soldiers' monument watching the crowd of people and the marching men with wide, wondering eyes. She did not know what it was all for. She knew very little, this tiny, ragged maid. Had you asked her name, she would have told you "Marguerite"; but she did not know she was named for the flowers she carried; she did not know that her hair was bright and sunny like their gold hearts; she did not know that they and her eyes were like the stars in their child-likeness, nor that the white petals were symbols of her own purity. She had not sold many flowers — she was so small and her daisies so simple that people scarcely noticed; but she did not seem to care — she was so busy with the new sights and sounds — and the child-soul was filled with a feeling she could not have told, and I doubt if we could express it for her, but I think she felt that there was something sweet and good in it all. I found this in her face as I watched her — for the little creature suddenly meant more to me than the ceremonies I had come to witness. After watching the drill of the uniformed men, she looked up at me wonderingly and said: "What does it mean?"

"It means, little one," said I, "that all this marching and music and this big monument trimmed with flowers, this great day of celebrating is for the brave soldiers who fought and died for our country, for you, and for me. Now, the men are going to put flowers on the soldiers' graves, because they were brave men."

"Ah!" said she, with a satisfied little look, "I'll go too. Will you come?"

I grasped the heavy basket and took the little hand in mine, and we trudged on toward the city of the dead. She scarcely spoke on the way, but clung to the bunch of daisies in her hand, and said softly to herself and to her blossoms: "Papa was a soldier."

When we reached the quiet city she looked about with more wonder than ever in the blue eyes, and asked me were the people who lived inside the white doors angels, and I said, "Yes."

Pointing to the lot of the unknown dead, she said:

"Who is over there under all those little flags?"

I explained to her, and she said:

"He must be there; they never knew where he was killed. I think he is there," and she drew me away from the crowd toward the rows of graves with the flag at each head.

"I don't know which is his, but I'll put the daisies here by this little flag."

She knelt at the head of one grave and laid her bunch of daisies down tenderly, then the large eyes looked up straight through the sunlight and blue sky, and with the little hands clasped on her breast, said:

"Can you see me, papa? I'm your own little girl. If this isn't your bed, you can look down and know the flowers are meant for you, and know this is your little girl, and she loves you."

Then, looking at the basket: "I could cover this brown bed all over, couldn't I? There are enough left, but then, perhaps, these other soldiers haven't any little girl to give them flowers, I guess I had better put one bunch on every grave." So the little Saint Marguerite went about on her own small flower mission, and only regretted that her daisies would not go "all around," and then said:

"I hope they all know we are proud of them."

As I looked at the hopeful face, I thought that if the soldier-father could not see his little one, the Great Father saw and blessed a new sweetness in life even in this tiny nature, whose true little heart had found the very deepest meaning of this Decoration Day.

———

THE WHISTLING REGIMENT

James Clarence Harvey

WHEN the North and South had parted, and the
    boom of the signal gun
Had wakened the Northern heroes, for the great
    deeds to be done,
When the nation's cry for soldiers had echoed o'er
    hill and dale,
When hot youth flushed with courage, while the
    mother's cheek turned pale,
In the woods of old New England, as the day sank
    down the west,
A loved one stood beside me, her brown head on
    my breast.
From the earliest hours of childhood our paths had
    been as one,
Her heart was in my keeping, though I knew not
    when 'twas won ;
We had learned to love each other, in a half un
    spoken way,

But it ripened to full completeness when the parting
    came that day,
Not a tear in the eyes of azure, but a deep and
    fervent prayer,
That seemed to say: "God bless you, and guard
    you, everywhere."
At the call for volunteers, her face was like drifted
    snow;
She read in my eyes a question and her loyal heart
    said, "Go,"
As the roll of the drums drew nearer, through the
    leaves of the rustling trees,
The strains of Annie Laurie were borne to us on
    the breeze.
Then I drew her pale face nearer and said: "Brave
    heart and true,
Your tender love and prayers shall bring me back
    to you."
And I called her my Annie Laurie and whispered
    to her that I
For her sweet sake was willing — to lay me down
    and die.
And I said: "Through the days of danger, that
    little song shall be
Like a pass-word from this hillside, to bring your
    love to me."
Oh! many a time, at nightfall, in the very shades
    of death,

When the picket lines were pacing their rounds
      with bated breath,
The lips of strong men trembled and brave breasts
      heaved a sigh,
When some one whistled softly: "I'd lay me
      down and die."
The tender little ballad our watch-word soon
      became,
And in place of Annie Laurie each had a loved
      one's name.
In the very front of battle, where the bullets
      thickest fly,
The boys from old New England ofttimes went
      rushing by,
And the rebel lines before us gave way where'er
      we went,
For the gray coats fled in terror from the "whistling
      regiment."
Amidst the roar of the cannon, and the shriek of
      the shells on high,
You could hear the brave boys whistling: "I'd lay
      me down and die."
But, alas! though truth is mighty and right will,
      at last, prevail,
There are times when the best and bravest, by the
      wrong outnumbered, fail;
And thus, one day, in a skirmish, but a half-hour's
      fight at most,

A score of the whistling soldiers were caught by
    the rebel host.
With hands tied fast behind us, we were dragged to
    a prison pen,
Where hollow-eyed and starving, lay a thousand
    loyal men.
No roof but the vault of heaven, no bed save the
    beaten sod,
Shut in from the world around us, by a wall where
    the sentries trod,
For a time our Annie Laurie brought cheer to that
    prison pen;
A hope to the hearts of the living; a smile to the
    dying men.
But the spark of Hope burned dimly, when each
    day's setting sun
Dropped the pall of night o'er a comrade, whose
    sands of life were run.
One night, in a dismal corner, where the shadows
    darkest fell,
We huddled close together, to hear a soldier
    tell
The tales of dear New England and of loved ones
    waiting there,
When, Hark! a soft, low whistle pierced through
    the heavy air,
And the strain was Annie Laurie. Each caught
    the other's eye,

And with trembling lips we answered: "I'd lay
    me down and die."
From the earth, near the wall behind us, a hand
    came struggling through,
With a crumpled bit of paper for the captive boys
    in blue.
And the name! My God! 'Twas Annie, my Annie,
    true and brave,
From the hills of old New England she had followed
    me to save.
"Not a word or a sign, but follow where'er you may
    be led;
Bring four of your comrades with you," was all
    that the writing said.
Only eight were left of the twenty, and lots were
    quickly thrown,
Then our trembling fingers widened the space
    where the hand had shown.
With a stealthy glance at the sentries, the prisoners
    gathered round,
And the five whom fate had chosen stole silent
    underground,
On, on, through the damp earth creeping, we
    followed our dusky guide,
Till under a bank o'erhanging, we came to the
    riverside:
"Straight over," a low voice whispered, "where
    you see yon beacon light."

And ere we could say, "God bless you," he
vanished into the night.

Through the fog and damp of the river, when the
moon was hid from sight,

With a fond, old, faithful negro, brave Annie had
crossed each night;

And the long, dark, narrow passage had grown till
we heard close by

The notes of the dear old pass-word: "I'd lay me
down and die."

With oar-locks muffled and silent, we pushed out
into the stream,

When a shot rang out on the stillness.   We could
see by the musket gleam,

A single sentry firing, but the balls passed harmless by,

For the stars had hid their faces and clouds swept
o'er the sky.

O God! How that beacon burning, brought joy to
my heart, that night,

For I knew whose hand had kindled that fire to
guide our flight.

The new-born hope of freedom filled every arm
with strength,

And we pulled at the oars like giants till the shore
was reached at length.

We sprang from the skiff, half fainting, once more
in the land of the free,

And the lips of my love were waiting to welcome
    and comfort me.
In my wasted arms I held her, while the weary
    boys close by
Breathed low, "For Annie Laurie, I'd lay me
    down and die."

———

FUTURE OF THE PHILIPPINES

William McKinley

I DO not know why in the year 1899 this republic
has unexpectedly had placed before it mighty
problems which it must face and meet. They
have come and are here, and they could not be
kept away. Many who were impatient for the conflict a year ago, apparently heedless of its larger
results, are the first to cry out against the far-
reaching consequences of their own act. Those
of us who dreaded war most, and whose every
effort was directed to prevent it, had fears of new
and grave problems which might follow its inaugu-
ration.

The evolution of events which no man could control has brought these problems upon us. Certain
it is that they have not come through any fault on
our own part, but as a high obligation, and we
meet them with clear conscience and unselfish

purpose, and with good heart resolve to undertake
their solution.

The Philippines, like Cuba and Porto Rico, were
intrusted to our hands by the war, and to that
great trust, under the providence of God and in
the name of human progress and civilization, we
are committed.   It is a trust we have not sought;
it is a trust from which we will not flinch.   The
American people will hold up the hands of their
servants at home to whom they commit its execution, while Dewey and Otis and the brave men
whom they command will have the support of the
country in upholding our flag where it now floats,
the symbol and assurance of liberty and justice.

What nation was ever able to write an accurate
programme of the war upon which it was entering,
much less decree in advance the scope of its
results?   Congress can declare war, but a higher
power decrees its bounds, and fixes its relations
and responsibilities.   The President can direct the
movements of soldiers on the field and fleets upon
the sea, but he cannot foresee the close of such
movements or prescribe their limits.   He cannot
anticipate or avoid the consequences, but he must
meet them.   No accurate map of nations engaged
in war can be traced until the war is over, nor can
the measure of responsibility be fixed till the last
gun is fired and the verdict embodied in the stipu-
lations of peace.

We have now ended the war with Spain. The treaty has been ratified by the votes of more than two-thirds of the Senate of the United States and by the judgment of nine-tenths of the people. No nation was ever more fortunate in war or more honorable in its negotiations in peace. Spain is now eliminated from the problem. It remains to ask what we shall now do. I do not intrude upon the duties of Congress, or seek to anticipate or forestall its action. I only say that the treaty of peace, honorably secured, having been ratified by the United States, and, as we confidently expect, shortly to be ratified in Spain, Congress will have the power, and, I am sure, the purpose, to do what in good morals is right and just and humane for these people in distant seas.

It is sometimes hard to determine what is best to do, and the best thing to do is oftentimes the hardest. The prophet of evil would do nothing because he flinches at sacrifice and effort, and to do nothing is easiest and involves the least cost. On those who have things to do there rests a responsibility which is not on those who have no obligations as doers. If the doubters were in a majority, there would, it is true, be no labor, no sacrifice, no anxiety, and no burden raised or carried; no contribution from our ease and purse and comfort to the welfare of others, or even to the extension of our resources to the welfare of ourselves. There would be ease, but, alas! there would be nothing done.

But grave problems come in the life of a nation, however much men may seek to avoid them. They come without our seeking, why, we do not know and it is not always given us to know; but the generation on which they are forced cannot avoid the responsibility of honestly striving for their solution. We may not know precisely how to solve them, but we can make an honest effort to that end, and if made in conscience, justice and honor, it will not be in vain.

The future of the Philippine Islands is now in the hands of the American people. Until the treaty was ratified or rejected the executive department of this Government could only preserve the peace and protect life and property. That treaty now commits the free and enfranchised Filipinos to the guiding hand and the liberalizing influences, the generous sympathies, the uplifting education, not of their American masters, but of their American emancipators.

Until Congress shall direct otherwise, it will be the duty of the executive to possess and hold the Philippines, giving to the people thereof peace and beneficent government, affording them every opportunity to prosecute their lawful pursuits, encouraging them in thrift and industry, making them feel and know that we are their friends, not their enemies, that their good is our aim, that their welfare is our welfare, but that neither their aspirations nor ours can be realized until our authority is recognized and unquestioned.

That the inhabitants of the Philippines will be benefited by this Republic is my unshaken belief. That they will have a kindlier government under our guidance, and that they will be aided in every possible way to be a self-respecting and self-governing people is as true as that the American people love liberty and have an abiding faith in their own government and in their own institutions.

No imperial designs lurk in the American mind. They are alien to American sentiment, thought and purpose. Our priceless principles undergo no change under a tropical sun. They go with the flag. They are wrought in every one of its sacred folds, and are indistinguishable as its shining stars.

> " Why read ye not the changeless truth,
> The free can conquer but to save."

If we can benefit these remote peoples, who will object? If in the years of the future they are established in government under law and liberty, who will regret our perils and sacrifices? Who will not rejoice in our heroism and humanity? Always perils, and always after them safety; always darkness and clouds, but always shining through them the light and the sunshine; always cost and sacrifice, but always after them the fruition of liberty, education and civilization.

I have no light or knowledge not common to my countrymen.   I do not prophesy.   The present is all-absorbing to me, but I cannot bound my vision by the blood-stained trenches around Manila, where every red drop, whether from the veins of an American soldier or a misguided Filipino, is anguish to my heart; but by the broad range of future years, when that group of islands, under the impulse of the year just past, shall have become the gems and glories of those tropical seas; a land of plenty and increasing possibilities; a people relieved from savage indolence and habits, devoted to the arts of peace, in touch with the commerce and trade of all nations, enjoying the blessings of freedom, of civil and religious liberty, of education and of homes, and whose children and children's children shall for ages hence bless the American Republic because it emancipated and redeemed their fatherland and set them in the pathway of the world's best civilization.

THE DISTRICT SCHOOL

Edwin H. Chapin

I would select as a symbol of our Republic whatever represents the privilege of free thought; and, as a sign and instrument of this, I would point to some district school-house, rough, weather-worn, standing in some bleak corner of New York or New Hampshire, through whose windows the passer-by catches the confused hum of recitation, or at whose door he sees children of all conditions mingling in motley play. Of all conditions so far as external peculiarities go, but of one condition as the recognized possessors of an immortal mind. Those who have helped mould the Republic have clearly seen that although intelligence is not the foundation of national greatness (for there is something deeper than that), still it is the discerning and directing power upon which depends the right use even of moral elements. They have scouted the notion that there is any ultimate evil in diffused knowledge, any such thing as "dangerous truth," and have affirmed that the best way to winnow the false from the true is to equip and set going the intellectual machine by which God has ordained that the work shall be done. It has been felt that if the State can properly extend its influence anywhere beyond the restrictive limits of evil or the punishment of overt wrong, if anywhere it may exercise a positive influence for good, it is here, where it does not interfere on the one hand with those outward pursuits which should be left to individual choice, nor on the other, with those inward sanctities which pertain to conscience and to God; it is here, in that region of our personality from which we can discern our duty and fill our place. For the intellect is the most neutral of all our qualities.

Man is swayed by the animal propensities of his nature; he is swayed by the moral and religious elements of his nature, but the intellect, by itself, is not a motive power. It is a light, and no one will object to its being kindled, except those who by that objection virtually confess that they fear the light. And this work of kindling is just what the State purposes to do for the child, leaving his religious convictions to such helps as conscience has chosen, and his position in life to the decision of circumstances. There is no way in which it can show so much impartiality, and exercise practically the most essential conception of freedom; for thus it recognizes a common inheritance — the possession of mind — something which is of more importance than any external condition; something on which rests the claim of human freedom; for the charter of man's liberty is his soul, not his estate. It says to the poorest child: "You are rich in this one endowment, before which all external possessions grow dim. No piled-up wealth, no social station, no throne, reaches as high as that spiritual plane upon which every human being stands by virtue of his humanity. And from that plane, mingling now in the common school with the lowliest and the lordliest, we give you the opportunity to ascend as high as you may. We put into your hands the key of knowledge, leaving your religious convictions, with which we dare not interfere, to your chosen guides. So far as the intellectual path may lead, it is open to you. Go free!" And when we consider the great principles which are thus practically confessed; when we consider the vast consequences which grow out of this, I think that little district school-house dilates, grows splendid, makes our hearts beat with admiration and gratitude, makes us resolve that, at all events, that must stand; for indeed it is one of the noblest symbols of the Republic, a sign and instrument of a great people having great power.

TRUE COURAGE

ADAPTED

It was during the famous battle of Chickamauga, at the time the Army of the Cumberland was almost routed, that General Rosecrans found it was necessary to send some one to inform General Thomas of his position, in order that he might be prepared to meet the Confederates under General Longstreet.

The Confederates held a position between two bodies of Federal forces and were preparing for the final charge that was to effect the complete destruction of the Union forces. It was at this critical moment that Garfield proved that he was a man of most extraordinary courage by volunteering to undertake that hazardous ride. There was only the barest possibility that he would escape with his life. Rosecrans, with reluctance, gave his hand to his brave staff officer, saying: "As you will, General," and then, his voice becoming stifled with his deep emotion, added: "We may not meet again, good-by; God bless you." Two orderlies went with him.

Although Thomas was only a few miles distant, they were forced to take a very circuitous route through tangled woods and open road, in order to reach him, and there was not a foot of this distance where they were not in danger of encountering the enemy.

They passed Rossville without meeting a rebel. Suddenly they encountered a volley of minie balls, as thick as hail, and the two orderlies and one horse dropped in their tracks, dead. Thank God, Garfield was mounted on a noble horse that knew his master's bridle hand as well as he knew the fence that he cleared at one bound. A hundred feet away the opposite fence was lined with gray blouses, and Garfield saw at a glance that they were loading for another volley. With a hero's determination he shut his teeth and put the spurs into his faithful horse's sides. His only chance was to zigzag across the cotton field, for, could they only get a steady aim at him, he was a dead man, and the Army of the Cumberland was lost. Up the hill he went, tacking from one side to the other. Another volley bellowed out from the woods below. His horse was struck — a flesh wound — but the noble animal only galloped forward the faster. He succeeded in reaching the summit and was half way over when another volley echoed along the hill, but it was too late, for he was already in the midst of a small body of bluecoats with his old friend, General McCook, at their head. He heard the welcome words: "My God, Garfield, I thought you were killed! How you have escaped is a miracle." Garfield's horse had been struck twice. At a breakneck speed they went forward through plowed fields and tangled woods, and over broken and rocky hills, for four weary miles, until they climbed a wooded crest and were within sight of Thomas. Shot and shell and canister plowed up the ground all about Garfield, but in the midst of it he halted, and with uplifted right arm, and eyes full of tears, he shouted, as he caught sight of Thomas: "There he is, God bless the old hero! he has saved the army!" Then he plunged down the hill through the fiery storm, and in five minutes more was by the side of Thomas, and had delivered his message.

Now, let us turn to another incident in the life of General Garfield. The war between the North and the South was over. It was the morning after Abraham Lincoln's assassination — the whole nation was excited. Even those who so recently wished to divide the land in twain were mourning the loss of him who was their best friend. New York was wild with frenzy, people feared that the nation would collapse, that the bloody scenes of the French Revolution would be reënacted. A great convention had been called in New York. Long before the hour set — eleven o'clock — an army of fifty thousand persons had assembled, cramming and jamming, wedged in as tight as men could be. Not a hurrah was heard; a deathly silence pervaded the whole place. Suddenly an ominous muttering arose and spread like a rising wave up the street toward Broadway, and again easterly toward the river. Soon two pieces of scantling, crossed at the top like the letter "X," stood out above the heads of the crowd. "Vengeance!" was the cry. On the right suddenly the shout arose: "*The World! The World!* The office of *The World!*" At this critical moment a man stepped forward, holding in one hand a small flag and with the other beckoning to the crowd. "Another telegram from Washington!" An awful silence ensued. A right hand was lifted toward the heavens, and a voice, clear and steady, rang out:

"Fellow citizens, clouds and darkness are round about Him. His pavilion is dark waters and thick clouds of the skies. Justice and judgment are the establishment of His throne. Mercy and Truth shall go before His face. Fellow citizens, God reigns, and the Government at Washington still lives."

That short message, delivered in a simple manner, did what all the police and military forces in New York could not have done. It calmed the frenzied, checked rashness, and preserved the dignity of the people. As the boiling wave subsides and settles to the sea when strong winds beat it down, so the tumult of the people sank and became still.

What might have happened had the swaying and maddened mob been let loose, no one can tell. The man for the crisis was on the spot. He was the hero of the famous ride of Chickamauga.

THE SOUL OF THE VIOLIN

Margaret Mantel Merrill

"IT has come at last, old comrade, it has come
at last — the time when you and I must say good-
bye. God knows I wish I could sell myself instead
of you. But I am worthless, while you — do you
know, my beauty? A Shylock down the street,
the man who has all else I own save you, has
offered me five hundred dollars if I will give you to
him — five hundred dollars to a man who has not
a coat to his back, a roof to cover him, or a crumb
of bread to eat! Why do I hesitate? You are
only some bits of wood and a few trumpery
strings — not much for a man to starve for. I
have only to run down the stairs with you — a few
steps more — hand you over the counter — the
thing is done; and I have five hundred dollars! I
can leave this wretched, rat-ridden hole. I can
have food to eat such as I have not tasted for a
year. I can mingle again with the men I used to
know. I can be one of them. Five hundred dollars! Why, that is wealth, wondrous wealth!
And all for you — you thing without a stomach.
You cannot know hunger, you, body without a
soul. Stay — am I sure of that?"

The man passes his fingers over the strings
and bends his head to listen. The soft vibrations

follow each other like sweet, half-forgotten thoughts.

"Your E-string is a trifle flat," says the man. "Well, it doesn't matter."

He rises hastily, possessed by a sudden determination, opens the case, and is about to thrust the violin inside, when he stops. A faint tremor of sound is still audible. It seems almost like a whisper of pain. The man lifts the violin again in his arms and lays his cheek upon it.

"What, old comrade, does it hurt you, too? Ah! I've wronged you. You have a heart. You can feel. I almost believe you can remember.

"Let me see. How long has it been? Twenty, thirty, thirty-five years. Think of that, old comrade. Thirty-five years! The average lifetime of man we have been together. And I knew you long before that. You were in a funny old shop, kept by a man who had owned you longer than I have. He would show you to the people who came, and allowed them to read your inscription, 'Cremona, 1731.' But he would not sell you. It is not probable that he was ever hungry. I loved you then, you inanimate thing of wood. I loved to hold you and hear you sing. I longed for you, as I had never longed for anything before. One day the old man sent for me.

"'Bring me your old violin,'" he said, 'and you shall have the Cremona.'

" ' To keep !' I exclaimed.

" ' Yes,' said the old man, ' to keep. For I am sure you will keep it. I'm old. Some one else will soon take possession here, and the Cremona might be sold into strange hands. I should not like that. I would rather give it to you.'

" So I took you home with me, and sat up half the night drawing the bow softly over your strings. I was the happiest boy in the world, I think. I laid you where, if I waked in the night, I could reach out and touch you. I would not have taken a kingdom in exchange for you then. Ah! but then I was not hungry. What animals we are, after all!"

The man still held the violin against his cheek, passing his hands gently along the strings, and talking on in a dreamy way, as if he scarcely knew that he spoke at all.

" Thirty-five years ! and we have seen the world together. We have tasted its sweets and its bitterness. Kings and beggars have listened to you, and both have loved you.

" Do you remember the night in Berlin, when we played *The Dream,* and the beautiful woman in the box at the right threw a great red rose ? It caught upon one of your strings — caught and hung by a thorn. And when I tried to release it, the blood-red petals fell in a shower at my feet. Then we played *The Last Rose of Summer.* I'm sure you had a heart that night. I could feel it vibrate with the quivering of your strings. There were tears in many eyes when we had finished, and she — I think the music had taken possession of her. For she rose, crying out :

" ' No, no ! It is not the last, the world is full of roses. See!' and she threw a great armful of white and red blossoms.

" I wonder if she loved me best, or you ? It was in the time of roses, when she, the rose of all the world, lay dead. You must remember that, old comrade. When it was dark, when all the rest had gone and left her, we went to say good-bye. The world was full of roses then, and I heaped them over her. Then you sang. Oh! how you sang! I have always believed that her soul was borne away on the wings of your song, carrying the perfume of the roses with it. The next time we played, some one threw a rose and I set my heel upon it. What right had roses to bloom when she was dead?

" We have done badly since then, you and I. Someway, things ceased to seem worth striving for. And you have been dearer, because you were the only one who knew and understood. And yet I said you had no soul. Forgive me, old comrade! A man is not to be blamed for what he says when he's hungry.

" Ah, what a fool I am ; maundering away to

an old fiddle when I might be filling my empty stomach!"

The man sprang up, thrust the violin rudely into its case, closed the lid with a bang, seized it and stopped, listening.   The strings were quivering from his rough handling.   He heard a sigh, faint as the farewell breath from the lips of a loved one dying.   The man set his feet hard, took another step, stopped again.   Then, suddenly, he clasped the violin in his arms.

"No, no, I cannot, I cannot!   I will not!   It may be folly; it is folly.   It is madness.   No matter.   I will not do it, I'm not hungry now."

The man opens the case, lifts the violin again, and holds it in his arms as if it were a child.

" To think that I ever dreamed of selling you, my treasure!   But a devil prompted me — the demon of hunger.   It is gone now.   I am quite content, quite satisfied.   Come, sing to me, and I shall be altogether happy."

The man raises the violin and draws the bow.

" Ah!   that E-string!   There — so — that is better.   Now we are all right.   And we are happy, are we not?   Sing to me of the rose and of her.   See!   she is in the box yonder, all among her blossoms.   She is smiling and throwing us handfuls, red and white.   We must do our best, our very best, when she listens."

The man's eyes kindle and burn.   His pale

cheeks flush. Starvation and rags are far away and forgotten things. He is again the master of music. The foul attic room has widened and brightened into a great, glittering amphitheater wherein thousands sit, breathless under the spell of that divine melody. The man's soul is breathing itself upon the strings; and how they respond! They shiver with sobs; they vibrate with laughter; they shout in exultation.

"Hear! hear! my comrade!" cries the man. "Bravos! encores! Ah, we have conquered the world to-night. How the lights glitter! This is ecstasy — this is heaven!"

Wilder and wilder grows the music. Faster and faster flies the bow.

Snap! a string breaks. Snap! another.

The weird strains sink to a wailing, minor key. The arm that holds the bow grows unsteady. The wild eyes cease their feverish shifting and fasten themselves upon one spot at the right. The tense features relax into a smile. The voice is very low and very tender:

"One more rose, my beauty, my queen of all the world. The lights are growing dim. My sight is failing. I can see only you, only you!"

Snap! The last string breaks.

AFTER THE BATTLE.

JAMES DAWSON

YOU have found me out at last, Will ; sit down
    beside me here —
It is not quite so hard to die when one we love is
    near ;
You and I have known each other since we ran
    about the glen,
When as boys we played as soldiers, and wished
    that we were men.

    *   *   *   *   *   *

But hark ! I hear the roll of drums, and at that
    stirring sound
The Angel of the Battle spreads its dusky wings
    around ;
I must tell you of the battle, tho' my breath is fail-
    ing fast,
For within my dying spirit sweeps the rousing
    battle blast.

Well, we scrambled through the vineyard, and we
    swam across the stream,
Above, from out the battery's smoke we saw the
    lightning's gleam ;
A few fell by the river, but we reached the farther
    banks,
And then we halted for a space to form our broken
    ranks.

Sir Colin passed along our line, our grand, old
      Highland chief;
He spoke, his words were few and stern, all soldier-
      like and brief:
" Now, Kilties, make me proud of this, my High-
      land plumed brigade,
We are going into battle, but let no one be afraid.

" Don't stay to tend the wounded, if any man shall
      shirk
I'll have his name placarded upon his parish kirk."
His parish kirk— at these two words the grim
      heights passed away,
And there, in all its quiet peace, our little village
      lay.

There were the well-known streets, and there the
      kirk upon the hill,
With the lowly graves of the loved and lost,
      around it calm and still —
That sight we ne'er may see again, there rose a
      smothered sob,
Along the line there seemed to pass a deep and
      passionate throb
Of eager yearning for the strife, each heart was
      all aflame
With courage high, to fight or die, for the dear
      land at hame.
We moved a little forward, then again, against our
      will,

We had to halt, for all this while the Russians on
    the hill
For us had true and deadly aim; each volley left
    its track,
And our fainted-hearted shouted that we might as
    well fall back.

Sir Colin heard the coward cry, and quick and fiery
    souled,
His pride flamed into fury, and his voice like thun-
    der rolled,
As to the cry he answer sent, a loud and thunder-
    ing " No !—
Better that every man should be upon the dust laid
    low
Than that we now should turn our backs to the
    proud, exulting foe !"
Still for a space we halted, still around the bullets
    flew,
And even as the moments fled our wild impatience
    grew.
At last the word was spoken, the long-looked-for
    signal made.
" Forward, Forty-second !" was all Sir Colin
    said,
But the visage of the veteran bore that strange
    and living light,
Which bespeaks the soldier's rapture at the com-
    ing of the fight.

As a steed bounds with his rider when at last he
    has got aim ;
As a stemmed up river rushes when it bursts
    toward the main,
As flies the unleashed hound or as 'scapes the
    caged bird,
So the Forty-second bounded when it heard its
    leader's word.

O Will! it is a splendid sight, a plumed and
    plaided host,
'Tis beautiful at home in peace, but its grandeur
    shines the most
When as then, in all the glory of its martial ardor
    dressed,
All swift and silent at the foe, the Forty-second
    pressed.
Our chieftain half restrained us, our headlong valor
    stayed,
Till we marched as firmly as we'd marched when
    home and on parade.

On in a grand, unbending line the plumes and
    tartan swept.
The bullets fell like hail, but still our stately step
    we kept.
Then when we felt the breath of the red-lipped
    Russian gun,

The deep tramp of a thousand men was as the
    tramp of one.
Before us loomed the foemen massed in columns
    dense and deep;
In a thin and slender British line, we climbed that
    deadly steep
As if it were some Highland hill our kilted lads
    upsprung,
While victory, like an eagle poised, between the
    armies hung;
But victory favored not the dense battalions of the
    Russ,
For soon we saw her gracious wings would fall
    that day on us.
Before our fire those foemen dense began to thin
    and sway.
Till with a groan, a wailing moan, they scattered
    in dismay.
Then we watched our brave Sir Colin, and we saw
    a signal given,
And from all along our slender line a shout went
    up to Heaven —
That shout which comes from free-born breasts,
    which foemen dread to hear,
And the Russian eagles vanished at a genuine
    British cheer!

Ah! war it is a glorious thing, but a deadly thing
    as well;

One face it wears is bright as Heaven, but one is
    dark as Hell ;
Deep wailing from full many a home of Russian,
    Frank and Turk,
And in England many tears shall be the fruit of
    this day's work.
Ah ! me — my pulse beats faintly, quicker and
    quicker comes my breath,
And chill and damp my forehead feels, damp with
    the dews of death.
Draw closer to my side, dear Will, and bend thine
    ear this way,
While I send by thee a last farewell to dear ones
    far away.
My father — tell my father that I lie by Alma's
    side —
That I like a soldier fought—that I like a soldier died;
Tell him ('twill give his manly heart a strange and
    stern delight)
That I was first across the stream, and foremost in
    the fight,
That though my mortal wound I got so early in the
    day,
I stemmed it up and would not yield, but strug-
    gled through the fray.
My mother — would that I could bear her sorrow
    and sharp pain ;
She'll dream at night that in the fight she sees her
    soldier slain ;

She'll wake at morn, with heavy heart, her sorrow
    to renew,
Suppressed by day, her tears will fall at even' like
    the dew.
But tell her to control her grief and wipe away her
    tears
When the joy-bells ring for victory and the air is
    rent with cheers ;
When old Scotland, 'mid her mourning for the
    wounded and the dead,
With calm and grand, yet tearful eyes, in pride
    uplifts her head,
That the Lion in her son's red blood, yet swift to
    battle leapt,
That thro' the long and peaceful years, he was not
    dead, but slept —
That still above her bannered host goes victory
    like a star,
And as England's first in peaceful acts, she still is
    first in war.
And all my friends and comrades, some I know
    will weep my fall,
Tell them I ne'er forgot them, give my kindest
    love to all.
Then, Will, with all things under heaven I now
    am almost done,
The silver chord is almost loosed — Life's sands
    are all but run ;

Sing to me *Auld Lang Syne,* then repeat that
    sweet old psalm
You and I once learned together in the Sabbath
    evening's calm.

———

FREEDOM AND PATRIOTISM

ORVILLE DEWEY

GOD has stamped upon our very humanity this
impress of freedom. It is the unchartered pre-
rogative of human nature. A soul ceases to be a
soul, in proportion as it ceases to be free. Strip it
of this, and you strip it of one of its essential
and characteristic attributes. It is this that draws
the footsteps of the wild Indian to his wide and
boundless desert-paths, and makes him prefer them
to the gay saloons and soft carpets of sumptuous
palaces. It is this that makes it so difficult to
bring him within the pale of artificial civilization.
Our roving tribes are perishing — a sad and solemn
sacrifice upon the altar of their wild freedom.
They come among us, and look with childish
wonder upon the perfection of our arts, and the
splendor of our habitations; they submit with
ennui and weariness, for a few days, to our burden-
some forms and restraints; and then turn their
faces to their forest homes, and resolve to push

those homes onward till they sink in the Pacific waves, rather than not be free.

It is thus that every people is attached to its country, just in proportion as it is free. No matter if that country be in the rocky fastnesses of Switzerland, amidst the snows of Tartary, or on the most barren and lonely island-shore; no matter if that country be so poor as to force away its children to other and richer lands, for employment and sustenance; yet when the songs of those free homes chance to fall upon the exile's ear, no soft and ravishing airs that wait upon the timid feastings of Asiatic opulence ever thrilled the heart with such mingled rapture and agony as those simple tones. Sad mementos might they be of poverty and want and toil; yet it was enough that they were mementos of happy freedom.

I have seen my countrymen, and I have been with them a fellow wanderer, in other lands; and little did I see or feel to warrant the apprehension, sometimes expressed, that foreign travel would weaken our patriotic attachments. One sigh for home — home, arose from all hearts. And why, from palaces and courts — why, from galleries of the arts, where the marble softens into life, and painting sheds an almost living presence of beauty around it — why, from the mountain's awful brow, and the lonely valleys and lakes touched with the sunset hues of old romance — why, from those

venerable and touching ruins to which our very
heart grows — why, from all these scenes, were
they looking beyond the swellings of the Atlantic
wave, to a dearer and holier spot of earth — their
own, own country? Doubtless, it was in part
because it *is* their country! But it was also, as
every one's experience will testify, because they
knew that *there* was no oppression, no pitiful ex-
action of petty tyranny; because that *there*, they
knew, was no accredited and irresistible religious
domination; because that *there*, they knew, they
should not meet the odious soldier at every corner,
nor swarms of imploring beggars, the victims of
misrule; that *there*, no curse causeless did fall, and
no blight, worse than plague and pestilence, did
descend amidst the pure dews of heaven; because,
in fine, that there, they knew, was liberty — upon
all the green hills, and amidst all the peaceful
villages — liberty, the wall of fire around the
humblest home; the crown of glory, studded with
her ever-blazing stars upon the proudest mansion!

CONSTANTIUS AND THE LION
George Croly

A PORTAL of the arena opened, and the combat-
ant, with a mantle thrown over his face and figure,
was led into the surroundery.   The lion roared
and ramped against the bars of his den at the
sight.   The guard put a sword and buckler into
the hands of the Christian, and he was left alone.
He drew the mantle from his face, and bent a
slow and firm look around the amphitheater.   His
fine countenance and lofty bearing raised a
universal shout of admiration.   He might have
stood for an Apollo encountering the Python.
His eye at last turned on mine.   Could I believe
my senses?   Constantius was before me.

All my rancor vanished.   An hour past I could
have struck the betrayer to the heart; I could
have called on the severest vengeance of man and
heaven to smite the destroyer of my child.   But
to see him hopelessly doomed, the man I had
honored for his noble qualities, whom I had even
loved, whose crime was, at the worst, but giving
way to the strongest temptation that can bewilder
the heart of man; to see that noble creature flung
to the savage beast, dying in tortures, torn
piecemeal before my eyes, and his misery wrought
by me! I would have obtested heaven and earth
to save him.   My limbs refused to stir.

The gate of the den was thrown back, and the lion rushed in with a roar and a bound that bore him half across the arena. I saw the sword glitter in the air; when it waved again it was covered with blood. A howl told that the blow had been driven home. The lion, one of the largest from Numidia, and made furious by thirst and hunger, an animal of prodigious power, crouched for an instant, as if to make sure of his prey, crept a few paces onward and sprang at the victim's throat. He was met by a second wound, but his impulse was irresistible. A cry of natural horror rang round the amphitheater. The struggle was now, for an instant, life or death. They rolled over each other; the lion, reared upon his hind feet, with gnashing teeth and distended talons, plunged on the man; again they rose together. Anxiety was now at its wildest height. The sword now swung around the champion's head in bloody circles. They fell again, covered with blood and dust. The hand of Constantius had grasped the lion's mane, and the furious bounds of the monster could not loose his hold; but his strength was evidently giving way; he still struck his terrible blows, but each was weaker than the one before; still, collecting his whole force for a last effort, he darted one mighty blow into the lion's throat and sank. The savage beast yelled, and, spouting out blood, fled around the

arena. But the hand still grasped the mane, and
the conqueror was dragged whirling through the
dust at his heels. A universal outcry now arose
to save him, if he were not already dead. But the
lion, though bleeding from every vein, was still
too terrible, and all shrank from the hazard. At
last the grasp gave way, and the body lay motionless on the ground.

What happened for some moments after I know
not. There was a struggle at the portal; a
female forced her way through the guards and
flung herself upon the victim. The sight of a
new prey roused the lion; he tore the ground with
his talons; he lashed his streaming sides with his
tail; he lifted up his mane and bared his fangs;
but his approaching was no longer with a bound;
he dreaded the sword, and came snuffing the blood
on the sand, and stealing round the body in
circuits still diminishing.

The confusion in the vast assemblage was now
extreme. Voices innumerable called for aid.
Women screamed and fainted, men burst into
indignant clamors at this prolonged cruelty. Even
the hard hearts of the populace, accustomed as
they were to the sacrifice of life, were roused to
honest curses. The guards grasped their arms,
and waited but for a sign from the Emperor.
But Nero gave no sign.

I looked upon the woman's face; it was

Salome! I sprang upon my feet. I called on her
name — called on her, by every feeling of nature,
to fly from that place of death, to come to my
arms, to think of the agonies of all that loved her.

She had raised the head of Constantius on her
knee, and was wiping the pale visage with her
hair. At the sound of my voice she looked up,
and calmly casting back the locks from her forehead, fixed her eyes upon me. She still knelt;
one hand supported the head — with the other she
pointed to it as her only answer. I again adjured
her. There was the silence of death among the
thousands around me. A fire flashed into her eye
— her cheek burned — she waved her hand with
an air of superb sorrow.

"I have come to die," she uttered, in a lofty
tone. "This bleeding body was my husband — I
have no father. The world contains to me but
this clay in my arms. Yet," and she kissed the
ashy lips before her, "yet, my Constantius, it was
to save that father that your generous heart defied
the peril of this hour. It was to redeem him from
the hand of evil that you abandoned your quiet
home! Yes, cruel father, here lies the noble
being that threw open your dungeon, that led
you safe through the conflagration; that, to the
last moment of his liberty, only sought how he
might serve and protect you." Tears at length
fell in floods from her eyes. "But," said she, in a

tone of wild power, "he was betrayed, and may the Power whose thunders avenge the cause of His people, pour down just retribution upon the head that dared ——"

I heard my own condemnation about to be pronounced by the lips of my own child. Wound up to the last degree of suffering, I tore my hair, leaped upon the bars before me, and plunged into the arena by her side. The height stunned me; I tottered a few paces and fell. The lion gave a roar and sprang upon me. I lay helpless under him; I heard the gnashing of his white fangs above.

An exulting shout arose. I saw him reel as if struck — gore filled his jaws. Another mighty blow was driven to his heart. He sprang high into the air with a howl. He dropped; he was dead. The amphitheater thundered with acclamations.

With Salome clinging to my bosom, Constantius raised me from the ground. The roar of the lion had roused him from his swoon, and two blows saved me. The falchion had broken in the heart of the monster. The whole multitude stood up, supplicating for our lives in the name of filial piety and heroism. Nero, devil as he was, dared not resist the strength of popular feeling. He waved a signal to the guards; the portal was opened, and my children, sustaining my feeble steps, showered with garlands from innumerable hands, slowly led me from the arena.

THE SCHOLAR OF THEBET BEN KHORAT

NATHANIEL P. WILLIS

NIGHT in Arabia. An hour ago,
Pale Dian had descended from the sky,
Flinging her cestus out upon the sea,
And at their watches, now, the solemn stars
Stood vigilant and lone ; and, dead asleep,
With not a shadow moving on its breast,
The breathing earth lay in its silver dew,
And, trembling on their myriad, viewless wings,
Th' imprisoned odors left the flowers to dream,
And stole away upon the yielding air.
Ben Khorat's tower stands shadowy and tall
In Mecca's loneliest street ; and ever there,
When night is at the deepest, burns his lamp
As constant as the Cynosure, and forth
From his loop'd window stretch the brazen tubes,
Pointing forever at the central star
Of that dim nebula just lifting now
Over Mount Arafat. The sky to-night
Is of a clearer blackness than is wont,
And far within its depths the colored stars
Sparkle like gems — capricious Antares
Flushing and paling in the Southern arch ;
And azure Lyra, like a woman's eye,
Burning with soft blue lustre ; and away

Over the desert the bright Polar star,
White as a flashing icicle ; and here,
Hung like a lamp above th' Arabian sea,
Mars with his dusky glow ; and fairer yet,
Mild Sirius, tinct with dewy violet,
Set like a flower upon the breast of Eve ;
And in the zenith sweet Pleiades
(Alas — that even a star may pass from heaven
And not be miss'd) — the linkéd Pleiades
Undimmed are there, though from the sister band
The fairest has gone down ; and, south away,
Hirundo with its little company ;
And white-browed Vesta, lamping on her path
Lonely and planet-calm, and, all through heaven,
Articulate almost, they troop to-night,
Like unrobed angels in a prophet's trance.

    *   *   *   *   Ben Khorat rose
And silently looked forth upon the East.
The dawn was stealing up into the sky
On its gray feet, the stars grew dim apace,
And faded, till the Morning Star alone,
Soft as a molten diamond's liquid fire,
Burn'd in the heavens.   The morn grew freshlier —
The upper clouds were faintly touched with gold ;
The fan-palms rustled in the open air ;
Daylight spread cool and broadly to the hills ;
And still the star was visible, and still
The young astronomer with straining eye

Drank its departing light into his soul.
It faded — melted — and the fiery rim
Of the clear sun came up, and painfully
The passionate scholar press'd upon his eyes
His dusky fingers, and, with limbs as weak
As a sick child's, turn'd fainting to his couch,
And slept.   *   *   *   *   *   *

*   *   It was the morning watch once more.
The clouds were drifting rapidly above,
And dim and fast the glimmering stars flew
        through,
And as the fitful gust sough'd mournfully,
The shutters shook, and on the sloping roof
Plash'd heavily large, single drops of rain —
And all was still again.   Ben Khorat sat
By the dim lamp, and, while his scholar slept,
Pored on the Chaldee wisdom.   At his feet,
Stretch'd on a pallet, lay the Arab boy,
Muttering fast in his unquiet sleep,
And working his dark fingers in his palms
Convulsively.   His sallow lips were pale,
And, as they moved, his teeth show'd ghastly
        through,
White as a charnel bone, and — closely drawn
Upon his sunken eyes, as if to press
Some frightful image from the bloodshot balls —
His lids a moment quiver'd, and again
Relax'd, half open in a calmer sleep.

Ben Khorat gazed upon the dropping sands
Of the departing hour.   The last white grain
Fell through, and with the tremulous hand of age
The old astrologer reversed the glass;
And, as the voiceless monitor went on,
Wasting and wasting with the precious hour,
He look'd upon it with a moving lip,
And, starting, turn'd his gaze up to the heavens,
Cursing the clouds impatiently.

                       "'Tis time!"
Mutter'd the dying scholar, and he dash'd
The tangled hair from his black eyes away,
And, seizing on Ben Khorat's mantle-folds,
He struggled to his feet, and falling prone
Upon the window ledge, gazed steadfastly
Into the East : —

        " There is a cloud between —
She sits this instant on the mountain's brow,
And that dusk veil hides all her glory now —
         Yet floats she as serene
Into the heavens !— O God, that even so
I could o'ermount *my* spirit-cloud, and go!

       " The cloud begins to drift !
Aha ! fling open ! 'tis the star — the sky!
Touch me, immortal mother ! and I fly !
         Wider ! thou cloudy rift

Let through ! — such glory should have radiant
      room !
Let through ! — a star-child on its light goes home!

    " Speak to me, brethren bright !
Ye who are floating in these living beams !
Ye who have come to me in starry dreams !
      Ye who have wing'd the light
Of our bright mother with its thoughts of flame --
(I *knew* it pass'd through spirits as it came) —

    " Tell me ! what power have ye?
What are the heights ye reach upon your wings ?
What know ye of the myriad wondrous things
      I perish but to see?
Are ye thought rapid ? — Can ye fly as far --
As instant as a thought, from star to star ?

    " Where has the Pleiad gone ?
Where have all missing stars found light and
      home ?
Who bids the Stella Mira go and come?
      Why sits the Pole-star lone ?
And why, like banded sisters, through the air
Go in bright troops the constellations fair ?

    " Ben Khorat ! dost thou mark?
The star ! the star ?   By heaven ! the cloud drifts
      o'er !

Gone — and I live! nay — will my heart beat
    more?
           Look! master! 'tis all dark —
Not a clear speck in heaven! — my eyeballs
    smother!
Break through the clouds once more! — oh, starry
    mother!

        " I will lie down!   Yet stay,
The rain beats out the odor from the gums,
And strangely soft to-night the spice-wind comes!
        I am a child alway
When it is on my forehead!   Abra sweet,
Would I were in the desert at thy feet!

        "My barb! my glorious steed!
Methinks my soul would mount upon its track
More fleetly, could I die upon thy back!
        How would thy thrilling speed
Quicken my pulse!   O, Allah!   I get wild!
Would that I were once more a desert child!

        " Nay — nay — I had forgot!
My mother! my star mother! — Ha! my breath
Stifles! — more air! — Ben Khorat, this is — death!
        Touch me! — I feel you not!
Dying! — Farewell! good master! — room! —
    more room!
Abra! I loved thee! star! bright star! I —
    come!"

TEACHINGS OF THE AMERICAN REVOLUTION

Jared Sparks

HAPPY was it for America, happy for the world, that a great name, a guardian genius, presided over her destinies in war, combining more than the virtues of the Roman Fabius and the Theban Epaminondas, and compared with whom the conquerors of the world, the Alexanders and Caesars, are but pageants crimsoned with blood and decked with the trophies of slaughter, objects equally of the wonder and the execration of mankind. The hero of America was the conqueror only of his country's foes, and the hearts of his countrymen. To the one he was a terror, and in the other he gained an ascendency, supreme, unrivalled, the tribute of admiring gratitude, the reward of a nation's love.

The American armies, compared with the en battled legions of the old world, were small in numbers, but the soul of a whole people centred in the bosom of those more than Spartan bands, and vibrated quickly and keenly with every incident that befell them, whether in their feats of valor, or the acuteness of their sufferings. The country itself was one wide battle-field, in which not merely the life-blood, but the dearest interests, the sustaining hopes, of every individual, were at stake. It

was not a war of pride and ambition between
monarchs, in which an island or a province might
be the award of success; it was a contest for
personal liberty and civil rights, coming down in
its principles to the very sanctuary of home and
the fireside, and determining for every man the
measure of responsibility he should hold over his
own condition, possessions and happiness. The
spectacle was grand and new, and may well be
cited as the most glowing page in the annals of
progressive man.

The instructive lesson of history, teaching by
example, can nowhere be studied with more profit,
or with a better promise, than in this revolutionary
period of America; and especially by us, who sit
under the tree our fathers have planted, enjoy its
shade, and are nourished by its fruits. But little
is our merit, or gain, that we applaud their deeds,
unless we emulate their virtues. Love of country
was in them an absorbing principle, an undivided
feeling; not of a fragment, a section, but of the
whole country. Union was the arch on which they
raised the strong tower of a nation's independence.
Let the arm be palsied, that would loosen one
stone in the basis of this fair structure, or mar its
beauty; the tongue mute, that would dishonor
their names, by calculating the value of that which
they deemed without price.

They have left us an example already inscribed

in the world's memory; an example portentous to the aims of tyranny in every land; an example that will console in all ages the drooping aspirations of oppressed humanity. They have left us a written charter as a legacy, and as a guide to our course. But every day convinces us, that a written charter may become powerless. Ignorance may misinterpret it; ambition may assail, and faction destroy its vital parts; and aspiring knavery may at last sing its requiem on the tomb of departed liberty. It is the spirit which lives; in this is our safety and our hope; the spirit of our fathers; and while this dwells deeply in our remembrance, and its flame is cherished, ever burning, ever pure, on the altar of our hearts; while it incites us to think as they have thought, and do as they have done, the honor and the praise will be ours, to have preserved unimpaired the rich inheritance which they so nobly achieved.

THE ENGINEER'S LAST RUN

"Pile in the diamonds, Tom, for the run is long,
  And the Lake Shore train from the east is a little
      late;
  And the minute we hear the tap of the depot
      gong,
    The old girl pants to strike her liveliest gait.

The night is black as death, and the wind is in
  the west,
  And the sky above us streaked with dusky
    bars;
Whether it storms or not, the night will be dark
  at best,
  For that climbing bank of clouds is blotting
    out the stars.

"I wish we could start on time, Tom, for we're
  pullin' a heavy train,
  Three coaches, a smoker, two Pullmans, bag-
    gage, express and mail;
And the old girl leans at the draw-bar as though
  she could feel the strain —
  I can see her holding her drivers awfully close
    to the rail.
There goes the gong; look out, Tom, the signal
  is on your side.
  'Afraid!' I hear him; what does he signal?
    'All right,' say you, 'go ahead!'
Now girlie, we'll give these folks in the sleepers
  an all-night ride,
  And we'll laugh at the Mississippi ere the
    eastern skies are red.

"Steady, old girl! Go easy; look out for yourself
  — don't slip;
  Look out you now!   Hold — that's right —
    there ain't no hurry just yet;

Here's a handful of sand for your drivers; it'll
    help you to hold your grip,
    Look out for that crossing — don't stub your
        toe — easy, old girl, don't fret.
Now then, you run a little; we haven't no time
    to dream;
    I'll just let you take a six-mile gait till we're
        well outside of the yards;
So we're past Grand Crossing — now rush right
    along — just help yourself to the steam,
    And we'll give old Time and distance our
        swiftest and best regards.
Ha, ha! Do you feel her quiver, Tom? It's a
    little too fast, I know;
    She knows she has time to make up — she is
        running so wild and glad;
And I haven't the heart to hold her, Tom, when
    I see she wants to go;
    When I know by the throb of her nervous
        pulse that she wants to run so bad.

"It must be nearly morning, Tom, the night has
    worn away,
    But the skies grow blacker and darker, it
        seems, as the weary night wears on;
And though I can tell by the smell of the air that
    it must be nearly day,
    Yet the clouds have blotted out the stars that
        should pale in the early dawn.

She shows two gauges, doesn't she, Tom?   This
    light, I can't half see —
    The very headlight shows dull and dim, falters
        as it flickers along the rails;
I reckon I'm nervous with this long run; and it
    always seems to me
    That along in the early morning a fellow
        weakens and fails.

"We must be near the river, Tom; I wish I could
    see it now;
    But we'll hear it sweep round the great stone
        piers, I reckon, by and by;
We're right on time, and I don't feel afraid of
    anything, but, somehow
    I wish I could see old Burlington's hills, up
        looming against the sky.
Just feel her spring!   How eager she seems!
    How faster than life she goes!
    Hear when I touch the whistle, what an agony
        in her scream;
And you cannot count the whirling miles that
    over her shoulders she throws —
    Why, the night's run seems to me, boy, like a
        strange, wild, unreal dream.

"My hand is heavy; the whistle I blew just now I
    could not hear;
    And your voice is so strange and distant, Tom,
    I can't tell where you are.

Have we dropped the train? It's roar is hushed
     — but murmuring cold and clear,
  I can hear the sweep of the river now — it
     can't be very far.
The headlight's out, and this air-brake, boy — it
     won't work any more;
    There's something wrong, but I'll drive ahead;
     there is no cause for fear —
It's dark and still as the grave behind, it's dark
     on the track before.
    But the signal lights are set all right — 'The
     block ahead is clear.'

"The river is close ahead, boy, I can hear its
     ceaseless flow,
    Tho' I cannot see in the darkness the rush of
     its chilling tide;
  It isn't the Mississippi, Tom; it's some river that
     I don't know,
    And the shadowy sweep of its waters is dark
     and cold and wide.
There ain't no bridge I can see, Tom, but I know
     the way is sure,
    And I'm going to pull right straight ahead,
     through the quiet, starless night,
For I see across the river, and white and clear
     and pure,
    The signal lights burn steadily, and they're set
     — 'Come ahead; all right!'"

THE CRIMSON SHROUD OF OLAF GULDMAR

Marie Corelli

Valdemar Svensen was conscious of staggering blindly onward, weighted with a heavy, helpless burden — he felt the slippery pier beneath his feet, the driving snow and icy wind on his face — but he was as one in a dream, realizing nothing plainly, till with a wild start he seemed to awake — and lo ! he stood on the glassy deck of the "Valkyrie" with the body of his "King" stretched senseless before him !   Had he brought him there?   There, most certainly, Olaf Guldmar lay— his pallid face upturned, his hair and beard as white as the snow that clung to the masts of his vessel — his hand clinched on the fur garment that enwrapped him as with a robe of royalty.

Dropping on his knees beside him, Valdemar felt his heart — it still throbbed fitfully and feebly. Watching the intense calm of the grand, rugged face, this stern, weather-worn sailor — this man of superstitious and heathen imaginations — gave way to womanish tears — tears that were the outcome of sincere and passionate grief.

As he knelt and wept unrestrainedly, a soft change, a delicate transparence, swept over the dark bosom of the sky. Pale pink streaks glittered on the dusky horizon — darts of light began to climb upward into the clouds, and to plunge downward into the water — the radiance spread, and gradually formed into a broad band of deep crimson, which burned with a fixed and intense glow—topaz-like rays flickered and streamed about it, as though uncertain what fantastic shape they should take to best display their brilliancy. This tremulous hesitation of varying color did not last long ; the whole jewel-like mass swept together, expanding and contracting with extraordinary swiftness for a few seconds—then, suddenly and clearly defined in the sky, a kingly crown blazed forth — a crown of perfect shape, its five points distinctly and separately outlined, and flashing as with a million rubies and diamonds. The red luster warmly tinged the pale features of the dying man, and startled Valdemar, who sprang to his feet and gazed at that mystic aureola with a cry of wonder. At the same moment Olaf Guldmar stirred. Suddenly he opened his eyes, and realizing his surroundings, raised himself half erect.

"Set sail!" he cried, pointing with a majestic motion of his arm to the diadem glittering in the sky. "Why do we linger? The wind favors us and the tide sweeps forward—forward ! See how the lights beckon from the harbor!" He bent his brows and looked angrily at Svensen. "Do what thou hast to do!" and his tones were sharp and imperious. "I must press on!"

An expression of terror, pain and pity passed over the sailor's countenance — for one instant he hesitated — the next he descended into the hold of the vessel. He was absent for a very little space — but when he returned his eyes were wild, as though he had been engaged in some dark and criminal deed. Olaf Guldmar was still gazing at the brilliancy in the heavens, which seemed to increase in size and luster as the wind rose higher. Svensen took his hand — it was icy cold, and damp with the dews of death.

"Let me go with thee!" he implored in broken accents. "I fear nothing! Why should I not venture also on the last voyage?"

Guldmar made a faint but decided sign of rejection.

"The Viking sails alone to the grave of his fathers!" he said, with a serene and proud smile. "Alone — alone! Neither wife nor child nor vassal may have place with him in his ship — even so have the gods willed it. Farewell, Valdemar! Loosen the ropes and let me go! — thou servest me ill — hasten — I am weary of waiting——"

His head fell back — that mysterious shadow which darkens the face of the dying a moment before dissolution was on him now.

Just then a strange, suffocating odor began to

permeate the air — little wreaths of pale smoke made their slow way through the boards of the deck — and a fierce gust of wind, blowing seaward from the mountains, swayed the "Valkyrie" uneasily to and fro. Slowly, and with evident reluctance, Svensen commenced the work of detaching her from the pier — feeling instinctively all the while that his master's dying eyes were fixed upon him. When but one slender rope remained to be cast off, he knelt by the old man's side and whispered tremblingly that all was done. At the same moment a small, stealthy tongue of red flame curled upward through the deck from the hold, and Guldmar, observing this, smiled.

"I see thou hast redeemed thine oath," he said, gratefully pressing Svensen's hand. "'Tis the last act of thine allegiance — may the gods reward thy faithfulness! Peace be with thee! — we shall meet hereafter. Already the light shines from the Rainbow Bridge — there — there are the golden peaks of the hills and the stretch of the wide sea! Go, Valdemar! — delay no longer, for my soul is impatient — it burns, it struggles to be free! Go! — and — farewell!"

Stricken to the heart, and full of anguish — yet serf-like in his submission and resignation to the inevitable — Svensen kissed his master's hand for the last time. Then with a sort of fierce, sobbing groan, wrung from the very depths of his despairing grief, he turned resolutely away, and sprang off the vessel.   Standing at the extreme edge of the pier, he let slip ·the last rope that bound her — her sails filled and bulged outward — her cordage creaked, she shuddered on the water — lurched a little — then paused.

In that brief moment, a loud, triumphant cry rang through the air.   Olaf   Guldmar leaped upright on the deck, as though lifted by some invisible hand, and confronted his terrified servant, who gazed at him in fascinated amazement and awe.   His white hair gleamed like spun silver — his face was transfigured, and wore a strange, rapt look of pale yet splendid majesty — the dark furs that clung about him trailed in regal folds to his feet.

"Hark!" he cried, and his voice vibrated with deep and mellow clearness.   "Hark to the thunder of the galloping hoofs! — see! — see the glitter of the shield and spear!   She comes — ah! Thelma! Thelma!"   He raised his arms as though in ecstasy.   "Glory! — joy! — victory!"

And, like a noble tree struck down by lightning, he fell — dead!

Even as he fell, the "Valkyrie" plunged forward, driven forcibly by a swooping gust of wind, and scudded out of the fjord like a wild bird flying before a tempest — and, while she thus fled, a sheet of flame burst through her sides and blazed upward, mingling a lurid, smoky glow with the clear crimson radiance of the still brilliant and crown-like aurora. Following the current, she made swift way across the dark water in the direction of the Island of Seiland, and presently became a wondrous ship of fire! Fire flashed from her masts — fire folded up her spars and sails in a devouring embrace — fire that leaped and played and sent forth a million showering sparks hissingly into the waves beneath.

Shivering, yet regardless of the snow that began to fall thickly, Valdemar kept his post, staring, staring in drear fascination across the fjord, where the "Valkyrie" drifted, now a mass of flame blown fiercely by the wind, and gleaming red through the flaky snow-storm. The aurora borealis faded by gradual degrees, and the blazing ship was more than ever distinctly visible. Farther and farther she receded — the flames around her waving like banners in a battle — farther and farther still — till Valdemar Svensen, from his station on the pier, began to lose sight of her blazing timbers. As he looked, a long, uptwisting snake of fire appeared to leap from the vanishing "Valkyrie" — a snake that twined its glittering coils rapidly round and round on the wind, and as rapidly sank — down — down — to one glimmering spark which glowed redly, like a floating lamp for a brief space, and then was quenched forever! The ship had vanished!

SIEGE OF THE ALAMO

Elizabeth L. Saxon

Come, gather round, my boys, to-night,
    And I will strive to tell
Of the Alamo's bloody fight,
    And how her heroes fell.
'Twas in the dark and bloody days
    When Santa Anna's men
Made havoc in our Texas lands,
    On every field and glen.

The little fort was manned by few,
    But they were tried and brave
As ever rammed a bullet home,
    Or filled a soldier's grave;
Travis, as brave a gentleman
    As ever rode a steed,
Commander of the little fort
    In all its desperate need;

Crockett, the gallant pioneer,
    Whose life so well is known,
And Edwin Bowie, round whose fame
    Such deadly lustre shone.
These, with some hundred men,
    Had made their last and fatal stand,
With none to succor or defend
    In all broad Texas land.

Three thousand Mexic demons made
  The air with yells resound,
As they gathered like the hungry wolves
  The little fort around.
Again, and yet again, had sent
  The still undaunted few
For fresh recruits, from the neighboring forts,
  To aid their venture through.

Into their walls the shot and shell
  Fell ceaseless like the rain,
While many a Texas bullet sank
  Deep in some Mexic brain.
Besieged, beset on every side,
  Within was sickness dire,
And fever burned within their veins,
  Hot as Vesuvian fire.

At last the fatal day had come,
  The cruel force is cast
With all its power upon the fort,
  Their latest hope is past.
It needs to die as brave men should,
  When life's last hope is done;
No piteous wail the soldier makes
  Because his course is run.

Within the courtyard, 'round their chief,
  The still undaunted few

Are met to say the latest words
    Of courage and adieu.
"My gallant boys," their leader said,
    "Our final hope is o'er;
Now let us fight as desperate men
    Who hope to fight no more.
As long as coming races
    Heroic deeds shall tell,
Let them recount Alamo's siege,
    And how its forces fell.

"Brave Crockett, you who never yet
    Have shunned a foe to meet,
Can give us deeds of courage now
    To make our death-pang sweet.
See yonder waves our Lone Star flag,
    Our Texan banner brave;
The hands that wave, the eyes that wept,
    Shall never see our grave.
It matters not, the deeds we do
    Fond lips at last will tell,
And boys unborn recount the fight,
    Where Bowie fought and fell.

Hark! hear that yell!   'They're ours now!'"
    The words were hardly said,
When rushed the red fiends to their work,
    'Mid dying and the dead.
With rifles clubbed the Texans fought
    For vengeance, not for life,

And many a Mexic home was reft
  Of sire, in that short strife.
The feet sank deep in crimson stain,
  The fight raged everywhere.
Fannin had led the murderers on,
  And in his last despair
Stood ready to fire the magazine —
  Death found the hero there.

THE SCALING OF PERCÉ ROCK

Ranulph Delagarde, an Englishman, has been seized by a press-gang and carried aboard a French frigate commissioned to ravage the coasts of British America. He is made gunner, and after sailing for weeks they land at Percé Bay at which point his friends Elie Mattingley, Carterette (his daughter) and Sebastian Alixandre live. He deserts the vessel and plans to make his escape by climbing Percé Rock, which no man has ever attempted to do. On his way he meets Carterette, who has long loved him and now offers to take him to a place of safety and pleads with him not to climb the mountain, but he does not heed her entreaties.

THE tide was well out, the moon shining brightly. Ranulph reached the point where, if the rock was to be scaled at all, the ascent must be made. For a distance there was shelving where foothold might be had by a fearless man with a steady hold and sure balance.   After that came about a hundred feet where he would have to draw himself up, by juttings and crevices, hand over hand, where was no natural pathway.   Woe be to him if head grew dizzy, foot slipped or strength gave out; he would be broken to pieces on the hard sand below.   That second stage once passed, the ascent thence to the top would be easier; for though nearly as steep, it had more ledges, and offered fair vantage to a man with a foot like a mountain goat.   Ranulph had been aloft all weathers in his time, and his toes were as strong as another man's foot, and surer.

He started.   The toes caught in crevices, held on to ledges, glued themselves on to smooth surfaces; the knees clung like a rough-rider's to a saddle; the big hands, when once they got a purchase, fastened like an air-cup.

Slowly, slowly up, foot by foot, yard by yard, until one-third of the distance was climbed.   The suspense and strain were immeasurable.   But he struggled on and on, and at last reached a sort of flying pinnacle of rock, like a hook for the shields of the gods.

Here he ventured to look below, expecting to see Carterette, but there was only the white sand, and no sound save the long wash of the gulf.   He drew a horn of arrack from his pocket and drank. He had two hundred feet more to climb, and the next hundred would be the great ordeal.

He started again. This was travail indeed. His rough fingers, his toes, hard as horn almost, began bleeding. Once or twice he swung quite clear of the wall, hanging by his fingers to catch a surer foothold to right or left, and just getting it sometimes by an inch or less. The tension was terrible. His head seemed to swell and fill with blood; on the top it throbbed till it was ready to burst. His neck was aching horribly with constant looking up, the skin of his knees was gone, his ankles bruised. But he must keep on till he got to the top, or until he fell.

He was fighting on now in a kind of dream, quite apart from all usual feelings of this world. The earth itself seemed far away and he was toiling among vastnesses, himself a giant with colossal frame and huge, sprawling limbs. It was like a gruesome vision of the night, when the body is an elusive, stupendous mass that falls into space after a confused struggle with immensities. It was all mechanical, vague, almost numb, this effort to overcome a mountain. Yet it was precise and hugely expert, too for though there was a strange mist on the brain, the body felt its way with a singular certainty, as might some molluscan dweller of the sea, sensitive like a plant, intuitive like an animal. Yet at times it seemed that this vast body overcoming the mountain must let go its hold and slide away into the darkness of the depths.

Now there was a strange, convulsive shiver in every nerve — God have mercy, the time was come! No, not yet. At the very instant when it seemed the panti..g flesh and blood would be shaken off by the granite force repelling it, the fingers, like long antennae, touched horns of rock jutting out from ledges on the third escarpment of the wall. Here was the last point of the worst stage of the journey. Slowly, heavily, the body drew up to the shelf of limestone, and crouched in an inert bundle. There it lay for a long time.

While the long minutes went by, a voice kept calling up from below; calling, calling, at first eagerly, then anxiously, then with terror. By and by the bundle of life stirred, took shape, raised itself, and was changed into a man again, a thinking, conscious being, who now understood the meaning of this sound coming up from the earth below — or was it the sea? A human voice had at last pierced the awful exhaustion of the deadly labor, the peril and strife, which had numbed the brain while the body, in its instinct for existence, still clung to the rocky ledges. It had called the man back to earth — he was no longer a great animal, and the rock a monster with skin and scales of stone.

"Ranulph! Maître Ranulph! Ah, Ranulph!" called the voice.

Now he knew, and he answered down:

"All right! all right, Garche Carterette."

"Are you at the top?"

"No, but the rest is easy."

"Hurry, hurry, Ranulph! If they should come before you reach the top!"

"I'll soon be there."

"Are you hurt, Ranulph?"

"No, but my fingers are in rags. I am going now. A bitôt, Carterette!"

"Ranulph!"

"'Sh, 'sh; do not speak. I am starting."

There was silence for what seemed hours to the girl below. Foot by foot the man climbed on, no less cautious because the ascent was easier, for he was now weaker. But he was on the monster's neck now, and soon he should set his heel on it; he was not to be shaken off.

At last the victorious moment came. Over a jutting ledge he drew himself up by sheer strength and the rubber-like grip of his lacerated fingers, and now he lay flat and breathless upon the ground.

How soft and cool it was! This was long, sweet grass touching his face, making a couch like down for the battered, wearied body. Surely such travail had been more than mortal. And what was this vast fluttering over his head, this million-voiced discord round him, like the buffetings and cries of spirits welcoming another to their torment? He raised his head and laughed in triumph. These were the cormorants, gulls and gannets of the Percé Rock.

Legions of birds circled over him with cries so shrill that at first he did not hear Carterette's voice calling up to him. At last, however, remembering, he leaned over the cliff and saw her standing in the moonlight far below.

Her voice came up to him indistinctly because of the clatter of the birds. "Maître Ranulph! Ranulph!" She could not see him, for this part of the rock was in shadow.

"Ah, bah; all right!" he said, and taking hold of one end of the twine he had brought, he let the roll fall. It dropped almost at Carterette's feet. She tied to the end of it three loose ropes she had brought from the Post. He drew them up quickly, tied them together firmly, and let the great coil down. Ranulph's bundle, a tent and many things Carterette had brought, were drawn up.

"Ranulph! Ranulph!" came Carterette's voice again.

"Garçon Carterette!"

"You must help Sebastian Alixandre up," she said.

"Sebastian Alixandre! Is he there? Why does he want to come?"

"That is no matter," she called softly. "He is coming. He has the rope round his waist. Pull away!"

It was better, Ranulph thought to himself, that he should be on Percé Rock alone, but the terrible strain had bewildered him, and he could make no protest now.

"Don't start yet," he called down; "I'll pull when all's ready!"

He fell back from the edge to a place in the grass, where, tying the rope round his body, and seating himself, he could brace his feet against a ledge of rock. Then he pulled on the rope. It was round Carterette's waist.

Carterette had told her falsehood without shame, for she was of those to whom the end is more than the means. She began climbing, and Ranulph pulled steadily. Twice he felt the rope suddenly jerk when she lost her footing, but it came in evenly still, and he used a nose of rock as a sort of winch.

The climber was nearly two-thirds of the way up when a cannon-shot boomed out over the water, frightening again the vast covey of birds which shrieked and honked till the air was a maelstrom of cries. Then came another cannon-shot.

Ranulph's desertion was discovered. The fight was begun between a single Jersey shipwright and a French warship.

His strength, however, could not last much longer. Every muscle of his body had been strained and tortured, and even this lighter task tried him beyond endurance. His legs stiffened against the ledge of rock, the tension numbed his arms. He wondered how near Alixandre was to the top. Suddenly there was a pause, then a heavy jerk. Love of God — the rope was shooting through his fingers, his legs were giving way! He gathered himself together, and then with teeth, hands and body rigid with enormous effort, he pulled and pulled. Now he could not see. A mist swam before his eyes. Everything grew black, but he pulled on and on.

He never knew how the climber reached the top. But when the mist cleared away from his eyes, Carterette was bending over him.

THE BOAT RACE

From "Tom Brown at Oxford"

THOMAS HUGHES

THE crew had just finished their early dinner. Hark! the first gun! The St. Ambrose crew fingered their oars, put a last dash of grease on their rowlocks, and settled their feet against the stretchers. "Shall we push her off?" asked "bow." "No, I can give you another minute," said the coxswain, who was sitting, watch in hand, in the stern; "only be smart when I give the word. Eight seconds more only. Look out for the flash. Remember, all eyes in the boat."

There it comes, at last — the flash of the starting gun. Long before the sound of the report can roll up the river the whole pent-up life and energy which has been held in leash, as it were, for the last six minutes is let loose, and breaks away with a bound and a dash which he who has felt it will remember for his life, but the like of which will he ever feel again? The starting ropes drop from the coxswain's hands, the oars flash into the water, and gleam on the feather, the spray flies from them, and the boats leap forward.

The crowds on the bank scatter and rush along, each keeping as near as it may be to its own boat. Some of the men on the towing path, some on the very edge of, often in, the water — some slightly in advance, as if they could help to drag their boat forward — some behind, where they can see the pulling better — but all at full speed, in wild excitement, and shouting at the top of their voices to those to whom the honor of the college is laid. "Well pulled, all!" "Pick her up there, five!" "You're gaining, every stroke!" "Time in the bows!" "Bravo, St. Ambrose!" On they rushed by the side of the boats, jostling one another, stumbling, struggling, and panting along.

For the first ten strokes Tom Brown was in too great fear of making a mistake to feel or hear or see. His whole soul was glued to the back of the man before him, his one thought to keep time, and get his strength into the stroke.   But as the crew settled down into the well-known long sweep, con-sciousness returned.   While every muscle in his body was straining, and his chest heaved, and his heart leaped, every nerve seemed to be gathering new life and his senses to wake into unwonted acuteness.   He caught the scent of the wild thyme in the air, and found room in his brain to wonder how it could have got there, as he had never seen the plant near the river or smelt it before. Though his eye never wandered from the back of the man in front of him, he seemed to see all things at once; and amid the Babel of voices, and the dash and pulse of the stroke, and the laboring of his own breathing he heard a voice coming to him again and again, and clear as if there had been no other sound in the air: "Steady, two! steady! well pulled! steady, steady!"

The voice seemed to give him strength and keep him to his work.   And what work it was!   He had had many a hard pull in the last six weeks, but "never aught like this."   But it can't last forever; men's muscles are not steel, or their lungs bull's hide, and hearts can't go on pumping a hundred miles an hour long without bursting. The St. Ambrose's boat is well away from the boat behind.   There is a great gap between the accompanying crowds.   And now, as they near the Gut, she hangs for a moment or two in hand, though the roar from the banks grows louder and louder, and Tom is already aware that the St. Ambrose crowd is melting into the one ahead of them.

"We must be close to Exeter!" The thought flashes into him and into the rest of the crew at the same moment. For, all at once, the strain seems taken off their arms again. There is no more drag. She springs to the stroke as she did at the start; and the coxswain's face, which had darkened for a few seconds, lightens up again. "You're gaining! you're gaining!" now and then he mutters to the captain, who responds with a look, keeping his breath for other matters. Isn't he grand, the captain, as he comes forward like lightning, stroke after stroke, his back flat, his teeth set, his whole frame working from the hips with the steadiness of a machine? As the space still narrows, the eyes of the fiery little coxswain flash with excitement.

The two crowds are mingled now, and no mistake; and the shouts come all in a heap over the water. "Now, St. Ambrose, six strokes more!" "Now, Exeter, you're gaining; pick her up!" "Mind the Gut, Exeter!" "Bravo, St. Ambrose!" The water rushes by, still eddying from the strokes of the boat ahead. Tom fancies now he can hear the voice of their coxswain. In another moment both boats are in the Gut, and a storm of shouts reaches them from the crowd. "Well steered, well steered, St. Ambrose!" is the cry. Then the coxswain, motionless as a statue till now, lifts his right hand and whirls the tassel round his head: "Give it her now, boys; six strokes and we are into them!"

And while a mighty sound of shouts, murmurs, and music went up into the evening sky, the coxswain shook the tiller ropes again, the captain shouted, "Now, then, pick her up!" and the St. Ambrose boat shot up between the swarming banks at racing pace to her landing-place, the lion of the evening.

———

"PRINCE"

I THINK you remember a man we knew, who
  went by the name of "Prince,"
With sinews of iron, and nerves of steel, that were
  never known to wince!
How came he to win that nickname? Well, that's
  more than I now can say:
Because, perhaps, he was given to rule, and all of
  us liked his sway;
Because he was free with his cash, perhaps, or
  maybe because, like Saul,
He looked a king, and stood, without boots, head
  and shoulders out-topping us all.

Oh! yes, there were stories afloat, I know; he
  was wicked and wild, they said.
'Tis slander, I tell you; and what so base as a
  slander against the dead?

I know how he trifled with shot and steel, and
  deaths have been laid at his door;
But he never was guilty of murderous deed to
  settle a private score.
He was quick to avenge a comrade's wrong, or a
  comrade's right defend,
And never was known to break his word, nor ever
  to fail a friend.
I see him now as I saw him then — and yet 'tis a
  long while since —
A hero, if ever a hero lived, was he whom we nick-
  named " Prince."

Well, "Prince" had a friend — his pal, his mate,
  A little chap, curly and brown;
They both of them hailed from Virginia State,
  And were born in the self-same town;
And "Prince" would have died for Charley, I
  know,
  And Charley'd have died for him;
And if luck was high, or if luck was low,
  Together they'd sink or swim.

But there came a time when their path was crossed
  By a girl with an angel face,

And the love of the friends was swamped and lost
    In the passion that filled its place ;
'Twas a secret at first each kept from each,
    And neither would dare disclose,
Till they broke the ice with a heedless speech,
    And fronted each other as foes.

It wasn't her fault, I will take my oath ;
    She didn't flirt, even in fun ;
She only tried to be kind to both
    For the love she bore to one.
'Twould have gone to her heart, I know, to offend
    By speaking the truth pat down ;
For she liked the " Prince," though she loved his
        friend,
    The little chap, curly and brown.

Oh, " Prince " was the better man of the two,
    By far, I don't deny ;
Yet her love for Charley was tender and true,
    And it's no good asking why.
But a letter was left at Charley's door
    In a hand he knew, which said :
" The days that are past can return no more,
    And nothing can raise what's dead ;
For Faith and Love they have lied to me,
    While I was the dupe of each,
And honor in woman or man, I see,
    Is only a figure of speech."

Hard words enough—they might have been worse;
  I am glad he stopped short there;
Thank God he didn't denounce or curse!
  For he went, and we knew not where;
To the Southerners' camp he went, they said,
  To the war that had just begun ;
If he couldn't love he would fight instead,
  For the joy of his life was done.

The war that ended in 'sixty-five
Maybe, if we could, we wouldn't revive.
In twenty-five years one has ceased to fret;
But there's one day's fighting I can't forget —
Balls and bullets, and shot and shell,
Musketry rattling, powder smell;
Horses and riders dying — dead,
And a scorching sun in the sky o'erhead;
And the van of our troops was led that day
By one whom nothing could stop nor stay.

When last I saw him — 'twas six months since—
He had changed in the time, yet I knew the
    " Prince."
The Virginia men were all to the front,
To lead their comrades, and bear the brunt;
But when the night fell, cold and damp,
There were twenty down in the enemy's camp ;
Ten to return in exchange for ten
The Southerners had of the Northerners' men —

Six for the prison, four to be shot —
And the fate of each to be drawn by lot!

And "Prince" was one of that fated row,
    Close-guarded the long night through;
And Charley, who'd joined but a week ago,
    Was one of the prisoners too.
'Twas strange that they thus should meet again,
    Each waiting for death or life;
None knew what the one was thinking then,
    But the other — he thought of his wife.

And never a word was spoke that night;
But when the day broke fair and bright,
    By the glare of the morning sky
The lots were drawn, and the "Prince" was free
To go once more to his home by the sea,
    And Charley was doomed to die!

Then "Prince," when he hears how the lots have
        gone, goes straight where the General he
        sees;
"A word with you, General" — says he, like a
        king — "apart from the rest, if you please.
There is one of our lot who is drawn for death — a
        little chap, curly and brown:
Now, 'tis nothing to you who goes or who stays,
        for your soldiers to shoot him down,

And whether I die or whether I live don't matter
    a curse to me ;
But, General, it matters a deal to him, for the little
    chap's married, you see.
So if it's a death you needs must have, there's
    mine — you can take my life ;
But tell him he's drawn for exchange, not death —
    and let him return to his wife."
I reckon the General did not demur ; from the
    soldier's point of view
The "Prince" was a nobler prize by far, as the
    better man of the two.
There were three led out in the sun that day, and
    shot by the men of the North,
And a fourth was shot in the rank with them —
    no, Charley was not that fourth.

He never was told till the deed was done, and
    "You're free to go," they said ;
And they bade him look, as he went his way, on
    his four companions dead ;
And he saw the corpse— they were strong in
    death, those arms and that sinewy chest —
Of the man he had loved, who loved him, too —
    and her — and he knew the rest !
Oh, aye ! the story is true enough ; I'm likely to
    know, you see,
For I was the little chap, curly and brown — his
    friend — and he died for me !

THE BOY IN BLUE

John D. Long

As if it were but yesterday, you recall the "boy in blue." He had but turned twenty. The exquisite tint of youthful health was in his cheek. His pure heart shone from frank, outspeaking eyes. He had pulled a stout oar in the college race, or walked the most graceful athlete on the village green. He had just entered on the vocation of his life. The unreckoned influences of the great discussion of human rights had insensibly moulded him into a champion of freedom. He had passed no solitary and sleepless night watching the armor which he was to wear when dubbed next day with the accolade of knighthood. But over the student's lamp or at the fireside's blaze he had passed the nobler initiate of a heart and mind trained to a fine sense of justice and to a resolution equal to the sacrifice of life itself in behalf of right and duty. He knew nothing of the web of politics, but he knew instinctively the needs of his country. His ideal was Philip Sidney, not Napoleon. And when the drum beat, he took his place in the ranks and went forward. You remember his ingenuous and glowing letters to his mother, written as though his pen were dipped in his very heart. How graphically he described his

sensation in the first battle, the pallor that he felt
creeping up his face, and then the utter fearless-
ness when once the charge began and his blood
was up! How gratefully he wrote of the days in
hospital, of the opening of the box from home, of
the generous distributing of delicacies that loving
ones had sent, of the gentle nurse whose eyes and
hands seemed to bring to his bedside the summer
freshness and health of the open window of his
home.

You remember when he came home on fur-
lough, how manly and war-worn he had grown.
But he soon returned to the ranks and to the
welcome of his comrades. They loved him for his
manliness, his high bearing, his fine sense of
honor. They recall him now alike with tears and
pride. In the rifle-pits around Petersburg they
heard his steady voice and firm command. It was
a forlorn hope, that charge of the brave regiment
to which he belonged, reduced now by three
years' long fighting to a hundred veterans, conscious that somebody had blundered, yet grimly
obedient to duty. But there was no flinching as
he charged. He had just turned to give a cheer
when the fatal ball struck him. His eyes, pleading and loyal, turned their last glance to the flag.
His lips parted. He fell dead, and at nightfall
lay with his face to the stars. Home they brought
him, fairer than Adonis, over whom the goddess

of Beauty wept.   They buried him in the village
church-yard under the green turf.   His picture
hangs on the old homestead walls.   Children look
up at it and ask to hear his story told.   It was
years ago; and the face is so young, so boyish, so
fair, that you cannot believe he was the hero of
twenty battles, a veteran in the war, a leader of
men, brave, cool, commanding, great.   Do you
ask who he was?   He was in every regiment and
every company.   He went out from every village,
from hundreds of quiet farm-houses.   He sleeps
in every Northern burying-ground.

Recall romance, recite the names of heroes of
legend and song: there is none that is his peer.

KISSED HIS MOTHER

Eben E. Rexford

She sat on the porch in the sunshine,
    As I went down the street —
A woman whose hair was silver,
    But whose face was blossom-sweet,
Making me think of a garden
    Where, in spite of frost and snow
Of bleak November weather,
    Late fragrant lilies grow.

I heard a footstep behind me,
    And a sound of a merry laugh,

And I knew the heart it came from
    Would be like a comforting staff
In the time and the hour of trouble,
    Hopeful, and brave, and strong,
One of the hearts to lean on
    When we think that things go wrong.

I turned at the click of the gate-latch,
    And met his manly look;
A face like his gives me pleasure,
    Like the page of a pleasant book.
It told of a steadfast purpose,
    Of a brave and daring will —
A face with a promise in it
    That God grant the years fulfill.

He went up the pathway singing;
    I saw the woman's eyes
Grow bright with a wordless welcome,
    As sunshine warms the skies.
"Back again, sweetheart mother!"
    He cried, and bent to kiss
The loving face that was lifted
    For what some mothers miss.

That boy will do to depend on;
    I hold that this is true;
From lads in love with their mothers
    Our bravest heroes grew.

Earth's grandest hearts have been loving hearts
　　Since time and earth began,
And the boy who kissed his mother
　　Is every inch a man!

THE TEACHER THE HOPE OF AMERICA

SAMUEL EELLS

LOOK abroad over this country; mark her extent, her wealth, her fertility, her boundless resources, the giant energies which every day develop, and which she seems already bending on that fatal race, tempting, yet always fatal to republics — the race for physical greatness and aggrandizement. Behold, too, that continuous and mighty tide of population, native and foreign, which is forever rushing through this great valley towards the setting sun, sweeping away the wilderness before it like grass before the mower; waking up industry and civilization in its progress; studding the solitary rivers of the West with marts and cities; dotting its boundless prairies with human habitations; penetrating every green nook and vale; climbing to every fertile ridge; and still gathering and pouring onward, to form new states in those vast and yet unpeopled solitudes, where the Oregon rolls his majestic flood, and

"Hears no sound save his own dashing."

Mark all this, and then say by what bonds will you hold together so mighty a people and so immense an empire? What safeguard will you give us against the dangers which must inevitably grow out of so vast and complicate an organization? In the swelling tide of our prosperity, what a field will open for political corruption! What a world of evil passions to control and jarring interests to reconcile! What temptations will there be to luxury and extravagance! What motives to private and official cupidity! What prizes will hang glittering at a thousand goals to dazzle and tempt ambition! Do we expect to find our security against these dangers in railroads and canals, in our circumvallations and ships of war? Alas! when shall we learn wisdom from the lessons of history? Our most dangerous enemies will grow up from our own bosom. We may erect bulwarks against foreign invasion, but what power shall we find in walls and armies to protect the people against themselves?

There is but one sort of "international improvement" (more thoroughly internal than that which is cried up by politicians), that is able to save this country. I mean the improvement of the minds and souls of her people. If this improvement shall be neglected, and shall fail to keep pace with the increase of our population and our physical advancement, one of two alternatives is certain:

either the nation must dissolve in anarchy under the rulers of its own choice; or, if held together at all, it must be by a government so strong and rigorous as to be utterly inconsistent with constitutional liberty. Let the one hundred millions which, at no very distant day, will swarm our cities and fill up our great interior, remain sunk in ignorance, and nothing short of an iron despotism will suffice to govern the nation, to reconcile its vast and conflicting interests, control its elements of agitation, and hold back its fiery and headlong energies from dismemberment and ruin.

How, then, is this improvement to be effected? Who are the agents of it? Who are they who shall stand perpetually as priests at the altar of freedom, and feed its sacred fires by dispensing that knowledge and cultivation on which hangs our political salvation? I repeat, they are our teachers, the masters of our schools, the instructors in our academies and colleges, and in all those institutions, of whatever name, which have for their object the intellectual and moral culture of our youth, and the diffusion of knowledge among our people.

Theirs is the moral dignity of stamping the great features of our national character; and, in the moral worth and intelligence which they give it, to erect a bulwark which shall prove impregnable in that hour of trial, when armies and fleets and fortifications shall be vain. And when those mighty and all-absorbing questions shall be heard, which are even now sending their bold demands into the ear of rulers and lawgivers, which are momentarily pressing forward to a solemn decision in the sight of God and of all nations, and which, when the hour of their decision shall come, will shake this country, the union, the constitution, as with the shaking of an earthquake, it is they who in that fearful hour will gather around the structure of our political organization, and, with uplifted hands, stay the reeling fabric till the storm and the convulsion be overpast.

BABY IN CHURCH

Winnie M. Gow

Aunt Nellie has fashioned a dainty thing,
    Of Hamburg and ribbon and lace,
And mamma has said, as she settled it 'round
    Our beautiful baby's face,
Where the dimples play and the laughter lies
Like sunbeams hid in her violet eyes:
"If the day is pleasant and baby is good,
    She may go to church and wear her new hood.

Then Ben, aged six, began to tell,
    In elder-brotherly way,
How very, very good she must be
    If she went to church next day.

He told of the church, the choir, and the crowd,
And the man up in front who talked so loud;
But she must not talk nor laugh nor sing,
But just sit as quiet as anything.

And so, on a beautiful Sabbath in May,
    When the fruit-buds burst into flowers
(There wasn't a blossom on bush or tree
    So fair as this blossom of ours),
All in her white dress, dainty and new,
Our baby sat in the family pew.
The grand, sweet music, the reverent air,
The solemn hush and the voice of prayer

Filled all her baby soul with awe,
    As she sat in her little place,
And the holy look that the angels wear
    Seemed pictured upon her face.
And the sweet words uttered so long ago
Came into my mind with a rhythmic flow:
"Of such is the Kingdom of Heaven," said He,
    And I knew that He spake of such as she.

The sweet-voiced organ pealed forth again,
    The collection-box came round,
And baby dropped her penny in,
    And smiled at the chinking sound.
Alone in the choir Aunt Nellie stood,
Waiting the close of the soft prelude,
To begin her solo.   High and strong
She struck the first note, clear and long.

She held it, and all were charmed but one,
    Who, with all the might she had,
Sprang to her little feet and cried:
    "Aunt Nellie, you's being bad."
The audience smiled, the minister coughed,
The little boys in the corner laughed,
The tenor-man shook like an aspen leaf
And hid his face in his handkerchief.

And poor Aunt Nellie never could tell
    How she finished that terrible strain,
But says that nothing on earth would tempt
    Her to go through the same scene again.
So, we have decided, perhaps 'tis best,
For her sake, ours and all the rest,
That we wait, maybe for a year or two,
Ere our baby re-enter the family pew.

THE STABILITY OF OUR GOVERNMENT

C. Sprague

IF there be on the earth one nation more than
another, whose institutions must draw their life-
blood from the individual purity of its citizens,
that nation is our own. Rulers by divine right,
and nobles by hereditary succession, may, perhaps,
tolerate with impunity those depraving indulgences
which keep the great mass abject. Where the
many enjoy little or no power, it were a trick of

policy to wink at those enervating vices which would rob them of both the ability and the inclination to enjoy it.   But in our country, where almost every man, however humble, bears to the omnipotent ballot-box his full portion of the sovereignty — where at regular periods the ministers of authority, who went forth to rule, return to be ruled, and lay down their dignities at the feet of the monarch multitude — where, in short, public sentiment is the absolute lever that moves the political world, the purity of the people is the rock of political safety.

We may boast, if we please, of our exalted privileges, and fondly imagine that they will be eternal; but whenever those vices shall abound which undeniably tend to debasement, steeping the poor and ignorant still lower in poverty and ignorance, and thereby destroying that wholesome mental equality which can alone sustain a self-ruled people, it will be found, by woeful experience, that our happy system of government, the best ever devised for the intelligent and good, is the very worst to be intrusted to the degraded and vicious. The great majority will then truly become a many-headed monster, to be tamed and led at will.   The tremendous power of suffrage, like the strength of the eyeless Nazarite, so far from being their protection, will but serve to pull down upon their heads the temple their ancestors reared for them.

Caballers and demagogues will find it an easy task to delude those who have deluded themselves; and the freedom of the people will finally be buried in the grave of their virtues. National greatness may survive; splendid talents and brilliant honors may fling their delusive luster abroad — these may illume the darkness that hangs round the throne of a monarch, but their light will be like the baleful flame that hovers over decaying mortality, and tells of the corruption that festers beneath. The immortal spirit will have gone; and along our shores, and among our hills — those shores made sacred by the sepulcher of the pilgrim, those hills hallowed by the uncoffined bones of the patriot — even there, in the ears of their degenerate descendants, shall ring the last knell of departed liberty!

THE KNIGHT'S TOAST

The Feast is o'er.   Now brimming wine
In lordly cup is seen to shine
  Before each eager guest;
And silence fills the crowded hall
As deep as when the herald's call
  Thrills in the loyal breast.

Then up arose the noble host,
And smiling, cried: "A toast! A toast!
  To all our ladies fair!

Here before all I pledge the name
Of Staunton's proud and beauteous dame,
  The Lady Gundamere."

Then to his feet each gallant sprung,
And joyous was the shout that rung,
  As Stanley gave the word;
And every cup was raised on high,
Nor ceased the loud and gladsome cry
  Till Stanley's voice was heard:

"Enough, Enough," he smiling said,
And lowly bent his haughty head,
  "That each may have his due,
Now each in turn must play his part,
And pledge the lady of his heart,
  Like gallant knight, and true."

Then, one by one, each guest sprang up,
And drained in turn the brimming cup,
  And called the loved one's name;
And each, as hand on high he raised,
His lady's grace or beauty praised,
  Her constancy and fame.

'T is now St. Leon's turn to rise;
On him are fixed those countless eyes;
  A gallant knight is he;
Envied by some, admired by all;
Far famed in lady's bower and hall,
  The power of chivalry.

St. Leon raised his kindling eye,
And lifts the sparkling cup on high.
　　"I drink to one," he said,
"Whose image never may depart,
Deep graven on this grateful heart,
　　Till memory be dead;

"To one whose love for me shall last
When lighter passions long have past,
　　So holy 't is and true;
To one whose love hath longer dwelt,
More deeply fixed, more keenly felt,
　　Than any pledged by you."

Each guest upstarted at the word,
And laid a hand upon his sword,
　　With fury-flashing eye;
And Stanley said: "We crave the name,
Proud knight, of this most peerless dame,
　　Whose love you count so high."

St. Leon paused, as if he would
Not breathe her name in careless mood,
　　Thus lightly to another;
Then bent his noble head as though
To give that word the reverence due,
　　And gently said: — "My mother."

THE LAST NIGHT OF MISOLONGHI

From "Andronike"

EDWIN A. GROSVENOR

IT was eight o'clock at night. The besieged, at the given signal, had gathered at the eastern batteries of Rhegas and Montalembert, from which they purposed to make their sortie.

Three thousand combatants, some of them wounded and convalescent, were to head the sally, and cut a way for the thousand artisans and five thousand women and children who followed.

"This is the plan of the sortie," said Notis Botsaris, the Nestor of the day. "By these four wooden bridges we shall pass out in the utmost silence. We shall collect in front of our bastions, Rhegas and Montalembert. You," he said, turning to the soldiers, "will fall on your faces and remain so until we give the signal to attack. Then rush against those two towers, which Ibrahim Pasha has built over against us. You," he said, turning to the guard, "as soon as you receive the signal, will divide into two bodies. One body, composed of all the guards on that side of the bastion of Montalembert, will cut through the middle of Reshid's camp. The Albanians are there, so it will be the most difficult part of the undertaking. The rest, with the women and children and the unarmed, are to strike through the Arabs of Ibrahim. All those who survive are to meet at the vineyard of Cotzicas, that is, at the foot of Mount Aracynthus near the Monastery of Saint Symeon.

"It is time to separate. Courage, brothers! Patience and courage! We stand alone, and yet all Europe admires our valor. Immortal is he who falls to-night, and thrice immortal whoever survives to take vengeance for the slain."

Only ten minutes later the pathetic scene of separation was enacted on the seashore. The aged, the sick, and many of the inhabitants, who, unwilling to leave the place of their birth, were to stay in the city, in tears were embracing and parting from their children, brothers, parents, kindred, and friends. Those moments were heartbreaking. Families were being torn asunder. Each last kiss was followed by a moan. The fiercest warriors wept upon that blood-stained soil, and many a stolid heart was moved, hesitated, and shrank back.

An aged, gray-haired man advanced and wished to speak. It was the primate Chrestos Capsalis. A sad silence for a moment interrupted the lamentations.

"Come, unconquered souls of my sacrifice, end all this! For the name of Christ, let the rest go out!" cried the primate. "These moments are precious. Follow me! I will lead you to a place where, if the barbarians dare approach, you shall find greater glory than these kindred from whom you are now separated."

So ended this scene of parting. Chrestos Capsalis led the women and children and the few volunteers, who were to stay, inside the powder magazine, where were thirty kegs of powder. There he was prepared to make to Ares a burnt offering, not indeed of quadrupeds, of bulls and horses, but of human lives.

At that same moment the women and children, with the rest, issued from the city. The hail of hostile bullets whistled all around them. In the storm wide graves yawned for the vanguard of the Greeks. Yet neither the cannon balls nor the lances nor the hand-arms of the Arabs were able to check the onset of the first line. Quickly they swept beyond the place of greatest slaughter, dispersed the infantry, leaped upon the outworks, and cut down like cattle the Egyptian gunners and the French officers beside their own guns.

But on the way they came upon a thousand other inhabitants in a straggling rabble. While ready to divide into two sections, as Notis Botsaris had directed, and to follow their intrepid vanguard, they had suddenly become panic-stricken and fallen into confusion. Every tongue began to shout the fatal cry: "Back! back to Misolonghi!" No one knows who uttered it first, or why any heart gave way. Huddled together, they were crowding to the city as the Mussulman masses, rolling back and around, poured in from the other end or entered with them.

Picture those barbaric hordes, which through thirteen months had been thirsting for the city's blood! Each street became a slaughterhouse, each house a human altar.

The mothers of western Greece were not the Sciot women of Ionia. The old men and the sick still had drops of warlike blood in their veins. Three times the Mussulmans rushed upon them, and three times they were driven back by stones and sticks and the chance weapons of despair.

Here valor was pitted against valor, despair against ferocity, self-sacrifice against cruelty, heroism against rapine, scorn and contempt against threats and blasphemies. Intermittent pistol shots, clash of swords, conflagration of houses and bastions, moans of the expiring, wild yells of the conquerors, taunts of the despairing, repeated on earth the scenes of hell. There might be seen some barefooted maiden with marble bosom and bare arm intrepidly defending a dying brother. There, a mother was throwing a babe into a well and then springing after it, that she might not become the prey of the dissolute Mussulman who was seeking to enslave her. In those black streets, in the dust of the ground, on the balconies of the houses rolled Greek and Arab,

Greek and Turkoman, Greek and Albanian, locked in close embrace, teeth set in each other's flesh, struggling each to destroy the other, agonizing each to thrust his sword first into the other's breast.

During those crucial moments Capsalis passed from one end of the house containing the powder to the other, encouraging all.

The Turks thought that here were concealed all the treasures of the city. As they heard no gun-shots, but only women's voices, their idea became confirmed, and they rushed upon it in crowds from every direction. Some tried to get in by the windows, others by breaking down the doors, others by climbing on the roof, in hopes of cutting their way through, and so leaping in.

The doors were already broken through, the steel of the Mussulman clanged ominously, when Chrestos Capsalis, standing, said: "Remember us, Lord, in thy kingdom! To the everlasting life, brothers!"

He plunged in his torch and the awful explosion followed. The solid ground was torn open, and the sea from the lagoon poured in. Some were drowned, who, after being shot into the air, fell back, half burned to the earth. Two thousand Turks found death around Capsalis, and five hundred more in the neighboring houses. Out of the six thousand Greeks only twelve hundred mutilated beings survived to endure slavery.

" INASMUCH "

Wallace Bruce

You say that you want a meetin'-house for the
boys in the gulch up there,
And a Sunday-school with pictur'-books? Well,
put me down for a share.
I believe in little children; it's nice to hear 'em
read
As to wander round the ranch at noon and see the
cattle feed.

And I believe in preachin', too — by men for
preachin' born,
Who let alone the husks of creed, and measure out
the corn.
The pulpit's but a manger where the pews are
gospel-fed;
And they say 'twas to a manger that the star of
glory led.

So I'll subscribe a dollar toward the manger and
the stalls;
I always give the best I've got whenever my part-
ner calls.
And, stranger, let me tell you: I'm beginning to
suspect
That all the world are partners, whatever their
creed or sect;

That life is a kind of pilgrimage, a sort of Jericho
road,
And kindness to one's fellows the sweetest law in
the code.
No matter about the 'nitials; from a farmer, you
understand,
Who's generally had to play it alone from rather
an or'nary hand.

I've never struck it rich; for farmin', you see, is
slow,
And whenever the crops are fairly good, the prices
are always low.
A dollar isn't very much, but it helps to count the
same;
The lowest trump supports the ace, and sometimes
wins the game.

It assists a fellow's praying when he's down upon
his knees —
"Inasmuch as you have done it to one of the least
of these."
I know the verses, stranger, so you needn't stop
to quote;
It's a different thing to know them than to say
them off by rote.

I'll tell you where I learned them, if you'll step in
from the rain;
'Twas down in 'Frisco years ago; had been there
haulin' grain.

It was near the city limits, on the Sacramento
    pike,
Where the stores and sheds are rather mixed, and
    shanties scatterin' like.

Not the likeliest place to be in, I remember, the
    saloon,
With grocery, market, baker-shop, and bar-room all
    in one,
And this made up the picture — my hair was not
    then gray,
But everything still seems as real as if 'twere yes·
    terday.

A little girl with haggard face stood at the counter
    there,
Not more than ten or twelve at most, but worn
    with grief and care ;
And her voice was kind of raspy, like a sort of
    chronic cold —
Just the tone you find in children who are prema-
    turely old.

She said : "Two bits for bread and tea. Ma
    hasn't much to eat ;
She hopes next week to work again, and buy us
    all some meat.
We've been half-starved all winter, but spring will
    soon be here,
And she tells us, 'Keep up courage, for God is
    always near.' "

Just then a dozen men came in; the boy was called
    away
To shake the spotted cubes for drinks, as 'Forty-
    niners say,
I never heard from human lips such oaths and
    curses loud
As rose above the glasses of that crazed and reck-
    less crowd.

But the poor, tired girl sat waiting, lost at last to
    revels deep,
On a keg beside a barrel in the corner, fast
    asleep.
Well, I stood there, sort of waiting, until some
    one at the bar
Said, "Hello! I say, stranger, what have you
    over thar?"

The boy then told her story, and that crew so
    fierce and wild
Grew intent, and seemed to listen to the breathing
    of the child.
The glasses all were lowered; said the leader:
    "Boys, see here;
All day we've been pouring whisky, drinking deep
    our Christmas cheer.

"Here's two dollars — I've got feelings which are
    not entirely dead —
For this little girl and mother suffering for the
    want of bread."

"Here's a dollar." "Here's another." And they
    all chipped in their share,
And they planked the ringing metal down upon
    the counter there.

Then the spokesman took a golden double-eagle
    from his belt,
Softly stepped from bar to counter, and beside the
    sleeper knelt ;
Took the " two bits" from her fingers; changed
    her silver piece for gold.
"See there, boys, the girl is dreaming." Down
    her cheeks the tear-drops rolled.

One by one the swarthy miners passed in silence
    to the street.
Gently we awoke the sleeper, but she started to
    her feet
With a dazed and changed expression, saying :
    "Oh, I thought 'twas true!
Ma was well and we were happy ; round our door-
    stone roses grew.

" We had everything we wanted, food enough, and
    clothes to wear ;
And my hand burns where an angel touched it
    soft with fingers fair."
And she looked and saw the money in her fingers
    glistening bright,
" Well, now, Ma has long been praying, but she
    won't believe me quite,

How you've sent 'way up to heaven, where the
    golden treasures are,
And have also got an angel clerking at your
    grocery bar."

That's a Christmas story, stranger, which I thought
    you'd like to hear ;
True to fact and human nature, pointing out one's
    duty clear,
Hence to matters of subscription, you will see that
    I'm alive ;
Just mark off that dollar, stranger ; I think I'll
    make it five.

THE CORPORAL OF CHANCELLORS-VILLE

John R. Paxton

I REMEMBER when the fight was on and the field
was lost, and a beaten and broken army were
falling back at Chancellorsville. I remember a
regiment of soldiers in position behind batteries of
artillery, near the Chancellor home.   The wounded
cried piteously for aid; the shells crashed through
the woods; it was an hour of dread and despair for
the Union soldiers, of exultation and hope for the
Confederates.   All the troops had fallen back in
disorder; a new line was being formed more than
a mile to the rear.   The soldiers supporting the

batteries were alone on a lost and bloody field.
These troops and batteries were to be sacrificed to
the army. They were put there to hold the
victorious enemy in check until a new line could
be formed. The Confederates, flushed with victory
and enraged by resistance on a field they considered won, yelled like demons and poured an
incessant fire upon the Union guns. The regiment
supporting the batteries lay prone on the earth
very still, while our artillery returned the enemy's
fire. The shells came screaming over and into the
regiment, not singly, not as skirmishers, but as if
in columns. It was the first battle of the regiment.
Between the brief pauses of loading and firing, the
men could hear the sharp commands of the Confederate officers, "Load and fire!" It was the
mouth of hell or gate of heaven for many of them.

The men shivered and thrilled. It was appalling,
yet it was glorious — to be living this minute and
possibly dead the next. That was their situation.
Officer after officer, soldier after soldier, was struck
and heard no more on earth. The wounded moaned
and cried for water; the living — well, some tried
to pray; some shut their eyes and shivered as the
shells came crashing through; the crackling of the
flames consuming the Chancellor house were clearly
heard. What did they feel or fear, those men
being slaughtered score by score? What visions
of eternity, on the dizzy edge of which they were,

flashed up in their souls! What did death mean? Wait till you are there to know.

But in that regiment being rapidly thinned by the shells of the Confederates, I remember a man and his conduct. He was first corporal, and dressed the company on the right. Tall he was and goodly to look upon, a farmer's lad from Pennsylvania. We heard a voice, strong, clear, serene, confident; we looked, and then on the right of the company, sitting upright, firm, while all of us lay down flat, we saw the corporal. His face was cold; a smile played over his features. He was so cold, so serene! He seemed to be looking away beyond the enemy's lines to something we did not see — to be utterly indifferent to the death-dealing shells. Here is what I heard from this corporal amid the carnage of the battle: "God is our refuge and strength, a very present help in trouble; therefore will we not fear though the earth be removed and the mountains carried into the depths of the sea. For the Lord of Hosts is with us; the God of Jacob is our refuge." The voice and prayer of this corporal silenced many an oath, stifled many a groan, and nerved us to stand it out as no shriek of fife or battle-drum had ever done. What made our corporal the man he was, at peace in battle, with a smile upon his lips in the jaws of death? It was this: he was a God-fearing lad, reared in an old Convenanters' meeting-house. When the day came to show the stuff men were made of, it was the man with this fear of God in his soul, and no other fear, that put us all to shame and showed us how to die.

MILKING-TIME

PHILIP MORSE

"I'll tell you, Kate, that Lovejoy cow
  Is worth her weight in gold;
She gives a good eight-quarts o' milk,
  And isn't yet five years old.

"I see young White a comin' now;
  He wants her, I know that;
Be careful girl, you're spillin' it!
  An' save some for the cat.

"Good evenin', Richard, step right in."
  "I guess I couldn't, sir,
I've just come down" — "I know it, Dick;
  You've took a shine to her.

"She's kind and gentle as a lamb,
  Jest where I go she follers;
And though its cheap, I'll let her go;
  She's your'n for thirty dollars.

"You'll know her clear across the farm,
  By them two milk-white stars;

You needn't drive her home at night,
But just let down the bars.

"Then when you've own'd her, say a month,
And learnt her, as it were,
I'll bet — why, what's the matter, Dick?"
"'Tain't her I want — it's — her!"

"What? Not the girl! Well, I'll be bless'd! —
There, Kate, don't drop that pan —
You've took me mightily aback,
But then a man's a man.

"She's your'n my boy, but one word more
Kate's gentle as a dove;
She'll foller you the whole world round,
For nothin' else but love.

"But never try to drive the lass,
Her natur's like her ma's;
I've allus found it worked the best,
To just let down the bars."

CHARIOT RACE IN ALEXANDRIA

From "Serapis"

GEORG EBERS

THE spacious Hippodrome was filled with some
thousands of spectators. The number of chariots
entered for competition was by no means smaller

than on former occasions. The heathens had strained every nerve to show they were still a power worthy of consideration. The Christians did their utmost to outdo the idolaters on the same ground where, not long since, they had held quite the second place.

The four magnificent black Arabs in the quadriga with which Marcus made his appearance in the arena had never before been driven in the Hippodrome. These perfect creatures had excited much interest among the knowing judges, and were perhaps as fine as the famous team of golden bays belonging to Iphicrates, which had so often proved victorious. But the *agitatores*, or drivers, attracted even more interest than the horses. Marcus, though he knew how to handle the reins, could hardly hold his own against Hippias, the handsome young heathen, who was an *agitator* by profession.

The betting was freest and the wagers highest on Hippias and his team. Some few backed Marcus and his Arabs, but for smaller sums; and when they compared the tall but narrow-shouldered figure of the young Christian with the heroic breadth of Hippias' frame, and his delicate features, dreamy blue eyes and downy black moustache with the powerful Hermes head of his rival, they were anxious about their money.

Wild excitement, expectation strung to the highest pitch, and party-feeling, both for and

against, had been rife here; but to-day they were
manifest in an acuter form — hatred had added its
taint, and lent virulence to every emotion.   The
heathens were oppressed and angered, their rights
abridged and defied.   This was intolerable and
roused the idolaters to wrath and malice.   They
displayed their color in wreaths of scarlet poppies,
pomegranate flowers and red roses, with crimson
ribbons and dresses.

The Christians were robed in blue from head to
foot, their sandals being tied with blue ribbons.
They could hate too, and they hated the idolaters
and their traditions of a brilliant past.

The Alexandrians were not a patient race and
they were beginning to rebel against the delay,
when Cynegius rose and with his white handkerchief waved the signal for the races to begin.

Four *missus* or races were to be run.   In each
of the first three, twelve chariots were to start, and
in the fourth only the leaders in the three former
ones were to compete.   It was the fate of Marcus
to start among the first lot, and to the horror of
those who had backed his chances, Hippias, the
hero of the Hippodrome, was his rival with his four
famous bays.

Cynegius repeated his signal.   The sound of the
tuba rang through the air, and the first twelve
chariots were led into the starting-sheds.   In a few
short minutes Cynegius signalled the third time.

A golden dolphin, on which the eye of every charioteer was fixed, dropped to the ground; a blast on the war-trumpet was sounded, and forty-eight horses flew forth as though thrown forward by one impulsion.

Five blue and seven red competitors had drawn the first lots. (The eye rested with pleasure on the sinewy figures whose bare feet seemed rooted to the boards they stood on, while their eyes were riveted on the goal they were striving to reach. A close cap with floating ribbons confined their hair, and they wore short, sleeveless tunics. The reins were fastened around the hips so as to leave the hands free, not only to hold them but also to ply the whip and use the goad. Each charioteer had a knife in his gridle, to enable him to release himself, in case of accident, from a bond that might prove fatal.)

Before long the bay team was leading alone. Behind were two Christian drivers, followed by three red chariots; Marcus was last of all, but it was easy to see that it was by choice and not by necessity. He was holding in his fiery team with all his strength and weight — his body thrown back, his feet firmly set with his knees against the silver bar of the chariot, and his hands gripping the reins. In a few minutes he came flying past Dada and his brother, but he did not see them. He could only keep his eyes and mind fixed on his horses and on the goal.

The multitude clapped, roared, shouted encouragement to their party, hissed and whistled when they were disappointed — venting their utmost indignation on Marcus as he came past behind the others; but he either heard them not or would not hear. Dada's heart beat so wildly that she thought it would burst. When he had passed, she said sadly enough: "Poor fellow! — we have brought our wreaths for nothing, after all, Demetrius!"

But Demetrius shook his head and smiled.

"Nay," he said, "the boy has iron sinews in that slight body. Look how he holds the horses in! He is saving their strength till they need it. Seven times, child, seven times he has to go round this great circus and past the *nyssa*, the goal. You will see, he will catch up what he has lost yet. There — you see! They drive round from right to left and that throws most of the work on the left-hand beast; it has to turn almost in its own length. Aura, our first horse, is as supple as a panther, and I trained her to do it myself. Now look out there! — that bronze figure of a rearing horse — the *Taraxippos* they call it — is put there to frighten the horses, and Megaera, our third horse, is like a mad thing sometimes, though she can go like a stag; every time Marcus gets her past the Taraxippos we are nearer to success. Look, look! — the first chariot has got round the *nyssa!* It is Hippias! Yes, by Zeus, he has done it!

He is a detestable braggart, but he knows his business!"

Next to Hippias came a blue team, and close behind were three red ones. The Christian who had succeeded in reaching the *nyssa* second, boldly took his horses close round the obelisk, hoping to gain space and get past Hippias; but the left wheel of his chariot grazed the granite plinth, the light car was overset, and the horses of the red chariot, whose noses were almost on his shoulder, could not be pulled up short in time. They fell over the Christian's team which rolled on the ground; the red chariot, too, turned over, and eight snorting beasts lay struggling in the sand.

The rest had time and space enough to beware of the wreck and to give it a wide berth, among them Marcus. The mêlée at the *nyssa* had excited his steeds almost beyond control, and as they tore past the Taraxippos the third horse, Megaera, shied violently, as Demetrius had predicted. She flung herself on one side, thrust her hind quarters under the pole, and kicked desperately, lifting the chariot quite off the ground; the young charioteer lost his footing and slipped. Dada covered her face with her hands, and his mother turned pale and knit her brows with apprehension. The youth was still standing; his feet were on the sand of the arena; but he had a firm grip on the right-hand spiral ornament that terminated the bar round the chariot. Many a heart stood still with anxiety, and shouts of triumph and mockery broke from the red party; but in less than half a minute, by an effort of strength and agility, he had his knees on the foot-board, and then in the winking of an eye, he was on his feet in the chariot, had gathered up the reins and was rushing onward.

In the third round the chariot of the red driver in front of Marcus made too sharp a turn and ran up against the granite. The broken car was dragged on by the terrified beasts, and the charioteer with it, till, by the time they were stopped, he was a corpse. In the fifth circuit the Christian who till now had been second to Hippias shared the same fate, though he escaped with his life; and then Marcus drove past the starting-sheds next to Hippias.

During the sixth circuit Hippias was still a long way ahead of the young Christian; the distance which lay between Marcus and the team of bays seemed to have become a fixed quantity, for, do what he could, he could not diminish it by a hand-breadth. The two *agitatores* had now completely altered their tactics; instead of holding their horses in they urged them onward, leaning over the front of their chariots, speaking to the horses, shouting at them with hoarse, breathless cries, and flogging them unsparingly. Steamy sweat and lathering foam streaked the flanks of the desperate, laboring brutes, while clouds of dust were flung up from the dry, furrowed and trampled soil. The other chariots were left farther and farther behind those of Hippias and Marcus, and when, for the seventh and last time, these two were nearing the *nyssa*, the crowd for a moment held its breath, only to break out into louder and wilder cries, and then again to be hushed.

Dada spoke no more; pale and gasping, she sat with her eyes fixed on the tall obelisk and on the cloud of dust which, as the chariots neared the *nyssa*, seemed to grow denser. At about a hundred paces from the *nyssa* she saw above the sandy curtain the red cap of Hippias flash past, and then — close behind it — the blue cap worn by Marcus. Then a deafening, thundering roar from thousands of throats went up to heaven, while, round the obelisk — so close to it that not a horse, not a wheel could have found room between the plinth and the driver — the blue cap came forward out of the cloud, and, behind it now — no longer in front, through not more than a length behind — came the red cap of Hippias. When within a few feet of the *nyssa* Marcus had overtaken his antagonist, had passed the bold with a bold and perilously close turn, and had left the bays behind him.

Demetrius saw it all, as though his eye had power to pierce the dust-cloud, and now he too lost his phlegmatic calm. He threw up his arms as if in prayer, and shouted, as though his brother could hear him: "Well done, splendid boy! Now for the *kention* — the goad — drive it in, send it home if they die for it! Give it them well! Death and Hades! The other is catching him up. The dog, the sneak! If only the 'boy would use his goad! Give it them, Marcus! Give it them, lad! Never give in now! Great Father Poseidon! — there, there! — no! I can hardly stand. Yes, he is still in front, and now, now, this must settle it! Thunder and lightning! They are close together again — may the dust choke him! No — it is all right, my Arabs are in front! All is well; keep it up, lad, well done! We have won!"

The horses were pulled up, the dust settled; Marcus, the Christian, had won. Hippias flung down his whip in a rage, but the triumphant shouts of the Christians drowned the music, the trumpet-blasts and the angry murmurs of the defeated heathen.

A RELENTING MOB

Lucy H. Hooper

The mob was fierce and furious. They cried :
" Kill him!" the while they pressed from every
    side
Around a man, haughty, unmoved, and brave,
Too pitiless himself to pity crave.

"Down with the wretch!" on all sides rose the cry.
The captive found it natural to die,
The game is lost — he's on the weaker side,
Life, too, is lost, and so must Fate decide.

From out his home they dragged him to the street,
With fiercely clenching hands and hurrying feet,
And shouts of "Death to him!"   The crimson
        stain
Of recent carnage on his garb showed plain.

This man was one of those who blindly slay
At a king's bidding.   He'd shot men all day,
Killing he knew not whom, scarce knew why,
Now marching forth impassible to die,
Incapable of mercy or of fear,
Letting his powder-blackened hands appear.

A woman clutched his collar with a frown,
"He's a policeman — he has shot us down!"
"That's true," the man said. "Kill him!" "Shoot
        him!"   "Kill!"
"No, at the Arsenal" — "The Bastile!"   "Where
        you will,"
The captive answered.   And with fiercest breath,
Loading their guns, his captors still cried "Death!"
"We'll shoot him like a wolf!"   "A wolf am I?
Then you're the dogs," he calmly made reply.
"Hark, he insults us!" and from every side
Clenched fists were shaken, angry voices cried.

Ferocious threats were muttered deep and low.
With gall upon his lips, gloom on his brow,
And in his eyes a gleam of baffled hate,
He went, pursued by howlings, to his fate.

Treading with wearied and supreme disdain
'Midst forms of dead men he perchance had slain
Dread is that human storm, an angry crowd ;
He braved its wrath with head erect and proud.
He was not taken, but walled in with foes,
He hated them with hate the vanquished knows,
He would have shot them all had he the power.
" Kill him — he's fired upon us for an hour!"
" Down with the murderer — down with the spy!"
And suddenly a small voice made reply :
" No — no, he is my father!"   And a ray
Like to a sunbeam seemed to light the day.
A child appeared, a boy with golden hair,
His arm upraised in menace or in prayer.

All shouted : " Shoot the bandit, fell the spy!"
The little fellow clasped him with a cry
Of " Papa, papa, they'll not hurt you now!"
The light baptismal shone upon his brow.

From out the captive's home had come the child.
Meanwhile the shrieks of "Kill him — Death!" rose
        wild.
The cannon to the tocsin's voice replied,
Sinister men thronged close on every side,

And in the street ferocious shouts increased
Of "Slay each spy—each minister—each priest—
We'll kill them all!"   The little boy replied :
"I tell you this is papa."   One girl cried :
"A pretty fellow—see his curly head!"
"How old are you, my boy?" another said.
"Do not kill papa!" only he replies.
A soulful luster lights his streaming eyes,
Some glances from his gaze are turned away,
And the rude hands less fiercely grasp their prey.
Then one of the most pitiless says : "Go—
Get you back home, boy."   "Where—why?"
        "Don't you know?
Go to your mother."   Then the father said :
"He has no mother."   "What—his mother's
        dead?
Then you are all he has."   "That matters not,"
The captive answers, losing not a jot
Of his composure as he closely pressed
The little hands to warm them in his breast,
And says : "Our neighbor, Catherine, you know ;
Go to her."   "You'll come, too?"   "Not yet."
        "No, no!
Then I'll not leave you."   "Why?"   "These
        men, I fear,
Will hurt you, papa, when I am not here."

The father to the chieftain of the band
Says softly : "Loose your grasp and take my hand,

I'll tell the child to-morrow we shall meet,
Then you can shoot me in the nearest street,
Or farther off, just as you like."   "'Tis well!"
The words from those rough lips reluctant fell,
And, half unclasped, the hands less fierce appear.
The father says : "You see, we're all friends here;
I'm going with these gentlemen to walk ;
Go home.   Be good.   I have no time to talk."
The little fellow, reassured and gay,
Kisses his father and then runs away.

"Now he is gone, and we are at our ease,
And you can kill me how and where you please,"
The father says.   "Where is it I must go?"
Then through the crowd a long thrill seems to
        flow,
The lips, so late with cruel wrath afoam,
Relentingly and roughly cry : "Go home!"

ONE NICHE THE HIGHEST

Elihu Burritt

THE scene opens with a view of the great
Natural Bridge in Virginia.   There are three or
four lads standing in the channel below, looking
up with awe to that vast arch of unhewn rocks
which the Almighty bridged over those everlasting
butments "when the morning stars sang together."

The little piece of sky spanning those measureless
piers is full of stars, although it is midday. It is
almost five hundred feet from where they stand,
up those perpendicular bulwarks of limestone to
the key of that vast arch, which appears to them
only of the size of a man's hand. The silence of
death is rendered more impressive by the little
stream that falls from rock to rock down the
channel. The sun is darkened, and the boys have
uncovered their heads, as if standing in the
presence-chamber of the Majesty of the whole
earth. At last this feeling begins to wear away;
they look around them, and find that others have
been there before them. They see the names of
hundreds cut in the limestone butments. A new
feeling comes over their young hearts, and their
knives are in their hands in an instant. "What
man has done, man can do," is their watchword,
while they draw themselves up, and carve their
names a foot above those of a hundred full-grown
men who have been there before them.

They are all satisfied with this feat of physical
exertion, except one. This ambitious youth sees
a name just above his reach — a name which will
be green in the memory of the world when those
of Alexander, Caesar, and Bonaparte shall rot in
oblivion. It was the name of Washington.
Before he marched with Braddock to that fatal
field, he had been there and left his name a foot

above any of his predecessors.   It was a glorious thought to write his name side by side with that of the Father of his Country.   He grasps his knife with a firmer hand, and, clinging to a little jutting crag, he cuts a niche into the limestone, about a foot above where he stands; he then reaches up and cuts another for his hands.   'Tis a dangerous adventure; and, as he draws himself up carefully to his full length, he finds himself a foot above every name chronicled in that mighty wall.   While his companions are regarding him with concern and admiration, he cuts his name in wide capitals, large and deep, into that flinty album.   His knife is still in his hand, and strength in his sinews, and a new-created aspiration in his heart.   Again he cuts another niche, and again he carves his name in larger capitals.   This is not enough; heedless of the entreaties of his companions, he cuts and climbs again.   He measures his length at every gain he cuts.   The voices of his friends wax weaker and weaker, till their words are finally lost on his ear.   He now for the first time casts a look beneath him.   Had that glance lasted a moment more, that moment would have been his last.   He clings with a convulsive shudder to his little niche in the rock.   His knife is worn half way to the haft.   He can hear the voices of his terror-stricken companions below.   What a moment!   What a meagre chance to escape destruc tion! There is no retracing his steps. It is impossible to put his hands into the same niche with his feet and retain his slender hold a moment. His companions instantly perceive this new and fearful dilemma. He is too high to ask for his father and mother, his brothers and sisters. But one of his companions anticipates his desire. Swift as the wind he bounds down the channel, and the situation of the fated boy is told upon his father's hearthstone.

Minutes of almost eternal length roll on, and there are hundreds standing in that rocky channel and hundreds on the bridge above, all holding their breath, and awaiting the fearful catastrophe. The poor boy hears the hum of new and numerous voices, both above and below. He can just distinguish the tones of his father, who is shouting with all the energy of despair: "William! William! don't look down! Your mother, and Henry and Harriet are all here praying for you! Don't look down! Keep your eyes toward the top!" The boy didn't look down. His eye is fixed like a flint toward heaven, and his young heart on Him who reigns there. He grasps again his knife. He cuts another niche, and another foot is added to the hundreds that remove him from the reach of human help from below. How carefully he uses his wasting blade! How anxiously he selects the softest places in that vast pier! How he avoids every flinty grain! How he economizes his physical powers, resting a moment at each gain he cuts! How every motion is watched from below! There stand his father, mother, brother, and sister on the very spot where, if he falls, he will not fall alone.

The sun is half-way down in the west. The lad has made fifty additional niches in that mighty wall. Fifty more must be cut before the longest rope can reach him. His wasting blade strikes again into the limestone. The boy is emerging painfully, foot by foot from under that lofty arch. Spliced ropes are ready in the hands of those who are leaning over the outer edge of the bridge above. Two minutes more and all must be over. The blade is worn to the last half-inch. The boy's head reels; his eyes are starting from their sockets. His last hope is dying in his heart; his life must hang on the next gain he cuts. That niche is his last.

At the last faint gash he makes, his knife — his faithful knife — falls from his little, nerveless hand, and, ringing along the precipice, falls at his mother's feet. An involuntary groan of despair runs like a death-knell through the channel below, and all is as still as the grave. At the height of nearly three hundred feet the devoted boy lifts his hopeless heart and closes his eyes to commend his soul to God.

'Tis but a moment — there! one foot swings off — he is reeling — trembling — toppling over into eternity! Hark! a shout falls on his ear from above. The man who is lying with half his length over the bridge, has caught a glimpse of the boy's head and shoulders. Quick as thought the noosed rope is within reach of the sinking youth. With a faint, convulsive effort the swooning boy drops his arms into the noose. Darkness comes over him, and with the words "God — mother" — whispered on his lips just loud enough to be heard in heaven — the tightening rope lifts him out of his last shallow niche. Not a lip moves while he is dangling over that fearful abyss; but when a sturdy Virginian reaches down and draws up the lad and holds him up in his arms before the tearful, breathless multitude, such shouting — such weeping and leaping for joy — never greeted the ear of a human being so recovered from the yawning gulf of eternity.

A PATHETIC INCIDENT OF THE REBELLION

ADAPTED

It was in the valley of the Shenandoah. General Stewart, with his rebel mob, had pitched his camp on a hillside. At the top of the hill lay an

old farmhouse, torn by the shot and shell of yesterday's fight, with a few haystacks standing near.

While General Stewart was inspecting his camp,
he came across a little child, a boy, four or five
years old. Turning to his sergeant, he asked in a
tone indicating displeasure : " Sergeant, where did
this child come from? Take it at once to its
mother." "Its mother is dead," replied the sergeant. "Dead?" "Yes, killed in the battle yesterday. When you led the boys over the stone
fence by the farmhouse on the hill, I found this
little chap in a corner, a-shivering with fear."

While the sergeant was giving this information,
the little fellow reached out a tiny Union flag, evidently trying to make friends with the general,
who was turning away as if to avoid him.

" Sergeant, where did that flag come from?"
"The boy had it in his hand when I found him.
He said that his father gave it to him for the
Fourth of July." This was sufficient. The general stooped and lifted the child in his arms.
" Keep your little flag, my boy," said he. " You
don't know the difference, and would that I didn't
know and never had known the difference. Here,
sergeant, take care of this child. We killed his
father yesterday ; let us take care of him. Perhaps he will bring luck to some of us. What do
you say, boys?"

The sergeant bent over and hoisted the little

fellow to his great, broad shoulders. Hark!
What's that noise? A shout from down the hill
and a whistle of bullets from the direction of the
farmhouse warned the sergeant that the Federals
were about to make another midnight attack.
There was only one thing to do, and that was to
gain the summit, where the haystacks would afford
some protection. So up the hill, over the brush,
through the woods, with the child on his shoulders, he led the flight. Suddenly midnight was
turned into daylight; the Federals had fired the
haystacks. Every move of the rebel raiders was
now discernible. Whither should they fly? Yankees in front of them, Yankees behind them,
Yankees all around them! There seemed to be
nothing but death awaiting them. During this
terrible scene the little fellow was full of excitement. The brilliant fire, and the sight of those
blue-clad men, with their glistening guns, delighted
him. Little did he know the deadly meaning of
those terrible machines of war. Look! The Federal officer draws his saber and his lips are framing
the command, "Fire!" when the little chap, holding
tightly to the sergeant's head, waved his little
Union flag over his head there in the glow and
light of those burning haystacks. And in that
awful stillness that comes before any dreadful
catastrophe, the child, raising himself higher on
the sergeant's shoulders, shouted in his brave little

voice: " Fourth of July! Hurrah! Hurrah! Fourth of July!"

When the little fellow ceased his boyish shouting, the sergeant stood there as firm as a rock, awaiting the volley that would hurl him to his death. But put it on record, in gold and in red, that at the sight of that flag the line of blue divided, and the old, gray Confederate sergeant, with his precious charge on his shoulders, still waving his tiny flag, passed through the lines, saved by the child he bore, while cheer after cheer shook the bullet-ridden leaves of the old oaks overhead.

OVER THE ORCHARD FENCE

HARRY J. SHELLMAN

It 'peared to me I wa'ant no use out in the field
    to-day,
I somehow couldn't swing the scythe nor toss the
    new-mown hay,
An' so I thought I'd jest sit here among the apple
    trees,
To rest awhile beneath their shade an' watch the
    buzzin' bees.

Well, no! Can't say I'm tired, but somehow
    wanted rest,
To be away from everything seemed sorter to be
    best;

For every time I go around where there is human
      kind,
I kinder hunger after what I know I cannot find.

It's sing'lar how in natur' the sweet apple blossoms
      fall,
The breeze, it 'pears to know an' pick the purtiest
      of 'em all ;
It's only rugged ones, perhaps, can stand agin' the
      blast —
The frail and delicate are made too beautiful to
      last.

Why, right here in the orchard, among the oldest
      there,
I had a nice young apple tree jest startin' out to
      bear,
An' when the ekinoctial storm come tearin' cross
      the farm
It tore that up, while to the rest it didn't do no
      harm.

An' so you've been away a spell ? Well, how is
      things in town ?
Dare say it's gettin' close an' hot. To take it up
      an' down
I like the country best. I'm glad to see you're
      lookin' spry.
No! Things don't go jest right with me; I
      scarcely can say why.

Oh, yes! The crop is lookin' fair, I've no right to
　　complain,
My corn runs well, an' I have got a purty stand of
　　grain ;
My hay is almost made, an'— Well, yes! Betsy ?
　　She's so so —
She never is as hearty as she ought to be, you
　　know.

The boys?   They're in the medder lot down by
　　the old mill race ;
As fine a piece of grass ground as I've got upon
　　the place ;
It's queer how, when the grass grows up, an' gits
　　to lookin' best,
That then's the time to cut it down.   It's so with
　　all the rest

Of things in natur', I suppose.   The harvest comes
　　for all
Some day, but I can't understand jest why the
　　best fruit fall ;
The Lord knows best.   He fixes things to suit His
　　own wise laws ;
An' yet it's cur'ous oftentimes to figure out the
　　cause.

Mirandy?   Yes, she's doin' well ; she's helpin'
　　mother now
About the house.   A likely gal to bake, or milk a
　　cow.

An— No! I'm not half the man I were ten
      year ago ;
But then the years will tell upon the best of us,
      you know.

Another ? Yes, our Lizzie was the best one of
      them all ;
Our baby, only seventeen, so sweet, an' fair, an'
      tall,
Jest like a lily ; always good, yet cheerful, bright
      an' gay —
We laid her in the church yard, over yonder, yes-
      terday.

That's why I felt I wa'ant no use out in the field
      to-day.
I somehow couldn't swing the scythe nor toss the
      new-mown hay ;
An' so I thought I'd jest sit here among the trees
      an' rest ;
These things come harder when we're old ; but
      then the Lord knows best.

THE HOME IN THE GOVERNMENT

A FEW Sundays ago I stood on a hill in Washington. My heart thrilled as I looked on the towering marble of my country's Capitol, and a mist gathered in my eyes as, standing there, I thought of its tremendous significance and the powers there assembled, and the responsibilities there centered —its president, its congress, its courts, its gathered treasure, its army, its navy, and its 60,000,000 of citizens. It seemed to me the best and mightiest sight that the sun could find in its wheeling course — this majestic home of a Republic that has taught the world its best lessons of liberty — and I felt that if wisdom and justice and honor abided therein, the world would stand indebted to this temple on which my eyes rested, and in which the ark of my covenant was lodged for its final uplifting and regeneration.

A few days later I visited a country home. A modest, quiet house sheltered by great trees and set in a circle of field and meadow, gracious with the promise of harvest — barns and cribs well filled and the old smoke-house odorous with treasure — the fragrance of pink and hollyhock mingling with the aroma of garden and orchard, and resonant with the hum of bees and poultry's busy clucking — inside the house, thrift, comfort, and that cleanliness that is next to godliness — the restful beds, the open fireplace, the books and papers, and the old clock that had held its steadfast pace amid the frolic of weddings, that had welcomed in steady measure the new born babes of the family, and kept company with the watchers of the sick bed, and had ticked the solemn requiem of the dead; and the well-worn Bible that, thumbed by fingers long since stilled, and blurred with tears of eyes long since closed, held the simple annals of the family, and the heart and conscience of the home.   Outside stood the master, strong and wholesome and upright; wearing no man's collar; with no mortgage on his roof, and no lien on his ripening harvest; pitching his crops in his own wisdom, and selling them in his own time in his chosen market; master of his lands and master of himself.   Near by stood his aged father, happy in the heart and home of his son.   And as they started to the house the old man's hand rested on the young man's shoulder, touching it with the knighthood of the fourth commandment, and laying there the unspeakable blessing of an honored and grateful father.   As they drew near the door the old mother appeared; the sunset falling on her face, softening its wrinkles and its tenderness, lighting up her patient eyes, and the rich music of her heart trembling on her lips, as in simple phrase she welcomed her husband and son to their home. Beyond was the good wife, true of touch and tender, happy amid her household cares, clean of heart and conscience, the helpmate and the buckler of her husband. And the children, strong and sturdy, trooping down the lane with the lowing herd, or weary of simple sport, seeking, as truant birds do, the quiet of the old home nest. And I saw the night descend on that home, falling gently as from the wings of the unseen dove. And the stars swarmed in the bending skies — the trees thrilled with the cricket's cry — the restless bird called from the neighboring wood — and the father, a simple man of God, gathering the family about him, read from the Bible the old, old story of love and faith, and then went down in prayer, the baby hidden amid the folds of its mother's dress, and closed the record of that simple day by calling down the benediction of God on the family and the home.

And as I gazed the memory of the great Capitol faded from my brain. Forgotten its treasure and its splendor. And I said: "Surely here — here in the homes of the people is lodged the ark of the convenant of my country. Here is its majesty and its strength. Here the beginning of its power and the end of its responsibility." The homes of the people; let us keep them pure and independent, and all will be well with the Republic. Here is the lesson our foes may learn — here is work the humblest and weakest hands may do. Let us in simple thrift and economy make our homes independent. Let us in frugal industry make them self-sustaining. In sacrifice and denial let us keep them free from debt and obligation. Let us make them homes of refinement in which we shall teach our daughters that modesty and patience and gentleness are the charms of woman. Let us make them temples of liberty, and teach our sons that an honest conscience is every man's first political law. That his sovereignty rests beneath his hat, and that no splendor can rob him and no force justify the surrender of the simplest right of a free and independent citizen. And above all, let us honor God in our homes — anchor them close in His love. Build His altars above our hearthstones, uphold them in the set and simple faith of our fathers and crown them with the Bible — that book of books in which all the ways of life are made straight and the mystery of death is made plain. The home is the source of our national life. Back of the national Capitol and above it stands the home. Back of the President and above him stands the citizen. What the home is, this and nothing else will the Capitol be. What the citizen wills, this and nothing else will the President be.

GENERAL GRANT'S ENGLISH

MARK TWAIN

I WILL detain you with only just a few words — just a few thousand words — and then give place to a better man if he has been created. Lately a great and honored author, Matthew Arnold, has been finding fault with General Grant's English. That would be fair enough, maybe, if the examples of imperfect English averaged more instances to the page in General Grant's book than they do in Mr. Arnold's criticism upon the book; but they don't.   It would be fair enough, maybe, if such instances were commoner in General Grant's book than they are in the works of the average standard author; but they aren't.   In truth, General Grant's derelictions in the matter of grammar and construction are not more frequent than are such derelictions in the works of a majority of the professional authors of our time and all previous times — authors as exclusively and painstakingly trained to the literary trade as was General Grant to the trade of war.

This is not a random statement; it is a fact, and easily demonstrable.   I have at home a book called *Modern English Literature, Its Blemishes and Defects*, by Henry H. Breen, F. S. A., a countryman of Mr. Arnold.   In it I find examples of bad grammar and slovenly English from the pens of Sydney Smith, Sheridan, Hallam, Whately, Carlyle, both Disraelis, Alison, Junius, Blair, Macaulay, Shakespeare, Milton, Gibbon, Southey, Bulwer, Cobbett, Dr. Samuel Johnson, Trench, Lamb, Landor, Smollett, Walpole, Walker (of the dictionary), Christopher North, Kirke White, Mrs. Sigourney, Benjamin Franklin, Walter Scott, and Mr. Lindley Murray, who made the grammar.

In Mr. Arnold's paper on General Grant's book we find a couple of grammatical crimes and more than several examples of very crude and slovenly English — enough of them to easily entitle him to a lofty place in that illustrious list of delinquents just named. General Grant's grammar is as good as anybody's; but if this were not so, we might brush that inconsequential fact aside and hunt his great book for far higher game. To suppose that because a man is a poet or a historian he must be correct in his grammar, is to suppose that an architect must be a joiner, or a physician a compounder of medicines. If you should climb the mighty Matterhorn to look out over the kingdoms of the earth, it might be a pleasant incident to find strawberries up there; but you don't climb the Matterhorn for strawberries!

There is that about the sun which makes us forget his spots; and when we think of General Grant our pulses quicken and his grammar vanishes

We only remember that this is the simple soldier, who, all untaught of the silken phrase-mak-
ers, linked words together with an art surpass-
ing the art of the schools, and put into them a
something which will still bring to American ears,
as long as America shall last, the roll of his vanished drums and the tread of his marching hosts.
What do we care for his grammar when we think
of the man that put together that thunderous
phrase, " Unconditional and immediate surrender!" And those others: " I propose to move
immediately upon your works!" " I propose to
fight it out on this line if it takes all summer!"
Mr. Arnold would doubtless claim that that last
sentence is not strictly grammatical, and yet,
nevertheless, it did certainly wake up this nation as
a hundred million tons of A1, fourth proof, hard-
boiled, hide-bound grammar from another mouth
couldn't have done. And, finally, we have that gentler phrase, that one which shows you another true
side of the man; shows that in his soldier heart there
was room for other than gory war mottoes, and in
his tongue the gift to fitly phrase them: " Let us
have peace."

THE OLD ACTOR'S STORY

George R. Sims

Mine is a strange, wild story — the strangest you
    ever heard ;
There are many who won't believe it, but it's gos-
    pel, every word ;
It's the biggest drama of any in a long, adventurous
    life ;
The scene was a ship, and the actors — were my-
    self and my new-wed wife.

You mustn't mind if I ramble, and lose the thread
    now and then ;
I'm old, you know, and I wander — it's a way with
    old women and men,
For their lives lie all behind them, and their
    thoughts go far away,
And are tempted afield, like children lost on a sum-
    mer's day.

The years must be five and twenty that have
    passed since that awful night,
But I see it again this evening, I can never shut
    out the sight.
We were only a few weeks married, I and my wife,
    you know,
When we had an offer from Melbourne, and made
    up our minds to go.

We'd acted in England together, traveling up and
    down
With a band of strolling players, going from town
    to town ;
We played the lovers together — we were leading
    lady and gent —
And at last we played in earnest, and straight to
    the church we went.

The parson gave us his blessing, and I gave Nellie
    the ring,
And swore that I'd love and cherish, and endow
    her with everything ;
How we smiled at that part of the service when I
    said, "I thee endow!"
But as to the "love and cherish," I meant to keep
    that vow.

We were only a couple of strollers ; we had coin
    when the show was good,
When it wasn't, we went without it, and did the
    best we could ;
We were happy, and loved each other, and laughed
    at the shifts we made —
Where love makes plenty of sunshine, there pov-
    erty casts no shade.

Well, at last we got to London, and did pretty
    well for a bit ;

Then the business dropped to nothing, and the
    manager took a flit —
Stepped off one Sunday morning, forgetting the
    treasury call;
But our luck was in, and we managed right on our
    feet to fall.

We got an offer from Melbourne — got it that
    very week.
Those were the days when thousands went over,
    their fortunes to seek,
The days of the great gold fever, and a manager
    thought the spot
Good for a "spec," and took us as actors among
    the lot.

We hadn't a friend in England — we'd only our-
    selves to please —
And we jumped at the chance of trying our for-
    tune across the seas.
We went on a sailing vessel, and the journey was
    long and rough ;
We hadn't been out a fortnight before we had had
    enough.

But use is a second nature, and we'd learned not
    to mind the storm,
When misery came upon us, came in a hideous
    form.

My poor little wife fell ailing, grew worse, and at
    last so bad
That the doctor said she was dying — I thought
    'twould have sent me mad —

Dying where leagues of billows seemed to shriek
    for their prey,
And the nearest land was hundreds — aye, thou-
    sands — of miles away,
She raved one night in her fever, and the next lay
    still as death,
So still I'd to bend and listen for the faintest sign
    of breath.

She seemed in a sleep, and sleeping, with a smile
    on her thin, wan face,
She passed away one morning, while I prayed at
    the throne of grace.
I knelt in the little cabin, and prayer after prayer
    I said,
Till the surgeon came and told me it was useless —
    my wife was dead!

Dead! I wouldn't believe it. They forced me
    away that night,
For I raved in my wild despairing, the shock sent
    me mad outright.
I was shut in the farthest cabin, and I beat with
    my head on the side,
And all day long in my madness, "They've mur-
    dered her!" I cried.

They locked me away from my fellows — put me
    in cruel chains;
It seems I had seized a weapon to beat out the
    surgeon's brains.
I cried in my wild, mad frenzy that he was a
    demon sent
To gloat o'er the frenzied anguish with which my
    heart was rent.

I spent that night with the irons heavy upon my
    wrists,
And my wife lay dead quite near me.   I beat
    with my fettered fists,
Beat on my prison panels, and then — O God —
    and then
I heard the shrieks of women, and the tramp of
    hurrying men.

I heard the cry, "Ship afire!" caught up by a
    hundred throats,
And over the roar the captain shouting to lower
    the boats;
Then cry upon cry, and curses, and the crackle of
    burning wood,
And the place grew hot as a furnace, I could feel
    it where I stood.

I beat at the door and shouted, but never a sound
    came back.

The timbers above me started, till right through a
yawning crack
I could see the flames shoot upward, seizing on
mast and sail,
Fanned in their burning fury by the breath of the
howling gale.

I dashed at the door in my fury, shrieking : " I
will not die!
Die in this burning prison!" but I caught no answering cry.
Then suddenly, right upon me, the flames crept
up with a roar,
And their fiery tongues shot forward, cracking
my prison door.

I was free — with the heavy iron door dragging
me down to death;
I fought my way to the cabin, choked by the
burning breath
Of the flames that danced around me like men-
mocking demons at play,
And then — O God ! I can see it, and shall to my
dying day —

There lay my Nell as they'd left her, dead in her
berth that night;
The flames flung a smile on her features — a horrible, livid light.

God knows how I reached and touched her, but
    found myself by her side;
I thought she was living a moment, I forgot that
    my Nell had died.

The shock of those awful seconds sent reason
    back to my brain;
I heard a sound as of breathing, and then a low
    cry of pain;
Oh, was there mercy in heaven? Was there a
    God in the skies?
The dead woman's lips were moving, the dead
    woman opened her eyes.

I cursed like a madman raving — I cried to her:
    " Nell! my Nell!"
They had left us alone and helpless, alone in that
    burning hell;
They had left us alone to perish — forgotten, me
    living — and she
Had been left to be borne to heaven by the
    flames instead of the sea.

I clutched at her, roused her shrieking, the stupor
    was on her still;
I seized her in spite of my fetters — fear gave me
    a giant's will.
God knows how I did it, but blindly I fought
    through the flames and the wreck

Up — up to the air, and brought her safe to the
    untouched deck.

We'd a moment of life together — a moment of
    life, the time
For one last word to each other — 'twas a mo-
    ment supreme, sublime.
From the trance we'd for death mistaken, the heat
    had brought her to life,
And I was fettered and helpless, so we lay there,
    husband and wife.

It was but a moment, but ages seemed to have
    passed away,
When a shout came over the water; I looked, and
    lo, there lay,
Right away from the vessel, a boat that was stand-
    ing by;
They had seen our forms on the vessel, as the
    flames lit up the sky.

I shouted a prayer to heaven, then called to my
    wife, and she
Tore with new strength at my fetters — God
    helped her, and I was free;
Then over the burning bulwarks we leaped for one
    chance of life.
Did they save us?   Well, here I am, sir, and yon-
    der's my dear old wife!

NOT GUILTY

ADAPTED

IT was about noon on a sultry day, that wore heavily on both court and jury, when the prosecution announced that it had finished its case. There was little excitement in the audience; it was evidently a clear case of murder, the chain of evidence presented by the state had completely entwined the prisoner. A man had been stabbed; had fallen dead, his hands clasped over his wound, with not an indication of defense on his part. From beneath his hand, when convulsively opened, a knife had fallen, which, it was shown, the prisoner's wife had seized and concealed. Why should she have concealed it if her husband was innocent of foul play?

There was marked lack of attention on the part of the jury when the dusky prisoner took the stand in his own behalf. He told his story in a straight-forward, simple manner; explained how he had killed the deceased in self-defense; that the knife had fallen from the dead man's hand and was the one with which he himself had been attacked. It was apparent that nothing he could say would make any impression on the jury; they were decided as to his guilt, so, with a sigh that permeated the whole room, he took his seat. While

the prisoner was on the stand, an elderly gentleman with iron-gray hair, and clad in a gray suit,
entered the room and stood silently by the door.
At the close of the prisoner's plea, the solicitor
arose and in a few cold words stated his case: The
man had stabbed another wantonly. If the knife
was the property of the deceased, why was it not
produced in court? The prisoner's wife had
picked it up. With this brief summary, he passed
the prisoner's life into the hands of the jury.
The judge had arisen, and in solemn style was
saying: "Mr. Foreman, and Gentlemen of the
Jury," when suddenly from the old gentleman in
gray came the sharp but decisive words: "If it
please your Honor, the prisoner is entitled to the
closing argument, and, in the absence of other
counsel, I beg you will allow me to speak for the
defense." "Mr. Clerk," said the Court, "mark
General Robert Thomas for the defense." The
court-room, which before had been astir with the
murmur of those present, was now deathly still.
General Thomas for the defense! What could it
all mean? Had any new evidence been discovered? Only the old man, grim, gray, and
majestically defiant, stood between the prisoner
and the gallows. After standing a moment and
gazing about the court-room with an air of disgust,
he said with quick but quiet energy: "The knife
that was found by the dead man's side was his

own. He had drawn it before he was stabbed. Ben Thomas is a brave man; a strong man; he would never have used a weapon, if his antagonist had been unarmed. A brave man who is full of strength never draws a weapon to repel a simple attack. The defendant drew his knife when he saw a knife in the hand of his foe, not from fear, but to equalize the combat. Why do I say he was brave? Every man upon this jury shouldered his musket during the war. Some of you were perhaps at Gettysburg; I was there too." It was evident that the General had aroused a deepfelt interest by his allusion to the old days when all the men for miles about entered the army, and many had served under the old General, whose war record was a household legend. "I and the only brother that God ever gave me. I well remember that fight. The enemy met our onslaught with a courage and grit that could not be shaken. Line after line melted away, and at last came Pickett's charge.

"You know the result. Out of that vortex of flame and that storm of lead and iron a handful drifted back. From one to another a man of black skin was seen to run. On, on he went; gone one moment and in sight the next, on, up to the flaming cannon themselves. There he stooped and lifted a form from the ground; and then, stumbling, staggering under his load, made his

way back across that field of death, until, meeting
him halfway, I took the burden myself from the
hero and bore it myself to safety.   That burden
was the senseless form of my brother" — here the
General paused, and walking rapidly towards the
prisoner, he raised his arm on high, and his voice
rang out like a trumpet, — "gashed and bleeding
and mangled, but alive, thank God!   And the man
who bore him out, who brought him to me in his
arms as a mother would a sick child, himself torn
by a fragment of a shell until the great heart was
almost dropping from his breast, that man, my
friends, sits here accused of murder."   To add
emphasis to his plea, he tore open the prisoner's
shirt and laid bare his breast on which were the
scars of that terrible day.   "Look!" he cried,
"and bless the sight, for that scar was won by a
slave in an hour that tried the courage of free men
and put to its highest test the best manhood of the
South.   No man who won such wounds could
thrust a knife into an unarmed assailant.   I have
come seventy miles in my old age to say this."

The jury did not even retire, but instantly
returned a verdict of "Not guilty!"   Some may
say that this was contrary to the evidence, but
if one could judge from the appearance of the
spectators, as they left the court-house, they
were content.   Even the apparently cold-hearted
solicitor, who bore a scar on his forehead that

dated back to the old days when North and South were estranged, received the verdict with a smile that indicated his approval.

———

THE PHILIPPINE ISLANDS

John D. Long

THE treaty of peace with Spain, thank heaven, has been ratified. And while, unfortunately, the delay in its ratification may be accountable for the recent bloodshed at Manila, the discussions which preceded it have not been without their value in an honest presentation of all phases of the situation, and in holding the country to the highest ideals of national duty and honor.

As an outside observer, I have been struck with the various methods in which this subject of the Philippines has been discussed. One of these methods may be styled as the oratorical declamatory. On the one hand this method has found expression in saying that the duty of the American eagle is to hold on to everything on which he puts his claws, reminding one of Abraham Lincoln's story of the modest farmer, who said that all the land he wanted to own was only what adjoined his farm. Under this head, also, comes the stirring cry, which never fails to capitivate the popular ear, that wherever the flag has once been let loose,

there it must always float. All of which sounds
well, but needs a second thought.

On the other hand is the equally extravagant
talk about the greed of conquest and the reduction
of the Filipino to the wretched condition of vas-
salage and slavery. Those who indulge in this
exuberance of rhetoric forget that our war was
with Spain and that we have simply transferred to
the United States, as the result of our victory in
that war, the sovereignty which Spain had over the
Philippines; that this transfer was incidentally very
much in the interest of the islanders — more, many
think, than in our own; and that it relieved them
from a yoke under which they groaned, giving
them the fairest promise on which their eyes ever
opened — a promise which the American people
will redeem.

The second method of discussion may be called
the judicial deliberate. Here, too, on the one hand
are those of whom the most distinguished is, perhaps, our revered Gov. Boutwell, who, I sometimes
think, is the noblest Roman of us all. He is
thoroughly logical and consistent. I do not believe
he is much troubled with the constitutional refine-
ments which the moment they were stated faded
into thin air. He is troubled by no notion that it
is our solemn duty not to permit these islands to
be restored to Spain, and at the same time our
equally solemn duty, which it is rather puzzling to

reconcile with the other, that the United States is not to accept the disposition of them. He puts his feet on the substantial rock of letting them absolutely alone, withdrawing our soldiers and our ships of war, and returning to the integrity and simplicity of our old-time American continental establishment. He presents clearly and emphatically the risks of the increased costs to our revenues, and of the increased strain upon our national system which their retention will bring. His objections are weighty and entitled to the most deliberate consideration.

But on the other hand is the view held, I think, by the great majority of our people, that we cannot thus easily, having once put our hands to the plough, look back, and that events not within our control have brought us to responsibilities which we cannot disregard and let alone, but which we must face and meet. The matter is one of great moment. I most heartily wish it had never confronted us. I wish the world would kindly let up for a while and not move so fast. I wish, also, that youth would stay. I would rather be a boy again than to be secretary of the navy, as I am. But I think it is a mistake to say that it is beyond the ability of the American people to deal with a problem with which other nations have successfully dealt, or that it is a harder problem than many problems which are upon us already.

God has so ordered the laws of growth that no life, of plant or man or nation, works out its destiny and bears its fruit except by ripening to its completion. First the blade, then the ear, then the full corn in the ear. The glory of Greece and of Rome is in the culmination of their civilization, art, literature and political power; and therein is their contribution to the higher civilizations which have succeeded.

So it must needs be with the great powers of to-day, Great Britain and Germany and America. "Thou fool, that which thou sowest is not quickened except it die." Of what infinitely greater value in the formation of all standards of character and service are the lives of Washington and Lincoln because they are mighty shadows of the past, rather than lean and slippered figures lingering on the thresholds of to-day. There never was a more beautiful triumph of the poetry of architecture, or a finer realization of the patriotism and genius of our country embodied in material shape and outline, than that White City on the borders of Lake Michigan, in which was held the World's Fair. But the impressiveness and untiring delight of that scene, which now lingers like an exquisite strain of music on the memory, would be lost if it had lasted longer. The flames consumed it, and it became eternal, and that mortal put on immortality.

It is a poor philosophy that peers hopelessly into the future only to learn how far off is the day, not of ruin and dissolution, for that will never come, but of transition to some new form of civilization, some new form of national life, some new arrangement of national boundaries, all of which are necessary accompaniments of the enlarging and advancing progress of mankind. Meantime, our duty is to meet the responsibility that is upon us. Undoubtedly it would be easier if we could shift it from our shoulders, and lay it down. It is with a wrench that any man, especially any son of New England familiar with its traditions and recalling its charms of provincial life, becomes aware that these must, betimes, give way to larger demands and more trying exigencies.

And yet, the fields that are before us are not altogether untrodden. It is not a new thing in the history of the world for an enlightened and civilized nation to deal with the less fortunate islands of remote seas. A Christian nation should not lose heart at the opportunity of carrying its education, its industries, its institutions and its untold. blessings to other less fortunate people.

The imagination kindles as it recognizes what those islands of the East may yet become. They are almost an unknown land. We have not yet begun to estimate the variety and opulence of their material wealth; their splendid forests, rich with every variety of wood in almost incalculable abundance; their mines of ore of every sort; their valleys teeming with luxuriant productiveness, and capable of supplying the food of the world.

Why doubt and repine, when the time of doubting and repining is inexorably past, and when doubting and repining can now do no good? Why shall not the United States, now that these lands and tribes have been intrusted to its disposition, enter upon the trust thus imposed upon it with the determination that, as it began by freeing them from the yoke of oppression, it will go on and insure them still larger blessings of liberty and civilization, and will so bear itself toward them that in securing their welfare it shall also promote its own, and, as always happens when men or nations coöperate in the spirit of justice and good will, the reward shall come to both in their mutual increase? Is not that the statesmanship of the great Master who limited not his mission or that of his disciples to his own chosen people, but proclaimed that his gospel should be preached in all the world unto all nations — that greatest statesman of all time, Jesus Christ?

THE SERGEANT'S STORY

I TELL you, pard, in this Western wild,
As a general thing, the dirt's jest piled
In a rather promiscuous sort of way
On top of a soldier's mortal clay;
An' a person'd think by the marble shaft
An' the flowers a-waving above the " graft "
That a major-general holds that tomb,
But the corpse down there wore a private's plume.

I remember the day they swore Mead in;
He was pale complected an' rather thin;
He'd bin what they call a trampin' beat,
An' enlisted for want o' somethin' to eat.
It's always the case that a new recruit
Is the butt o' the tricks from the older fruit,
An' the way the boys tormented the cuss
Was real down wicked an' scandalous.

He took it all with a sickly smile,
An' said if they'd wait till after awhile,
Till he got fed up in some sort o' trim,
It mightn't be healthy to fool with him;
An' I know'd by the look o' the fellow's eye —
For all he was backward an' rather shy —
That behind his skeleton sort o' breast
A heart like a lion's found a nest.

One night as the guard, at twelve o'clock,
Relieved the sentinel over the stock,
The corp'ral seen a kind o' glare
From toward the officers' quarters there;
The alarm was raised, an' the big gun fir'd,
An' the soldiers, not more'n half attired,
Come a-rushin' out on the barrack ground
With a wild an' excited sort of a bound.

The colonel's headquarters was all on fire,
An' the flames a-mountin' higher an' higher;
An' what with the yells o' men, an' shrieks
O' the officers' wives with their whitish cheeks,
An' the roar o' the flames an' demon's light
Illuminatin' the pitch-dark night,
'Twas sich a sight as I've often thought
You would see in hell, where it's bilin' hot.

An' then, with a wild, despairin' yell,
The colonel shouted: "*My God! Where's Nell?*"
His wife responded: "She's in her bed!"
Then fell to the ground like a person dead.
Up through the roof the mad flames roared,
An' the blindin' smoke in a dense mass poured
Through every crevice an' crack, till the cloud
Hung above like a death-black shroud.

(It mightn't be out o' place to state —
A kinder accountin' for this Mead's fate —
That Nell was an angel, ten years old,

With a heart as pure as the virgin gold ;
An' she had a kind of an angel trick
Of readin' an' sich like to the sick ;
An' many's the dainty her hands 'd bear
To Mead, one time, in the hospital there !)

My God ! it was 'nough to raise the hair
On the head of a marble statue.   There
Stood a crowd of at least two hundred men,
None darin' to enter that fiery pen —
Men that war brave on an Injun trail,
Whose courage was never known to fail —
But to enter that buildin' was certain death !
So they stood there starin' an' held their breath.

Then all to once, with an eager cry,
An' a bull-dog look in his flashin' eye,
This Mead rushes up to the wailin' band,
An' a paper thrust in the colonel's hand ;
"My mother's address!" he said, an' then
He sort o' smiled on the crowd o' men,
An' jest like a flash o' lightnin' shot
Through the door right into the seethin' pot.

With a yell o' horror the crowd looked on,
For they felt with him it was " Good-bye, John!"
But a half a minute after the dash
An upstairs window burst with a crash !
An' there stood Mead, like a smilin' saint,
The gal in his arms in a death-like faint.

He yelled for a rope, an' let her down
To *terra firma*, which means the ground.

Then he tied the rope to the window sash
Fur to follow down — but there came a crash,
An' the blazin' roof, with a fearful din,
Throwed the boy to the ground as it tumbled in.
We carried him 'way from the fearful heat,
A-hopin' the noble heart still beat,
But the old post surgeon shook his head,
An' said with a sigh that Mead was dead!

It wasn't long afore little Nell
Got over the shock, an' as soon as well
She circulated among the men,
With a sheet o' paper an' ink an' pen,
An' axed each one fur to give his mite
In remembrance o' Mead's brave work that night!
An' as a result, this monument stands
Among flowers planted by Nellie's hands.

An' every evenin' she walks up here,
The boys all say fur to drop a tear,
An' I've seen her, too, on her knees right there,
With her face turned upwards as if in prayer!
You see, that line up above's to tell
As how the stone was " Erected by Nell,"
An' down at the bottom, there, you'll see
Some Bible quotin' — "He died for me."

LOCHINVAR

ADAPTED

Kate McGhie, at the command of her father, was to wed Black Murdo, the Lord of Barra. She had long loved Wat Gordon, the young Lord of Lochinvar, who had rescued her from many perilous situations. Lochinvar heard from afar the day of the wedding and rose from a sick bed to snatch her from another man's hands.

As Lochinvar rode through the glinting, dewy woodlands he saw youths and damsels parading the glades in couples — keeping, however, their faces carefully towards the house for the signal that the bride was coming. Already the bride-groom had arrived with his company, and, indeed, most of them were even now in the hall drinking prosperity and posterity to the wedding.

"Haste you, my lord!" cried one malapert damsel to Wat, as he rode past a group of chattering minxes, "or you'll be too late to win your loving-cup of luck from the hands of the bride ere she goes to don her veil."

To her Wat Gordon bowed with his gayest air, and so passed by. The company was just coming out of the hall as he rode up. There, first of all, was Lady Wellwood, now wife of the bride's father. Behind her came Roger McGhie, looking wan and frail, but carrying himself with his old dignity and gentle courtesy. And there, talking gayly to my lady, was Murdo, Lord of Barra, now proud and elate, having come to the height of his estate, and with the cup of desire at his lip.

These three stopped dead when they saw the gay rider on the black horse, reining his steed at the foot of the steps of the house of Balmaghie. For a space they stood speechless.   But the master of the house, Roger McGhie, it was who spoke first :

" 'Tis a marvel and a pleasure to see you here, my Lord Lochinvar, on this, our bridal day — a welcome guest, indeed, if you come in peace to the house which once gave you shelter in time of need."

" Or come you to visit your ancient friends, who have not wholly cast you off, Lochinvar, though you have forgotten them?" added my lady, dimpling with a pleasure more than half malicious, on the broad terrace above him.

But Murdo said no word, as he stood on the upper steps gnawing his thin mustache and talking aside to his groomsman, as though that which was happening below were but some trifling matter which concerned him not.

" Light down and lead the dance, my lord," said Roger McGhie, courteously.   " None like you, they say, can tread a measure, none so readily win a lady's favor — so runs the repute of you."

" I thank you, Balmaghie," answered Wat,

courteously; "but I came without invitation, without summons, to ask but that last favor — the loving-cup of good luck from the bride's fair hands ere I ride to meet my fate. For I must needs ride fast and far this day."

"It is well and knightly asked, and shall be granted," said Roger McGhie. "Bid Kate bring hither a loving-cup of wine for my Lord of Lochinvar, who bides her coming at the hall door."

Black Murdo of Barra moved his hand impatiently.

"Let a bridesmaid fetch it," he said. "The bride is doubtless at her dressing and brooks not to be disturbed."

"Give me but the moment, and to you I leave the rest," said Wat Gordon, looking up at him with the light of a desperate challenge shining clear in his eye.

Then the maidens of the bridal standing about whispered eagerly to each other:

"Ah, that were a bridegroom, indeed! See him sit in the saddle like a god — fitter for our bonny Kate than you, black, scowling Murdo."

Then out through the open doorway of the hall there came a vision of delight. The young bride came forth, clad in white, daintily slender, divinely fair. Not yet had she assumed her bridal veil. In simple white she moved, her hair rippling in sunlit curls to her neck; her maiden snood still for

the last time binding it up. A silver beaker,
brimmed with the red claret wine, in her hand.
And as she came bearing it in, the wedding guests
opened a way for her to pass, murmuring content
and admiration.   Barra stepped forward as if to
relieve her of the burden, but she passed him by
as though she had not seen him.

Suddenly she stood at the side of Wat Gordon's
charger, which looked back at her over his shoulder, as though he, too, marveled at her beauty.

The true lovers were met for the last time.

"Would that they need never part!" said a
wise bridesmaid, leaning over and whispering to
her mate.   For their story was known, and all the
young were very pitiful.

"Amen to that!   Look at Murdo, how black
and gash he glowers at them!" said her companion.

Wat Gordon took the cup and held it high in
one brown gauntlet, still keeping the hand that
gave it in his other.

"I pledge the bride — the bride and her own
true love!" he said, loud enough for all to hear.

Then he drank, and leaned towards Kate as
though to return the cup with courteous salu-
tation.

None had heard the word he whispered.   None,
save she who loved him, can ever know, for Kate
has not revealed it.   But the word was heard.   A

moment only the bride's eyes sought her lover's. The next his arm was about her waist, and her foot left the gravel with a spring airy as a bird's first morning flight. The reins were gathered in Wat's hand; his love was safe on the saddle before him. The spurs were set in Drumclog's dark flanks, the brave horse sprang forward, and, before even so much as a cry could go up from that watching assembly, Wat Gordon was riding straight for Dee Water with his love between his arms.

"SWORE OFF"

J. N. FOOT

(Sit on chair at right side of a table.)

Boys, take another! To-night we'll be gay;
For to-morrow, you know, is the New Year's Day
And I promised my Bessie to-night should be
The very last night I stayed on this spree.
I've been a good fellow — spent lots of "tin"
In sampling and drinking both whiskey and gin;
And yet I remember, a long while ago,
When the sight of a drunken man frightened me so
I ran for a square.   I remember quite well
When I even detested the very smell
Of the accursed stuff.   I sometimes think
'Twas the devil tempted me to take the first drink.

But why look back with remorse or regret?
I must not remember — I want to forget.
Landlord, the bottle!   That's pretty good stuff;
Though I reckon I've seen and tasted enough.
It's a year since I've drawn a sober breath.
The doctors all say I will go to my death
If I do not leave off — you may laugh and scoff;
But somehow or other, between me and you,
I believe what the doctors tell me is true,
For at night when I try to be closing my eyes,
Such horrible visions before me arise
That I cannot rest, and I walk the floor
And long for the sleep that is mine no more.
To-night it winds up.   Laugh on, but you'll see
That this is the very last night of my spree.
I've promised my Bessie, and further, I swore —
She's got the paper — to take it no more
After to-night.   When I told her I'd sign,
The look on her face made me think of the time
When she stood at the altar, a beautiful bride,
And I looked on my choice with a good deal of
        pride.
Ah! many's the time, since I've been on this spree,
I've seen this good woman get down on her knee
And ask God, in His goodness, have mercy on me.
To-night it ends up.   Do you hear what I say? —
I'm a man once again from the New Year's Day.
Take one with you?   Why, I certainly will —
To-night is my last, and I'll be drinking my fill.

"Good luck and good health!" — strange wishes
    to make
O'er each glass of whiskey and gin that we take.
Good luck! Well, now, fellows, be still, and we'll
    see
The good luck I've had since I started this spree.
What with losing the job where I first learned my
    trade —
I've had twenty since, and I'm much afraid
The reason for losing them all is this glass.
The story of shame and disgrace let us pass;
I'll sum up the whole : You all know it's true
I would own a nice house — now the rent's
    overdue,
Yet, during this time — it is true what I say —
I wished myself luck at least ten times a day,
And as for good health! Now, do you think it
    right,
When you know it's destroying your appetite,
To call it good health? Why, I've not tasted food
For days at a time. Do you call my health good?
One with the landlord? To be sure, every time —
His till has held many a dollar of mine.
Come! Set up the poison! To-night is the last —
Well, here's to you, land — Ah! you'd play me a
    trick!
Take off that red wig with the horns very quick,
Or I'll put down this glass and be leaving the place.
Boys, look at the way he's distorting his face!

Look! look! it's the devil — a good masquerade
For those who engage in the rum-selling trade.
Go on with the game! — you'll find I'm not
　　afraid —
Ha, ha, ha, ha! at your by-play I scoff —
Whose blood-hound is this? Keep him off! — keep
　　him off!
Get out, you big brute! Don't you fellows see
He's wicked? Will bite? That he's snapping at
　　me?
My God! see the fangs! all reeking with gore —
Help! landlord, help! — fell this brute to the floor.
Ah! — he's gone! Take another! My nerves are
　　unstrung;
Quick! Give me the bottle ere the midnight is
　　rung.
Ah! — whiskey's the stuff that will make me feel
　　gay,
And I've said I've sworn off from the New Year's
　　Day —
Quick! — give me the bottle! Curse you! Don't
　　refuse,
Or I'll pull you apart, if my temper I lose —
Now give me a glass! Come, boys, take a drink!
It's the last you'll be taking with me, so I think —
O God! what is this? See, boys, it's a snake!
Look! — the bottle is full — hear the hissing they
　　make —
They crawl from its neck! For God's sake a drink!

Thanks! Boys, here's luck! (midnight hour strikes)
            'Tis the New Year, I think!
My oath — yes my oath! Is this sound I hear
The hour of midnight? Aye, it is the New Year.
         (throws the glass from him)
Begone from my sight, thou demon of hell!
Boys, here they come! there they go! Ah, the spell
Is o'er. I'm afire! See! It shoots from my eyes!
I am burning within! There the red demon lies.
What angel is this? 'Tis my Bessie to see
If my word has been kept about ending the spree —
No, no, it is black! 'Tis the devil's device —
He's claiming a soul as a sacrifice.
Great God! Is this death? The blood-hound
    again!
Take him off! Take him off! Do I call you in
    vain?
He clutches my throat — he chokes out my life!
Won't some of you fellows go after my wife!
Must I die here alone? See! They beckon to me!
Oh! if Bessie, my heart-broken wife could but see
That I kept my word. Won't — you — kindly —
    say
I "swore off" for good on the New Year's Day?

SERGEANT PRENTISS' FIRST PLEA

N. L. F. BACHMAN

IT was noon in the Crescent City.   Strolling up the broad walks of the courtyard, among the orange trees, were two men.   The one was the State's Attorney, a genial old man ; the other a mere boy, the old man's clerk.   Suddenly the old man turned to his companion and said : "Prentiss, would you like to make a speech on the case to-day?"   "I, sir! Why?"   "Well, I'll tell you. It is a bad thing for a young man to begin life with a success.   He is too apt to stop there.   This case is beyond doubt lost.   We have no evidence against the prisoner; but then, ' we must not give up the ship' until it sinks, you know.   Now here is a splendid chance to win glory, and all that sort of thing.   Pay no attention to blunders; I'll see to them.   Will you speak?"   "Yes, sir," said he, "I will."

It was a case of murder.   A man was missing ; no one knew what had become of him.   At last suspicion fell upon a man in high position in society, and he was arrested.   The community was astounded.   They knew the prisoner was not guilty.   That he was seen to go into the forest with the missing man did not prove anything.   This was the public verdict.   At the trial, nothing directly proving the prisoner's guilt was produced. Everything positive and direct seemed to point toward his innocence.

There was a smile of contempt on the prisoner's face when young Prentiss rose to speak. What could this stripling do against the giants of the law? It was David going out with a sling, the sling of Conscience, that sinks deep the pebbles of truth into the mailed forehead of guilt and crime. Prentiss stammered through a few sentences amid the derisive smiles of his opponents; then it seemed as though a wild spirit had fired his imagination, and he spoke with such power as was never before witnessed within that court-room. He caught up the merest shreds of evidence, and wove them into convicting arguments. He pictured the scene : the two men in the dark forest, the attack, the struggle, the death wound, the victim a moment gasping, and in a moment still; the hidden grave; and, trembling from head to foot, he pointed to the prisoner and fairly hissed : *"That man is the murderer!"*

The smile was gone from the prisoner's lips now. His counsel moved uneasily in their places; the thronged court-room was hushed. "Hold!" cried his opponent. "You have proved no such thing! You speak your piece extremely well; but we want facts here, my son." Prentiss turned upon him. "Hold, did you say? Hold? My

God!—if I should hold my peace the very stones
would stand witnesses; the walls would cry out
'*Murder!*' Aye, the spirit of the dead would rise
up before you; throwing back its crimsoned ves-
ture, it would disclose the cruel wound; holding
up the bloody dagger before your eyes, it would
point to him and whisper: '*He did this!*' Sir, can
you go with me out into that forest, and, standing
by that grave, known only to you and God, lift up
your hand to Heaven and swear you did not the
heinous deed?   Can you swear away your guilt?"

The prisoner had arisen.   "Stop, Prentiss!   I
had rather endure the pangs of Hell than of Conscience!   *I killed that man!*"

THE SONG OF THE MARKET–PLACE

James Buckham

Gay was the throng that poured through the streets
   of the old French town;
The walls with bunting streamed, and the flags
   tossed up and down.
"Vive l'roi!   Vive l'roi!" the shout of the people
   rent the air,
And the cannon shook and roared, and the bells
   were all ablare.

But, crouched by St. Peter's fount, a beggar with
   her child,

Weary and faint and starved, with eyes that were
    sad and wild,
Gazed on the passing crowd, and cried, as it went
    and came,
"Alms, for the love of God! Pity in Jesu's name!"

Few were the coins that fell in the little cup she
    bore;
But she looked at her starving babe, and cried
    from her heart the more:
"Alms, for the love of God! Mother of Jesu, hear!"
The steeples shook with bells, and the prayer was
    drowned in a cheer.

But see! Through the thoughtless crowd comes
    one with a regal face;
He catches the beggar's prayer, and turns with a
    gentle grace:
"Alms thou shalt have, poor soul! Alas! not a
    soul to share!
But stay!" — and he doffs his hat, and stands in
    the crowded square.

Then from his heart he sang a little song of the
    South,
A far-off cradle song, that fell from his mother's
    mouth,
And the din was hushed in the square, and the
    people stood as mute

As the beasts in the Thracian wood, when Orpheus
   touched his lute.

The melting tenor ceased, and a sob from the
   list'ners came;
"Mario!" cried a voice, and the throng caught up
   the name;
"Mario!" and the coins rained like a shower of
   gold,
Till the singer's hat o'erflowed, like Midas' chests
   of old.

"Sister," he said, and turned to the beggar crouching there,
"Take it; the gold is thine; Jesu hath heard thy
   prayer";
Then kissed the white-faced child, and smiling
   went his way,
Gladdened with kindly thoughts, and the joy of
   holiday.

That night, when the footlights shone on the
   famous tenor's face,
And he bowed to the splendid throng with his
   wonted princely grace,
Cheer after cheer went up, and, stormed at with
   flowers, he stood
Like a dark and noble pine, when the blossoms
   blow through the wood.

Wilder the tumult grew, till out of his fine despair
The thought of the beggar rose, and the song he
    had sung in the square.
Raising his hand, he smiled, and a silence filled
    the place,
While he sang that simple air, with the love-light
    on his face.

Wet were the singer's cheeks when the last note
    died away;
Brightest of all his bays, the wreath that he won
    that day!
Sung for the love of God, sung for sweet pity's
    sake,
Song of the market-place, tribute of laurel take.

THE GREAT AMERICAN REPUBLIC
A CHRISTIAN STATE

CARDINAL GIBBONS

AT first sight it might seem that religious principles were entirely ignored by the fathers of the
Republic in framing the Constitution, as it contains no reference to God, and makes no appeal to
religion.   And so strongly have certain religious
sects been impressed with this fact that they have
tried to get the name of God incorporated into
that document.   But the omission of God's holy

name affords no just criterion of the religious character of the founders of the Republic, or of the
Constitution which they framed.   Nor should we
have any concern to have the name of God
imprinted in the Constitution, so long as the Instrument itself is interpreted by the light of Christian revelation.   I would rather sail under the
guidance of a living captain than of a figure-head
at the prow of the ship.   Far better for the nation
that His Spirit should animate our laws, that He
should be invoked in our Courts of Justice, that He
should be worshipped in our Sabbaths and Thanks-
givings, and that His guidance should be implored
in the opening of our Congressional proceedings.

But the Declaration of Independence is one of
the most solemn and memorable professions of
political faith that ever emanated from the leading
minds of any country.   It has exerted as much influence in foreshadowing the spirit and character
of our Constitution and public policy as the Magna
Charta exercised on the Constitution of Great
Britain.   A devout recognition of God and of His
overruling Providence pervades that momentous
document from beginning to end.   God's holy
name greets us in the opening paragraph, and is
piously invoked in the last sentence of the Declaration; and thus it is, at the same time, the corner-
stone and the keystone of this great monument to
freedom.   The illustrious signers declared that

"when, in the course of human events, it becomes necessary for one people to dissolve the political bands that have connected them with another, and to assume among the powers of the earth the separate and equal station to which the laws of nature and of nature's God entitle them, a decent respect for the opinions of mankind requires that they should declare the causes that impel them to the separation." They acknowledge one Creator, the source of "life, liberty, and of happiness." They "appeal to the Supreme Judge of the world" for the rectitude of their intentions and they conclude in this solemn language: "For the support of this declaration, with a firm reliance on the protection of Divine Providence, we mutually pledge to each other our lives, our fortunes and our sacred honor."

The laws of the United States are so intimately interwoven with the Christian religion that they cannot be adequately expounded without the light of revelation. "The common law," says Kent, "is the common jurisprudence of the United States, and was brought from England and established here, so far as it was adapted to our institutions and circumstances. It is an incontrovertible fact that the common law of England is, to a great extent, founded on the principles of Christian ethics. The maxims of the Holy Scriptures form the great criterion of right and wrong in the civil courts.

The Puritans who founded New England, the

Dutch who settled in New York, the Quakers and
Irish who established themselves in Pennsylvania,
the Swedes in Delaware, the English Catholics who
colonized Maryland, the English Episcopalians
who colonized Virginia, Georgia, and North Carolina, the Irish Presbyterians who also emigrated to
the last-named State, the French Huguenots and
the English colonists who planted themselves in
South Carolina, the French and Spanish who took
possession of Louisiana and Florida — all these
colonists made an open profession of Christianity
in one form or other, and recognized religion as the
basis of society. The same remark applies with
equal truth to that stream of population which,
from the beginning of the present century, has
been constantly flowing into this country from Ire-
land and Germany, and extending itself over the
entire land. We have grown up, not as distinct,
independent, and conflicting communities, but as
one corporate body, breathing the same atmosphere of freedom, governed by the same political
rights.

I see in all this a wonderful manifestation of the
humanizing and elevating influence of Christian
civilization. What is the secret of our social stability
and order? It results from wise laws, based on
Christian principles, and which are the echo of
God's eternal law. What is the cohesive power
that makes us one body politic out of so many

heterogeneous elements? It is the religion of Christ. We live as brothers, because we recognize the brotherhood of humanity — one Father in Heaven, one origin, one destiny.

THE TRAITOR'S DEATHBED

GEORGE LIPPARD

FIFTY years ago, in a rude garret near the loneliest suburbs of the city of London, lay a dying man. He was but half dressed, though his legs were concealed in long military boots. An aged minister stood beside the rough couch. The form was that of a strong man grown old through care more than age. There was a face that you might look upon but once, and yet wear it in your memory forever. Aye, there was something terrible in that face, something so full of unnatural loneliness, unspeakable despair, that the aged minister started back in horror. But look! those strong arms are clutching at the vacant air; the death sweat stands in drops on that bold brow; the man is dying. Throb, throb, throb, beats the death watch in the shattered wall. "Would you die in the faith of the Christian?" faltered the preacher, as he knelt there on the damp floor.

The white lips of the death-stricken man trembled, but made no sound. Then, with the strong agony of death upon him, he rose into a sitting posture. For the first time he spoke. "Christian!" he echoed, in that deep tone which thrilled the preacher to the heart; "will that give me back my honor? Come with me, old man, come with me, far over the waters. Ha! we are there! This is my native town. Yonder is the church in which I knelt in childhood; yonder the green on which I sported when a boy. But another flag waves there, in the place of the flag that waved when I was a child. And listen, old man. Were I to pass along the streets, as I passed when but a child, the very babes in their cradles would raise their tiny hands and curse me! The graves in yonder churchyard would shrink from my footsteps, and yonder flag would rain a baptism of blood upon my head!"

Suddenly the dying man arose; he tottered along the floor, threw open a valise, and drew thence a faded coat of blue, faced with silver, and the wreck of a battle-flag.

"Look ye, priest! This faded coat is spotted with my blood!" he cried, as old memories seemed stirring at his heart. "This coat I wore when I first heard the news of Lexington; this coat I wore when I planted the banner of the stars on Ticonderoga! That bullet hole was pierced in the fight of Quebec; and now I am a — let me whisper it in your ear!" He hissed that single burning word into the minister's ear. "Now help me, priest! help me to put on this coat of blue; for you to see." — and a ghastly smile came over his face — "there is no one here to wipe the cold drops from my brow, no wife, no child. I must meet death alone; but I will meet him, as I have met him in battle, without a fear."

And while he stood arraying his limbs in that worm-eaten coat of blue and silver the good minister spoke to him of that great faith which pierces the clouds of human guilt and rolls them back from the face of God. "Faith!" echoed that strange man who stood there erect with the death chill on his brow; "Faith! Can it give me back my honor? Look ye, priest! There, over the waves, sits George Washington, telling to his comrades the pleasant story of the eight years' war! There, in his royal halls, sits George of England, bewailing, in his idiotic voice, the loss of the colonies! And here am I — I, who was the first to raise the flag of freedom, the first to strike a blow against that king — here am I dying! oh, dying like a dog!"

The awe-stricken preacher started back from the look of the dying man, while throb, throb, throb, beats the death watch in the shattered wall. "Hush! silence along the lines there!" he muttered in that wild, absent tone, as though speaking to the dead. "Silence along the lines! not a word

— not a word on peril of your lives! Hark you,
Montgomery! we will meet in the center of the
town; we will meet there in victory, or die! —
Hist — Hist! silence, my men; not a whisper as
we move up those steep rocks! Now on, my
boys; now on! Men of the wilderness, we will
gain the town! Now up with the banner of the
stars! Up with the flag of freedom, though the
night is dark and the snow falls! Now, now one
more blow, and Quebec is ours!"

The aged minister unrolls that faded flag; it is
a blue banner gleaming with thirteen stars. He
unrolls that parchment; it is a colonel's commis-
sion in the Continental Army, addressed to *Benedict Arnold.* And there, in that rude hut, while
the death watch throbbed like a heart in the shattered wall, there, unknown, unwept, in all the bitterness of desolation, lay the corpse of the patriot
and the traitor.

THE BENEDICTION

François Coppée

IT was in eighteen hundred — yes — and nine,
That we took Saragossa. What a day
Of untold horrors! I was sergeant then.
The city carried, we laid siege to houses,
All shut up close, and with a treacherous look,
Raining down shots upon us from the windows.

"'Tis the priests' doing!" was the word passed
    round;
So, that, although since daybreak under arms —
Our eyes with powder smarting, and our mouths
Bitter with kissing cartridge-ends — piff! paff!
Rattled the musketry with ready aim,
If shovel hat and long black coat were seen
Flying in the distance.   Up a narrow street
My company worked on.   I kept an eye
On every house-top, right and left, and saw
From many a roof flames suddenly burst forth;
Coloring the sky, as from the chimney-tops
Among the forges.   Low our fellows stooped,
Entering the low-pitched dens.   When they came
    out,
With bayonets dripping red, their bloody fingers
Signed crosses on the wall; for we were bound,
In such a dangerous defile, not to leave
Foes lurking in our rear. There was no drum-beat,
No ordered march.   Our officers looked grave;
The rank and file uneasy, jogging elbows
As do recruits when flinching.
                All at once,
Rounding a corner, we are hailed in French
With cries for help.   At double-quick we join
Our hard-pressed comrades. They were grenadiers,
A gallant company, but beaten back
Inglorious from the raised and flag-paved square,
Fronting a convent.   Twenty stalwart monks

Defended it, black demons with shaved crowns,
The cross in white embroidered on their frocks,
Barefoot, their sleeves tucked up, their only weapons
Enormous crucifixes, so well brandished
Our men went down before them.   By platoons
Firing we swept the place; in fact, we slaughtered
This terrible group of heroes, no more soul
Being in us than in executioners.

The foul deed done — deliberately done —
And the thick smoke rolling away, we noted
Under the huddled masses of the dead,
Rivulets of blood run trickling down the steps;
While in the background solemnly the church
Loomed up, its doors wide open.   We went in.
It was a desert.   Lighted tapers starred
The inner gloom with points of gold.   The incense
Gave out its perfume.   At the upper end,
Turned to the altar, as though unconcerned
In the fierce battle that had raged, a priest,
White-haired and tall of stature, to a close
Was bringing tranquilly the mass.   So stamped
Upon my memory is that thrilling scene,
That, as I speak, it comes before me now —
The convent, built in old time by the Moors;
The huge, brown corpses of the monks; the sun
Making the red blood on the pavement steam;
And there, framed in by the low porch, the priest;
And there the altar, brilliant as a shrine;

And here ourselves, all halting, hesitating,
Almost afraid.

            I, certes, in those days
Was a confirmed blasphemer. 'Tis on record
That once, by way of sacrilegious joke,
A chapel being sacked, I lit my pipe
At a wax candle burning on the altar.
This time, however, I was awed — so blanched
Was that old man!

            "Shoot him!" our captain cried.
Not a soul budged.   The priest beyond all doubt
Heard; but, as though he heard not, turning round,
He faced us with the elevated Host,
Having that period of the service reached
When on the faithful benediction falls.
His lifted arms seemed as the spread of wings;
And as he raised the pyx, and in the air
With it described the cross, each man of us
Fell back, aware the priest no more was trembling
Than if before him the devout were ranged.
But when, intoned with clear and mellow voice,
The words came to us —

            Vos benedicat!
Deus Omnipotens!

            The captain's order
Rang out again and sharply, "Shoot him down,
Or I shall swear!"   Then one of ours, a dastard,
Leveled his gun and fired.   Upstanding still,
The priest changed color, though with steadfast look

Set upwards, and indomitably stern.
Pater et Filius!

                    Came the words.   What frenzy,
What maddening thirst for blood, sent from our
      ranks
Another shot, I know not; but 'twas done.
The monk, with one hand on the altar's ledge,
Held himself up; and strenuous to complete
His benediction, in the other raised
The consecrated Host.   For the third time
Tracing in air the symbol of forgiveness,
With eyes closed, and in tones exceeding low,
But in the general hush distinctly heard,
Et Sanctus Spiritus!

                    He said; and ending
His service, fell down dead.

THE PERMANENCE OF GRANT'S FAME

James G. Blaine

THE monopoly of fame by the few in this world comes from an instinct of human nature. Heroes cannot be multiplied. The millions pass into oblivion; only the units survive. Who aided the great leader of Israel to conduct the chosen people over the sands of the desert and through the waters of the sea unto the Promised Land? Who marched with Alexander from the Bosphorus to

India? Who commanded the legions under Caesar in the conquest of Gaul? Who crossed the Alps with the Conqueror of Italy? Who fought with Wellington at Waterloo? Alas! how soon it may be asked, Who marched with Sherman from the mountain to the sea? Who stood with Meade on the victorious field of Gettysburg? Who went with Sheridan through the trials and triumphs of the blood-stained valley?

Napoleon said: "The rarest attribute among generals is two–o'clock–in–the–morning courage." "I mean," he added, "unprepared courage, that which is necessary on an unexpected occasion and which, in spite of the most unforeseen events, leaves full freedom of judgment and promptness of decision." No better description could be given of the type of courage which distinguished General Grant.

His constant readiness to fight was another quality which, according to the same high authority, established his rank as a commander. "Generals," said the exile at St. Helena, "are rarely found eager to give battle; they choose their positions, consider their combinations, and then indecision begins." "Nothing," added this greatest warrior of modern times, "nothing is so difficult as to decide." General Grant, in his services in the field, never once exhibited indecision. This was the quality which gave him his crowning characteristic as a military leader; he inspired his men with a sense of their invincibility, and they were thenceforth invincible!

General Grant's name will survive because it is indissolubly connected with the greatest military and moral triumph in the history of his country. If the armies of the Union had ultimately failed, the vast and beneficent designs of Mr. Lincoln would have been frustrated. General Grant would then have taken his place with that long and always increasing array of able men who are found wanting in the supreme hour of trial. But a higher power controlled the result. In the reverent expression of Mr. Lincoln, "No human counsel devised, nor did any mortal hand work out these great things." In their accomplishment these human agents were sustained by more than human power, and through them great salvation was wrought for the land.

As long, therefore, as the American Union shall abide, with its blessings of law and liberty, Grant's name shall be remembered with honor; as long as the slavery of human beings shall be abhorred and the freedom of man cherished, Grant's name shall be recalled with gratitude; and in the cycles of the future the story of Lincoln's life can never be told without associating Grant in the enduring splendor of his own fame.

THE HOME CONCERT

WELL, Tom, my boy, I must say good-bye,
  I've had a wonderful visit here;
Enjoyed it, too, as well as I could
  Away from all that my heart holds dear.
Maybe I've been a trifle rough —
  A little awkward, your wife would say —
And very likely I've missed the hint
  Of your city polish day by day.

But somehow, Tom, though the same old roof
  Sheltered us both when we were boys,
And the same dear mother-love watched us both,
  Sharing our childish griefs and joys,
Yet you are almost a stranger now;
  Your ways and mine are as far apart
As though we had never thrown an arm
  About each other with loving heart.

Your city home is a palace, Tom;
  Your wife and children are fair to see;
You couldn't breathe in the little cot,
  The little home that belongs to me.
And I am lost in your grand, large house,
  And dazed with the wealth on every side,
And I hardly know my brother Tom,
  In the midst of so much stately pride.

Yes, the concert was grand, last night.
  The singing splendid; but, do you know,

My heart kept longing, the evening through,
　For another concert so sweet and low
That maybe it wouldn't please the ear
　Of one so cultured and grand as you;
But to its music — laugh if you will —
　My heart and thoughts must ever be true.

I shut my eyes in the hall last night
　(For the clash of the music wearied me),
And close to my heart this vision came —
　The same sweet picture I always see:
In the vine-clad porch of a cottage home,
　Half in shadow and half in sun,
A mother chanting her lullaby,
　Rocking to rest her little one.

And soft and sweet as the music fell
　From the mother's lips, I heard the coo
Of my baby girl, as with drowsy tongue
　She echoed the song with "Goo-a-goo."
Together they sang, the mother and babe,
　My wife and child, by the cottage door.
Ah! that is the concert, brother Tom,
　My ears are aching to hear once more.

So, now, good-bye.　And I wish you well,
　And many a year of wealth and gain.
You were born to be rich and gay;
　I am content to be poor and plain.
And I go back to my country home

With a love that absence has strengthened, too—
Back to the concert all my own —
Mother's singing and baby's coo.

———

MIDNIGHT IN LONDON

ARDENNES JONES-FOSTER

THERE it lies before you, that moving panorama, that ever-shifting kaleidoscope, dazing, bewildering in its myriad of mystic changes. Startling romances stride over the vast scene like pawns upon a boundless chess-board. Wealth and poverty jostling side by side in the great highways. Millionaire and beggar touching elbows in the surging crowd. Money-kings in carriages riding past hunger-haunted hovels. Women, mothers, children, dying of cold and destitution. Everywhere bustle; "pêle-mêle," confusion; city arteries throbbing with agitation; the rush, the race, the hurry of women and men; droning of countless wires, carrying electric messages of life, death, sorrow, peace, joy, happiness, engagement, battle, loss, victory, fortune into the home, the public house, the counting-room, the offices of the great journals.

The rumbling tram-car, carrying home the belated, dozing passenger; cabbie, urgently rousing his groggy fare; cautious landlord, artfully closing

the shutters to cheat the excise law and accom-
modate the all-night toper; screech of boatman's
whistle; river pirates lugging away their booty;
prison deputies guarding their sleeping charge;
condemned, penitent criminal, with feverish anxiety clutching the crucifix and trying to make
peace with God, before the golden sun dawns
upon his execution day; glum doctor, bobbing
about, post-haste, in answer to his patient's call;
crafty, designing solicitor, drawing up the last
testament of the old miser; modest maiden kneeling beside the couch of innocence, entrusting her
pure soul to the keeping of her Maker; the Sister
of Charity speaking words of cheer to a poor
woman; a life-lamp going out in a near-by garret;
child of nobility opening his eyes to the world in
yonder palace; child of poverty born within the
lowly manger; drunken man reeling home to his
pallid, starving, martyr-wife, who fondles in her
trembling arms her puny babe, so like a parcel of
unwelcome death; jolly companions tripping to the
strains of merry music; gay thespians clinking
glasses and toasting public favorites in rousing
bumpers; sly, treacherous burglar helping the lad
through the window; highwaymen, foot-pads, way-
laying the lonely traveller; a cry in the night, a
struggle, sharp crack of the robber's pistol, a
shriek, murder, escape; bold elopement of lad and
lassie thwarting the stern parental protest; tipsy

serenaders waking the welkin with laughter and song. Clang! Clang! Clang! the fire-bells! Bing! Bing! Bing! the alarm! In an instant quiet turns to uproar — an outburst of noise, excitement, clamor — bedlam broke loose; Bing! Bing! Bing! Rattle, clash and clatter. Open fly the doors; brave men mount their boxes. Bing! Bing! Bing! They're off! The horses tear down the street like mad. Bing! Bing! Bing! goes the gong!

"Get out of the track! The engines are coming! For God's sake, snatch that child from the road!"

On, on, wildly, resolutely, madly fly the steeds. Bing! Bing! the gong. Away dash the horses on the wings of fevered fury. On whirls the machine, down streets, around corners, up this avenue and across that one, out into the very bowels of darkness, whiffing, wheezing, shooting a million stars from the stack, paving the breath of startled night with a galaxy of stars. Over the house-tops to the north, a volcanic burst of flame shoots out, belching with blinding effect. The sky is ablaze. A tenement house is burning. Five hundred souls are in peril. Merciful Heaven! Spare the victims. Are the engines coming? Yes, here they are, dashing down the street. Look! the horses ride upon the wind. Eyes bulging like balls of fire; nostrils wide open. A palpitating billow of blaze,

rolling, plunging, bounding, rising, falling, swelling, heaving, and with mad passion bursting its
red-hot sides asunder, reaching out its arms, encircling, squeezing, grabbing up, swallowing everything before it with the hot, greedy mouth of an
appalling monster.

How the horses dash around the corner!   Animal instinct, say you? Aye, more. Brute reason.

"Up the ladders, men!"

The towering building is buried in bloated
banks of savage, biting elements. Forked tongues
dart out and in, dodge here and there, up and
down and wind, their cutting edges around every
object. A crash, a dull, explosive sound, and a
puff of smoke leaps out. At the highest point
upon the roof stands a dark figure in a desperate
strait, the hands making frantic gestures, the arms
swinging wildly — and then the body shoots off
into frightful space, plunging upon the pavement
with a revolting thud. The man's arm strikes a
bystander as he darts down. The crowd shudders,
sways, and utters a low murmur of pity and horror.
The faint-hearted lookers-on hide their faces. One
woman swoons away.

"Poor fellow! Dead!" exclaims a laborer, as
he looks upon the man's body.

"Aye, Joe, and I knew him well, too! He lived
next door to me, five flights back. He leaves a
widowed mother and two wee bits of orphans. I

helped him bury his wife a fortnight ago. Ah, Joe! but it's hard lines for the orphans."

A ghastly hour moves on, dragging its regiment of panic in its trail and leaving crimson blotches of cruelty along the path of night.

"Are they all out, firemen?"

"Aye, aye, sir!"

"No, they're not! There's a woman in the top window holding a child in her arms — over yonder in the right-hand corner! The ladders, there! A hundred pounds to the man who makes the rescue!"

A dozen start. One man more supple than the others, and reckless in his bravery, clambers to the top rung of the ladder.

"Too short!" he cries. "Hoist another!"

Up it goes. He mounts to the window, fastens the rope, lashes mother and babe, swings them off into ugly emptiness and lets them down to be rescued by his comrades.

"Bravo, fireman!" shouts the crowd.

A crash breaks through the uproar of crackling timbers.

"Look alive, up there! Great God! The roof has fallen!"

The walls sway, rock, and tumble in with a deafening roar. The spectators cease to breathe. The cold truth reveals itself. The fireman has been carried into the seething furnace. An old woman, bent with the weight of age, rushes through the fire line, shrieking, raving, and wringing her hands and opening her heart of grief.

"Poor John! He was all I had! And a brave lad he was, too! But he's gone, now. He lost his own life in savin' two more, and now — now he's there, away in there!" she repeats, pointing to the cruel oven.

The engines do their work. The flames die out. An eerie gloom hangs over the ruins like a formidable, blackened pall.

And the noon of night is passed.

THE UNKNOWN RIDER

George Lippard

It was the 7th of October, 1777. Horatio Gates stood before his tent, gazing steadfastly upon the two armies, now arrayed in order of battle. It was a clear bracing day, mellow with the richness of autumn. The sky was cloudless; the foliage of the woods scarce tinged with purple and gold. But the tread of legions shook the ground; from every bush shot the glimmer of the rifle barrel; on every hillside blazed the sharpened bayonet. But all at once a smoke arose, a thunder shook the ground, and a chorus of shouts and groans yelled along the darkened air. The play ɔf death had begun. The two flags, this of the stars, that of the red cross, tossed amid the smoke of battle, while the sky was clouded with leaden folds, and the earth throbbed with the pulsations of a mighty heart.

Suddenly, Gates and his officers were startled. Along the height on which they stood came a rider upon a black horse rushing toward the distant battle. Look! he draws his sword, the sharp blade quivers through the air; he points to the distant battle, and lo! he is gone, gone through those clouds, while his shout echoes over the plains. Wherever the fight is thickest, there, through intervals of cannon smoke, you may see, riding madly forward, that strange soldier, mounted on his steed black as death. Look at him as, with face red with British blood, he waves his sword and shouts to his legions. Now you may see him fighting in that cannon's glare, and in the next moment he is away off yonder, leading the forlorn hope up that steep cliff.

Look for a moment into those clouds of battle. There bursts a band of American militiamen, fleeing before that company of redcoat hirelings, who came rushing forward, their solid front of bayonets gleaming in the battle light. In the moment of their flight a horse comes crashing over the plain. The unknown rider reins his steed back on his haunches, right in the path of these broad-shouldered militiamen. "What! are you Americans, men, and flee before British soldiers?" he shouts. "Back again, and face them once more, or I myself will ride you down!" Their leader turns; his comrades, as if by one impulse, follow his example. In one line, but thirty men in all, they confront thirty sharp bayonets. The British advance. "Now upon the rebels, charge!" shouts the red-coat officer. They spring forward at the same bound. At this moment the voice of the unknown rider is heard! "Now let them have it! Fire!" A sound is heard, a smoke is seen, twenty Britons are down. The remaining ten start back. "Club your rifles and charge them home!" shouts the unknown. That black horse springs forward, followed by the militiamen. Then a confused conflict, a cry for quarter, and a vision of twenty farmers grouped around the rider of the black horse, greeting him with cheers.

Thus it was all the day long. Wherever that black horse and his rider went, there followed victory. At last, toward the setting of the sun, the crisis of the conflict came. That fortress yonder on Bemis' Heights must be won, or the American cause is lost! That cliff is too steep, that death is too certain. The officers cannot persuade the men to advance. The Americans have lost the field. Even Morgan, that iron man among iron men, leans on his rifle and despairs of the field. But look yonder! In this moment, when all is dismay and horror, here, crashing on, comes the black horse and his rider. And now look! as that black steed crashes up that steep cliff. That steed quivers! he totters! he falls! No! No! Still on, still up the cliff, still on toward the fortress. The rider turns his face and shouts: "Come on, men of Quebec! come on!" That call is needless. Already the bold riflemen are on the rock. Now, British cannon, pour your fires, and lay your dead in tens and twenties on the rock. Now, redcoat hirelings, shout your battle cry if you can! For look, there, in the gate of the fortress, as the smoke clears away, stands the black horse and his rider. That steed falls dead, pierced by a hundred balls; but his rider, as the British cry for quarter, lifts up his voice and shouts afar to Horatio Gates, waiting yonder in his tent: "Saratoga is won!" As that cry goes up to heaven he falls, with his leg shattered by a cannon ball.

Who was the rider of the black horse? Do you not guess his name? Then bend down and gaze on that shattered limb, and you will see that it bears the mark of a former wound. That wound was received in the storming of Quebec. That rider of the black horse was — Benedict Arnold.

EDELWEISS

MARY LOWE DICKINSON

By Alpine road, beneath an old fir-tree,
  Two children waited patiently for hours;
One slept, and then the elder on her knee
  Made place for baby head among her flowers.

And to the strangers, climbing tired and slow,
  She called, "Buy roses, please," in accents mild,
As if she feared the echo, soft and low,
  Of her own voice might wake the sleeping child.

And many came and passed, and answered not
  The pleading of that young, uplifted face,
While in each loiterer's memory of the spot,
  Dwelt this fair picture full of patient grace.

And one took offered flowers with gentle hand,
  And met with kindly glance the timid eyes,
And said, in tones that children understand,
  "My little girl, have you the Edelweiss?"

"Oh! not to-day, dear lady," said the child,
  "I cannot leave my little sister long;
I cannot carry her across the wild;
  She grows large faster than my arms grow strong.

"If you stay on the mountain all the night,
  At morning I will run across the steep
And get the mossy flowers ere sun is bright,
  And while my baby still is fast asleep."

"Your baby, little one?"   "Oh! yes," she said,
  "Yonder, you see that old stone tower shine?
There, in the churchyard, lies my mother, dead,
  And since she died the baby has been mine."

Soft shone the lady's eyes with tender mist,
  And ever, as she pressed toward fields of ice,
She pondered in her heart the half-made tryst
  With this young seeker of the Edelweiss.

At night, safe sheltered in the convent's fold,
  Where white peaks stand in ermined majesty,
Where sunsets pour great throbbing waves of gold
  Across the white caps of a mountain sea;

At morn, with face subdued and reverent tone,
  Slow winding down, with spirit hushed and awed,
As from a vision of the great white throne,
  Or veil half-lifted from the face of God.

The blessing of the hills her soul had caught
  Made all the mountain-track a path of prayer,
Along which angel forms of loving thought
  Led to the trysting-place; — no child was there!

The wind was moaning in the old fir-tree,
  The lizards crawling o'er the mossy seat;
But no fair child, with baby at her knee,
  And in the mold no track of little feet.

No faded flowers strewing the stunted grass;
  No young voice singing clear its woodland strain;

No brown eyes lifted as the strangers pass;
    A murmur in the air, like far-off rain;

A black cloud, creeping downward swift and still,
    Answered her listening heart, a far-off knell,
Almost before there swept along the hill
    The slow, deep tolling of the valley bell.

Once more there drifted 'cross the face the mist;
    Once more, with trembling soul and tender eyes,
She hurried on to keep the half-made tryst,
    To meet the child, to claim the Edelweiss.

Nearer she came and nearer every hour,
    Her heart-beat answering quick the deep bell's
        call;
It led her to the shadow of the tower,
    The shining tower beside the churchyard wall.

She found her there — a cross rose at her feet,
    And burning tapers glimmered at her head:
Her white hands clinging still to blossoms sweet,
    And God's peace on her face; the child was dead.

Quaint carven saints and martyrs stood around.
    Each clasped the symbol of his sacrifice;
But this fair child, in saintly sweetness crowned,
    Held, as they held the cross, her Edelweiss.

Early that morn a shepherd, on the height,
    In cleft of rocks sought shelter from the cold,
And there he found this lamb, all still and white,
    Entered already to the heavenly fold.

The Edelweiss grew on that rocky steep;
 The brave child-feet had climbed too fast and far
And so had come to her this blessed sleep,
 This blessed waking 'neath the morning star.

The light within the little church grew dim,
 And, ere the last gleam faded in the west,
While childish voices sang the vesper hymn,
 A lady, with a babe upon her breast,

Crept silently adown the shadowy aisle,
 And, kneeling, bathed with tears the hand of ice,
And laid it on the babe, and saw it smile,
 And whispered, "I have named her Edelweiss!"

When one more day had seen its shadows fall,
 That old stone tower gleaming in the sun,
And the great olive by the western wall,
 Shaded two humble graves where had been one.

And by and by, above the dear child's head,
 Arose a little stone with quaint device.
When summer blossoms died around the bed,
 A marble hand grasped still the Edelweiss.

WATERLOO

J. T. HEADLEY

THE whole continental struggle exhibits no sublimer spectacle than this last effort of Napoleon to save his sinking empire. The greatest military energy and skill the world possessed had been tasked to the utmost during the day. Thrones were tottering on the turbulent field, and the shadows of fugitive kings flitted through the smoke of battle. Bonaparte's star trembled in the zenith, now blazing out in its ancient splendor, now suddenly paling before his anxious eye. At last he staked his empire on one bold throw.

Nothing could be more imposing than the movement of the Old Guard to the assault. It had never recoiled before a human foe, and the allied forces beheld with awe its firm and steady advance to the final charge. For a moment the batteries stopped playing and the firing ceased along the British lines, as, without the beating of a drum or a bugle note to cheer their steady courage, they moved in dead silence over the field. The next moment the artillery opened, and the head of that gallant column seemed to sink into the earth. Rank after rank went down; yet they neither stopped nor faltered. Dissolving squadrons and whole battalions disappearing one after another in the destructive fire affected not their steady courage. In vain did the artillery hurl its storm of fire and lead into that living mass. Up to the very muzzles they pressed, and, driving the artillerymen from their pieces, pushed on through the English lines.

But just as the victory seemed won, a file of soldiers who had lain flat on the ground behind a low ridge of earth suddenly rose and poured a volley in their very faces. Another and another followed, till one broad sheet of flame rolled on their bosoms, and in such a fierce and unexpected flow that they staggered back before it. Before the guard had time to rally again and advance, a heavy column of infantry fell on its left flank in close and deadly volleys, causing it in its unsettled state to swerve to the right. At that instant a whole brigade of cavalry thundered on the right flank, and penetrated where cavalry had never gone before. It was then that the army, seized with despair, shrieked out: "The Guard recoils! the Guard recoils!" and turned and fled in wild dismay.

Still those veterans refused to fly; rallying from their disorder, they formed into two immense squares of eight battalions and turned fiercely on the enemy, and nobly strove to stem the reversed tide of battle. Michel, at the head of those brave battalions, fought like a lion. To every command of the enemy to surrender he replied: "The Guard

dies; it never surrenders," and, with his last breath
bequeathing this glorious motto to the Guard, he
fell a witness to its truth.

Death traversed those eight battalions with such
a rapid footstep that but a single battalion, the
débris of the "column of granite" at Marengo, was
left. Into this Napoleon flung himself. Cam-
bronne, its brave commander, saw with terror the
emperor in its frail keeping. Approaching the
emperor, he cried out: "Retire! do you not see
that death has no need of you?" and, closing
mournfully yet sternly round their expiring eagles,
those brave hearts bade Napoleon an eternal adieu,
and, flinging themselves on the enemy, were soon
piled with the dead at their feet.

THE DIGNITY OF LABOR

Newman Hall

There is dignity in toil; in toil of the hand as
well as toil of the head; in toil to provide for the
bodily wants of an individual life, as well as in toil
to promote some enterprise of world-wide fame.
All labor that tends to supply man's wants, to
increase man's happiness, in a word, all labor that
is honest, is honorable too.

The Dignity of Labor! Consider its achievements. Dismayed by no difficulty, shrinking from

no exertion, exhausted by no struggle, "clamorous Labor knocks with its hundred hands at the golden gate of the morning," obtaining each day, through succeeding centuries, fresh benefactions for the world.

Labor clears the forest, and drains the morass, and makes the wilderness rejoice and blossom as the rose. Labor drives the plough, and scatters the seeds, and reaps the harvest, and grinds the corn, and converts it into bread, the staff of life. Labor gathers the gossamer web of the caterpillar, the cotton from the field, and the fleece from the flock, and weaves them into raiment, soft, and warm, and beautiful — the purple robe of the prince and the gray gown of the peasant being alike its handiwork. Labor moulds the brick, and splits the slate, and quarries the stone, and shapes the column, and rears, not only the humble cottage, but the gorgeous palace, and the tapering spire, and the stately dome.

Labor, diving deep into the solid earth, brings up its long-hidden stores of coal, to feed ten thousand furnaces, and in millions of habitations to defy the winter's cold. Labor explores the rich veins of deeply-buried rocks, extracting the gold, the silver, the copper, and the tin. Labor smelts the iron, and moulds it into a thousand shapes for use and ornament. Labor cuts down the gnarled oak, and hews the timber, and builds the ship, and guides it over the deep, to bear to our shores the produce of every clime.

Labor, laughing at difficulties, spans majestic rivers, carries viaducts over marshy swamps, suspends bridges over deep ravines, pierces the solid mountains with its dark tunnel, blasting rocks, filling hollows, and linking together with its iron but loving grasp all nations of the earth.

Labor, a mighty magician, walks forth into a region uninhabited and waste; he looks earnestly at the scene, so quiet in its desolation; then waving his wonder-working wand, those dreary valleys smile with golden harvests; those barren mountain slopes are clothed with foliage; the furnace blazes; the anvil rings; the busy wheel whirls round; the town appears; the mart of commerce, the hall of science, the temple of religion, rear high their lofty fronts; a forest of masts, gay with varied pennons, rises from the harbor. Science enlists the elements of earth and heaven in its service; Art, awaking, clothes its strength with beauty; Civilization smiles; Liberty is glad; Humanity rejoices; Piety exults; for the voice of industry and gladness is heard on every side.

> "Work for some good, be it ever so slowly;
> Work for some hope, be it ever so lowly;
> Work! for all labor is noble and holy!"

WOLFE AT QUEBEC

FRANK D. BUDLONG

ON a bright June morning, 1759, Wolfe, sailing proudly up the St. Lawrence River, landed at Quebec. Continual victory had thus far rested on the banners of the English. Louisburg had been taken by storm, Ticonderoga and Crown Point evacuated, Fort Niagara surrendered, and now the eager eyes of the British were turned toward Wolfe and Quebec.

But Wolfe had no sluggard with whom to deal. Quebec, almost impregnable from its position on the bluff, had been rendered doubly secure by the wary Montcalm. For a dozen miles above the city every landing-place was intrenched and protected, while for a dozen miles below it the shore was guarded, to where the impetuous Montmorency, leaping and whirling down the steps of its rocky bed, rushes headlong over the ledge and pours its fiery cataract into the chasm. But the young and heroic Wolfe was not to be checked by an appearance of strength. Mortars were stationed, hot shot and shell thrown into the city, and a rally was made to force a landing; but nowhere was a point left unguarded. Again and again the brave Grenadiers rush forward, only to be met with a withering fire which mows them down like grass. Flesh and blood cannot stand it, and reluctantly Wolfe orders a retreat.

Day after day the general studied the position of the enemy; seemingly every avenue of approach was reconnoitered. So the days crept into weeks, the weeks into months, and still the citadel of Quebec stood there on the cliff, — bold, silent, impregnable, — the Gibraltar of America; and above floated the banner of the Bourbons.

Worn down by care and constant watching, fighting fire rafts by night and studying the shore by day, the feeble frame of Wolfe sunk under the energy of his resistless spirit. But his purpose was unchanged. He knew that far across the water Pitt was watching him with anxious eyes. To his comrades in arms, who loved their leader and were ready to follow him to death, he said: "While a man is able to do his duty and can stand and hold arms, it is infamous to retire." At length perseverance is crowned with success. A narrow bridle path is discovered winding from a little cove to the plateau above; and up this path, under cover of the night, Wolfe determined to lead his army, offer battle to Montcalm, or carry the town by assault.

On the evening of September 12 the final preparations were made. What a scene spread out before the English general on the clear, starlight evening, — the spacious harbor, so far from the sea, his own fleet and army gathering under way, and in the distance the gray walls and towering cliffs of Quebec! Impressed by the sight as he passed along from ship to ship, the general spoke of the poet Gray and his "Elegy in a Country Churchyard." "Ah, yes," he said, "I would rather be the author of that poem than to take Quebec." Then the oars struck the river. As it rippled in the silence of the night, with almost prophetic tenderness he repeated:

> The boast of heraldry, the pomp of power,
> And all that beauty, all that wealth e'er gave
> Await alike th' inevitable hour: —
> The paths of glory lead but to the grave.

At one o'clock the little band of five thousand men glide down the river, reach the landing-place, leap ashore, climb foot by foot up the precipitous height, and daylight finds Wolfe and his invincible battalions on the plains of Abraham — "the battle-field of empires." Montcalm was astounded. "'T is impossible!" he exclaimed. But there in the distance were the redcoats; there the gleaming bayonets to assure him of the fact.

The bugle sounds to arms, and soon the fast-falling death shot, the boom of guns, and the roar of battle tell of another "harvest of death," another day to be lost or won. Twice Montcalm leads his merry Frenchmen in the charge, and twice the bleeding line falls back shattered and broken.

Again and again they rush forward reënforced and more determined than ever. The English line wavers, falters; will it break and the day be lost for England? No, no. Wolfe is here, and his rallying cry is heard high above the din of battle. With a cheer the soldiers rush forward, and, catching the inspiration of his cry, on they go, over the uneven ground, over the bogs and brushwood, over the dead and dying, pursuing the enemy to the very gates of the city.

But their leader? Ah! The warrior had verified the words of the poet. For as the shouts of the victorious army came ringing over the plains of Abraham the spirit of their valorous leader, who had crowded into a few hours actions that would lend luster to length of days, went out in a blaze of glory.

HILDA

James H. Rayhill

Beneath the summer moon, the city lies
Bathed in a flood of light that rivals day,
Each columned temple and star-striking spire
Has now an added beauty, which the noon
In all its glory could not give.
The many fountained courts and colonnades,
The flowered lawns, and lofty dim-arched halls
Seem chosen haunts of soft-eyed dreamy Peace.

But on the ear there falls the measured tread
Of armed men; and from each moonlit spot
Is flashed the silver sheen of spear and shield
That know not peace; the mighty gates are closed:
And from the walls the weary warders watch.

Before the seaward gates a verdant plain
Extends in grassy billows to the shore,
From which in other days was heard the plash
Of waves upon the beach, or low-voiced cry
Of some sad sea-bird, and no other sound.
And thro' the plains a placid river winds,
Its banks enriched with fairy fretted ferns
And water plants, that whisper to the winds,
And bow before the stream that ripples by,
Half loth to leave the meadows for the sea:
Time was, the plains re-echoed with the shouts
Of children at their play, and on the stream
They sailed their masted toys from noon till eve.
A host now lies encamped beneath the walls:
Huge ships of war float at the river's mouth,
And all men deem the city near its doom.
How otherwise, when half its folks are slain,
And famine, hollow-eyed, broods in its midst?
Yet on this night, despite the silver moon,
The 'leagured folks have planned one more assault
Upon the camp outside, if by some chance
The God of battle might prove on their side,
And they might conquer this last time or die.

What tender partings are there this sad night!
Pale wives and famished children clasping hands
Of men half mad with hunger and despair!
See near the walls the youthful Sigurd stands.
His crest is ever in the battle's van —
His glittering helm now lies upon the ground
And he bare-headed, stands beneath the stars,
Heedless of all, except the dark-eyed maid
He clasps with loving arms, and on whose cheeks,
Tear-stained and blushing, he lets kisses fall
Like summer showers on a thirsting rose.
"Nay, sweet," he whispers "have no fear for me.
Have I not fought a hundred fights ere now,
And each time brought you back myself and love?
But hark! the tramp of men and clash of steel
Breaks on the peaceful night, and I must go —
Farewell, sweet Hilda, once again, farewell!"

Dim-eyed she watched the warriors slowly pass
And vanish 'neath the shadow of the gates
That groaned as if forewarned of coming woe —
Then to the battlements the women ran,
To watch with anxious eyes the battle-whirl;
For ere the camp was reached, the serried ranks
Of foemen hurried forth in strengthening lines
To meet this last assault of desperate men.
Sharp was the conflict, but the struggle short,
For worn and weak, the townsmen turned and fled
Leaving one-half their number on the ground.

In vain did Sigurd and his brother chiefs
Attempt to stem the tide; the men swept past
Like some tumultuous current to the sea.
Straight to the gates, they, panic-stricken, rushed,
And fearful that the foe was close behind
Shut the gates, nor waited to discern
If any comrades were without or not.

Retreating slowly, one heroic band
With Sigurd at its head, still faced the foe,
And scorned to turn; but cried upon the men
To rally once again and conquer yet.
This Hilda saw from where she watching stood
Gazing with scorn upon the hurrying men,
And thus with flashing eyes, addressed the crowd :—
"Are you so many now that you could spare
The friends you have shut out, or do you deem
You are so few you can no longer fight as hitherto?
Cowards, the foeman's steel had once no terrors for
        you.
Is his blade more keen, his arm more strong than
        erst it was?
Have you no shame to leave your chiefs outside,
While you in careless safety stand afar?
Open the gates there, warder, and let those
Who love their gods and friends now follow me."
Thus speaking she passed through the silent crowd,
Scorn on her lip and courage in her eye.
With spear and shield she hurried through the gates,

Nor paused to see if any followed her;
And wonder fell on all the weary folk.

Like to a star that shoots across the sky,
Bright for a while, then lost in utter gloom,
She darted o'er the plain engulphed
Within the struggling mass of raging men.
Heedless of all — save one — she forced her way
Until she found her Sigurd, worn and hurt.
No time for words had they; the battle storm
Raged hotly 'round them, and none heeded them
In the uncertain light and press of war
Whether it was a man or maid they fought.
In vain did Sigurd try to shield the maid;
For weary with the fight and many wounds,
His strong arm failed him, and his eye grew dim,
And with one last great stroke he reeled and fell.
Hilda beheld him, and with hasty hands,
Careless of all men, staunched his bleeding wounds,
But as she knelt, a man with dying hand
Hurled at a venture, through the empty air,
His hurtling spear, which struck the maiden's
          breast
And laid her dead in dying Sigurd's arms.

No city now lies on the widowed plain,
And through rank grass, the lonely river creeps
In silence to the sad deserted shore.
How many summer suns have risen and set!

How many winter winds have swept the plain
Since those two lovers were laid breast to breast!
The memory of the city has long since died;
But this bright picture of a woman's love
Shines down the vista of the years gone by
Dim with the gathered mist of human tears,
Like slanting sunbeams through the rain-cloud's
      gloom,
Or moonlight bursting through the screen of night.

CENTRALIZATION IN THE UNITED STATES

Henry W. Grady

THE unmistakable dånger that threatens free government in America is the increasing tendency to concentrate in the federal government powers and privileges that should be left with the states, and to create powers that neither the state nor federal government should have.

Concurrent with this political drift is another movement, less formal, perhaps, but not less dangerous, — the consolidation of capital. The world has not seen nor has the mind of man conceived of such miraculous wealth gathering as are everyday tales to us. Aladdin's lamp is dimmed, and Monte Cristo becomes commonplace when compared to our magicians of finance and trade.

I do not denounce the newly rich. Our great wealth has brought us profit and splendor. But the status itself is a menace. A home that costs three million dollars and a breakfast that costs five thousand dollars are disquieting facts to the millions who live in a hut and dine on a crust. The fact that a man ten years from poverty has an income of twenty million dollars falls strangely on the ears of those who hear it, as they sit empty-handed while children cry for bread.

But the abuse of this amazing power of consolidated wealth is its bitterest result and its pressing danger. We have read of the robber barons of the Rhine, who from their castles sent a shot across the bow of every passing craft, and, descending as hawks from the crags, tore and robbed and plundered the voyagers until their greed was glutted or the strength of their victims spent. Shall this shame of Europe against which the world revolted, shall it be repeated in this free country? And yet, when a syndicate or a trust can arbitrarily add twenty-five per cent to the cost of a single article of common use, and safely gather forced tribute from the people, until from its surplus it could buy every castle on the Rhine, or requite every baron's debauchery from its kitchen account, where is the difference — save that the castle is changed to a broker's office, and the picturesque river to the teeming streets and the broad fields of this government "of the people, by the people, and for the people?"

I do not overstate the case. Economists have held that wheat, grown everywhere, could never be cornered by capital. And yet one man in Chicago tied the wheat crop in his handkerchief, and held it until a sewing woman in my city, working for ninety cents a week, had to pay him twenty cents tax on the sack of flour she bore home in her famished hands. Three men held the cotton until the English spindles stopped and the lights went out in three million English homes. Recently one man cornered pork until he had levied a tax of three dollars per barrel on every consumer, and pocketed a profit of millions. The Czar of Russia would not have dared to do these things. And yet they are no secrets in this free government of ours! They are known of all men, and, my countrymen, no argument can follow them, and no plea excuse them, when they fall on the men who, toiling, yet suffer, who hunger at their work, and who cannot find food for their wives with which to feed the infants that hang famishing at their breasts.

What is the remedy? To exalt the hearthstone, to strengthen the home, to build up the individual, to magnify and defend the principle of local self-government. Not in deprecation of the federal government, but to its glory — not to weaken the Republic, but to strengthen it.

Let it be understood in my parting words to you that I am no pessimist as to this Republic. I always bet on sunshine in America. I know that my country has reached the point of perilous greatness; but I know that beyond the uttermost glory is enthroned the Lord God Almighty, and that when the hour of her trial has come he will lift up his everlasting gates and bend down above her in mercy and in love.

And, bending down humbly as Elisha did, and praying that my eyes shall be made to see, I catch the vision of this Republic — plenty streaming from its borders, and light from its mountain tops — working out its mission under God's approving eye, until the dark continents are opened, and under one language, one liberty, and one God all the nations of the world, hearkening to the American drumbeat, and girding up their loins, shall march amid the breaking of the millennium dawn into the paths of righteousness and of peace!

OPINIONS STRONGER THAN ARMIES

Luther A. Ostrander

There is a vignette representing a heavy sword thrown across a dozen quills, crushing and destroying them. In the thrilling times of war, the picture seems the illustration of truth, rather than the artist's fancy. When governments lay their hands on their sword-hilts, and nations marshal themselves in battle array, it is natural to believe the sword mightier than the pen, armies stronger than opinions. Strength is a force known only in its results. An army is a gigantic force. It marches forth with roll of drums, and proud banners streaming, bayonets gleaming in the sunlight. Earth trembles under its measured tread, and it is full of grandeur. It sweeps to the battle with the fury of the tempest; dark battalions roll together; squadrons charge with flashing sabres, and dense sulphurous clouds hail iron. It returns with honored scars, torn battle flags and shouts of victory.

Military strength is physical strength. It defies reason; hews congenial states asunder; chains, in repulsive union, the deadliest enemies. What is the strength of opinions? Opinions are ideas, condensed thoughts. They, too, are force; but a force intellectual and enduring. Inventing a press, they print a Bible, and stamp progress on every page of history. Under their influence, the hydra, terrible upon the waters, and the dragon, vomiting fire, are metamorphosed into the steamship and locomotive; the savage becomes a man; he dives into the profundity of philosophy, flashes his thoughts over magnetic wires, and, with the airy lightness of genius, soars to the farthest bounds of immensity. Are not opinions stronger than armies? The convulsed lips of the poisoned Socrates proclaim it; the classic periods of Tully proclaim it; the mute eloquence of the past and the fiery logic of the present proclaim it. It may be objected that Marathon, Yorktown and Gettysburg were glorious triumphs of arms. True; but were they not also glorious triumphs of opinions? What were those conquering armies but embodiments of a lofty patriotism, the genius of liberty, and the spirit of freedom? Our glorious victories — what are they but drumbeats that keep time to the march of opinions? Our armies — they are not composed of vassals, but of thinkers, voters, men — high minded men, who use the ballot as wisely as they wield the sword — sustaining with brain-sweat and heart-blood their grand opinions. Armies are the towers of strength which men have built; opinions are the surging waves of the ocean which God has made, beating against those towers, and crumbling them to dust.

The dim light of the past reveals to us the forms
of gigantic empires, whose mighty armies seem
omnipotent. A halo of martial glory surrounds
them, and then fades away; their marble thrones
crumble; their iron limbs are broken; their proud
navies are sunk. To-day, history dipping its pencil in sunlight, records the sublime triumphs of
opinions. The sword rounds the periods of the
pen; the ballot wings the bullet; school-houses
accompany cannon-balls; and principles bombard
forts and thunder from ironclads. Glorious is the
morning dawn! Science fringes the lands of darkness with a border of light; and the sun of Christianity, glowing along the eastern waters, arches
the bow of promise above the golden western hills.

KNIGHTS OF LABOR

T. V. POWDERLY

WE are Knights of Labor because we believe
that law and order should prevail, and that both
should be founded in equity. We are Knights of
Labor because we believe that the thief who
steals a dollar is no worse than the thief who steals
a railroad. To remedy the evils we complain of
is a difficult and dangerous undertaking. The
need of strong hearts and active brains was never
so great as at the present time. The slavery that

died twenty-two years ago was terrible, but the
lash in the hands of the old-time slave owner could
strike but one back at a time, and but one of
God's poor, suffering children felt the stroke.
The lash of gold in the hands of the new slave
owner falls not upon one slave alone, but upon the
backs of millions, and among the writhing, tortured
victims, side by side with the poor and the
ignorant, are to be found the well-to-do and the
educated.

The power of the new slave owner does not end
when the ordinary day laborer bends beneath his
rule; it reaches out still further, and controls the
mechanic, the farmer, the merchant, and the
manufacturer.   It dictates not alone what the
price of labor shall be, but regulates the price of
money as well.   Do I overestimate its power?
Have I made a single misstatement?   If my word
is not sufficient, turn to the pages of the history of
to-day, — the public press, — and you will find
the testimony to prove that what I have said is
true.   The lash was stricken from the hand of the
slave owner of twenty-five years ago, and it must
be taken from the hand of the new slave owner as
well.   The monopolist of to-day is more dangerous
than the slave owner of the past.   Monopoly takes
the land from the people in millionacre plots; it
sends its agents abroad, and brings hordes of un-
educated, desperate men to this country; it

imports ignorance, and scatters it broadcast throughout the land. While I condemn and denounce the deeds of violence committed in the name of labor during the present year, I am proud to say that the Knights of Labor, as an organization, is not in any way responsible for such conduct. He is the true Knight of Labor who with one hand clutches anarchy by the throat and with the other strangles monopoly.

The man who still believes in the "little red schoolhouse on the hill" should take one holiday and visit the mine, the factory, the coal breaker, and the mill. There, doing the work of men, he will find the future citizens of the Republic, breathing an atmosphere of dust, ignorance, and vice! The history of our country is not taught within these walls. The struggle for independence and causes leading to that struggle are not spoken of there; the name of Washington is unknown, and the words that rang out trumpet-tongued from the lips of Patrick Henry are never mentioned. The little red schoolhouse must fail to do its work properly, since the children of the poor must pass it by on the road to the workshop. How can they appreciate the duties of citizenship when we do not take the trouble to teach them that to be an American citizen is greater than to be a king, and that he upon whom the mantle of citizenship is bestowed should part with his life before surrendering one jot or tittle of the rights and liberties which belong to him.

Turn away from these hives of industry, stand for a moment on a street corner, and you will see gayly caparisoned horses driven by a coachman in livery; a footman occupying his place at the rear of the coach is also dressed in the garb of the serf. On the coach door you will find the crest or coat of arms of the illustrious family to whom it belongs. If you speak to the occupant of the coach concerning our country, her institutions, or her flag, you will be told that they do not compare with those of foreign countries. The child who graduates from the workshop dons the livery of a slave, covers his manhood, and climbs to the footman's place on the outside of the coach. The man who apes the manners and customs of foreign noblemen occupies the inside. The one who with strong heart and willing hands would defend the rights and liberties of his country has never learned what these rights or liberties are. The other does know, but has learned to love the atmosphere of monarchy better than that which he breathes in this land. Between these two our freedom is in danger, and that is why we as Knights of Labor most emphatically protest against the introduction of the child to the workshop until he has attained his fourteenth year, so that he may be enabled to secure for himself the benefits of an education that will enable him to understand and appreciate the blessings of our free institutions and, if necessary, defend them with his life.

THE PROVINCE OF HISTORY

JAMES RIDPATH

THE concluding paragraphs of a historical work may well be brief and simple. It is not permitted to the writer of history to moralize at length upon the events which are sketched by his pen. He is forbidden to conjecture, to imagine, to dream. He has learned, albeit against his will, to moderate his enthusiasm, to curb his fancy, to be humble in the presence of facts. To him the scenery on the shore of the stream that bears him onward — tall trees and giant rocks — must pass but half observed, and for him the sun and the south wind strive in vain to make enticing pictures on the playful eddies of human thought. None the less, he may occasionally pause to reflect; he may ever and anon throw out an honest deduction drawn from the events upon which his attention has been fixed. Particularly is this true when he has come to the end.

All of a sudden he anchors in the bay of the present, and realizes that his voyage is done. In such a moment there is a natural reversion of the thought from its long and devious track across the fields, valleys and wastes of the past, and a strong disposition to educe some lesson from the events which he has recorded. The first and most general truth in history is that men ought to be free. If happiness is the end of human race, then freedom is its condition. And this freedom is not to be a kind of half-escape from thraldom and tyranny, but ample and absolute. The emancipation in order to be emancipation at all, must be complete. To the historian it must ever appear strange that men have been so distrustful of this central principle in the philosophy of human history. The greatest fallacy with which the human intellect has ever been beguiled, is that the present has conceded to men all the freedom which they are fit to enjoy. On the contrary, no age has done so. Every age has been a Czar, and every reformer is threatened with Siberia. Nevertheless, in the face of all this baleful opposition and fierce hostility to the forward and freedom-seeking movement of the race, the fact remains that to be free is the prime condition of all the greatness, wisdom, and happiness in the world. Whatever force, therefore, contributes to widen the limits which timid fear or selfish despotism has set as the thus-far of freedom is a civilizing force and deserves to be augmented by the individual will and personal endeavor of every lover of mankind; and on the other hand, every force which tends to fix around the teeming brains and restless activities of men one of those so-called necessary barriers to their progress and ambition, is a force of barbarism and cruelty, meriting the relentless antagonism of every well-wisher of his kind. Let it be remembered, then, that the battle is not yet ended, the victory not yet won. The present is relatively — not absolutely, thanks to the great warriors of humanity — as much the victim of the enslaving forces as was the past; and it is the duty of the philanthropist, the sage, the statesman, to give the best of his life and genius to the work of breaking down, and not imposing, those bulwarks and barriers which superstition and conservatism have reared as the ramparts of civilization, and for which an enlightened people have no more need than for the Chinese wall.

Of all things that are incidentally needed to usher in the promised democracy and brotherhood of man — the coming new era of enlightenment and peace — one of the most essential is toleration. It is a thing which the world has never yet enjoyed — is just now beginning to enjoy. Almost every page of the ancient and mediæval history of mankind has been made bloody with some form of intolerance. Until the present day the baleful shadow of this sin against humanity has been upon the world. The proscriptive vices of the Middle Age have flowed down with the blood of the race and tainted the life that now is with a suspicion and distrust of freedom. Liberty in the minds of men has meant the privilege of agreeing with the majority. Men have desired free thought, but fear has stood at the door. It remains for the present to build a highway, broad and free, into every field of liberal inquiry, and to make the poorest of men who walks therein more secure in life and reputation than the soldier who sleeps behind the rampart. Proscription has no part nor lot in the modern government of the world. The stake, the gibbet, and the rack, thumbscrews, swords, and pillory have no place among the machinery of civilization. Nature is diversified; so are human faculties, beliefs, and practices. Essential freedom is the right to differ, and that right must be sacredly respected. Nor must the privilege of dissent be conceded with coldness and disdain, but openly, cordially, and with good will. No loss of rank, abatement of character, or ostracism from society must darken the pathway of the humblest of the seekers after truth. The right of free thought, free inquiry, and free speech to all men everywhere is as clear as the noonday and bounteous as the air and the sea. May the day soon dawn when every land, from Orient to Occident, from pole to pole, from mountain to shore, and from shore to the farthest island of the sounding sea, shall feel the glad sunshine of freedom in its breast; and when the people of all climes, arising at last from the heavy slumbers and barbarous dreams which have so long haunted the benighted minds of men, shall join in glad acclaim to usher in the Golden Era of Humanity and the universal Monarchy of Man!

THE OPENING OF THE MISSISSIPPI
IN 1862

WILLIAM E. LEWIS

RISING in the pine forests of the North, gathering with far extending arms the raindrops of a half continent, a royal river seeks the sea. The rebellion barred this river; so from the beginning of our civil war one purpose animated the great Northwest. It was the opening of the Mississippi. "On to Richmond!" was the battle cry of the East; "On to New Orleans!" the rallying shout of the West. Said General Sherman: "The possession of the Mississippi is the possession of America."

On the 14th of March, 1862, our fleet, accompanied by a land force of forty thousand infantry, moved southward. Forts Henry and Donelson, on the Tennessee and Cumberland, had been stormed and mastered; Columbus, "the

Gibraltar of the West," evacuated. Then followed other victories. Besieged Fort Pillow yielded; blustering Memphis capitulated; the Union colors floated once more from the Chickasaw Bluffs; and on the 1st of July the heroes of Island No. 10 and New Orleans mingled their cheers under the battlements of Vicksburg.

Let us glance at other struggles even fiercer and grander which consummated this meeting. About seventy miles below New Orleans stood two magnificent fortresses with bastions and casemates of solid masonry. Below, an immense chain boom locked up the river. Above, to make New Orleans secure, to preclude the possibility of ascent, rams, gunboats, and fire rafts were stationed. "No fleet," said the South, "can pass up the river without miraculous interposition." But Farragut was undaunted. "I came here to pass or reduce the forts and take New Orleans," he said, "and I shall try it."

On the 16th of April the mortar boats open fire on Fort Jackson. Thirteen-inch shells whirl athwart the sky like meteors. Thrice a thousand rise from forts and fleet before evening falls. Four days of dissonance — still the bombardment a failure. There is no sign of yielding. Farragut resolves on a desperate course, — to cut the cable, run the batteries, capture or sink the rebel navy, and subdue the city. A midnight attack severed the boom.

On the evening of April 23 all is in readiness. Up goes the signal to fall into line. Guided by the lurid glare of rebel beacon fires, the attacking squadrons breast the current in three columns. The forts open fire; as the fleet draws near they become volcanoes, their casemates crevices of continuous flame. The foremost vessel, the *Cayuga*, steams toward the break in the boom, encounters a volley of red-hot shot; reels; recovers; dashes through the chasm. One by one the armada follows. Now abreast, now above the forts. The pilots see beyond a gleam of light. It grows brighter. What is this new danger? A river all aflame! Turn back? Repass the batteries? Never! "Close action!" signals the *Hartford*, and leads the way. Nearer and nearer come the fire rafts. Higher and higher rise their billows of flame. The ram *Manassas* crowds a blazing raft against the flagship. Fiery flames lick the deck, leap up into the rigging, and envelop the frigate. Ashore and afire, sorely beset, yet her commander does not despair. The pumps are manned. The boarding flames are repelled. The *Manassas* is beaten off, and the "good old *Hartford*" dashes once more into the thickest of the fight.

Who can recount the heroic achievements of that eventful night? How the *Brooklyn* swept through the fight, all aglow with incessant broadsides! How the *Varuna* dashed into the midst of

the enemy, fired her last shot, and went down in
the turbid waters, — a fit casket for her noble
dead.   Titanic the conflict, decisive the victory.
The rebel squadron is destroyed, the strongholds
and city are conquered, the river is speedily opened
to Vicksburg.

The opening of the Mississippi terminated a
crisis in the war.   The North gained needed
inspiration; the South stood paralyzed before this
omen of final defeat.   The possession of the
Mississippi was indeed the possession of America.

THE PRESENT AGE

W. E. CHANNING

THE Present Age.   In those brief words what a
world of thought is comprehended!   What infinite
movements!   What joys and sorrows!   What hope
and despair!   What faith and doubt!   What silent
grief and loud lament!   What fierce conflicts and
subtle schemes of policy!   What private and public
revolutions!

In the period through which many of us have
passed, what thrones have been shaken!   What
hearts have bled!   What millions have been
butchered by their fellow men!   What hopes of
philanthropy have been blighted!

At the same time what magnificent enterprises

have been achieved! What new provinces won to
science and art! What rights and liberties secured
to nations! Aye — it is a privilege to have lived
in an age so stirring, so eventful! It is an age
never to be forgotten. Its voice of warning and
encouragement is never to die. Its impression on
history is indelible.

Amid its events the American Revolution — the
first distinct, solemn assertion of the rights of
men — and the French Revolution — that volcanic
force, which shook the earth to its very centre —
are never to pass from men's minds. Over this
age the night will indeed gather more and more
as time rolls away; but in that night two forms
will appear. Washington and Napoleon! The
one a lurid meteor, the other a benign, serene, and
undecaying star.

Another American name will appear in history.
Your Franklin; and the kite which brought lightning from heaven, will be seen sailing in the clouds
by remote posterity when the city where he dwelt
may be known only by its ruins.

There is, however, something greater in the age
than its greatest men; it is the appearance of a
new power in the world, the appearance of the
multitude on the stage, where as yet the few have
acted their parts alone. This influence is to endure to the end of time. What more of the present
is to survive? Perhaps much of which we now

take no note.   The glory of an age is often hidden from itself.   Perhaps some word has been spoken in our day which we have not deigned to hear, but which is to grow clearer and louder through all ages.   Perhaps some silent thinker among us is at work in his closet, whose name is to fill the earth. Perhaps there sleeps in his cradle some reformer who is to move the church, and the world; who is to open a new era in history, who is to fire the human soul with new hope and new daring.

What else is to survive the age?   That which the age has little thought of, but which is living in us all; I mean the soul, the immortal Spirit!   Of this, all ages are the unfoldings, and it is greater than all.   We must not feel in the contemplation of the vast movements in our own and former times, as if we ourselves were nothing.   I repeat it, we are greater than all.   We are to survive our age, to comprehend it, and to pronounce its sentence.

THE MYSTERIOUS GUEST

Fowler Bradnack

'T was night; the clock had just struck ten
    When, with a mighty din,
The stage-coach halted at the door
    Of Smith's Hotel in Lynn;
An inside passenger got out,
    Who straight went in the inn.

His portly figure was enwrapped
  In overcoat of shag,
While one hand grasped a traveling trunk,
  The other held a bag;
And in the twinkle of his eye
  You recognized a wag.

"Waiter," he cried, "show me a room;
  I'm tired and travel-sore."
The waiter showed him to a room
  Upon the second floor.
"Just stay a moment," said the man, —
  The waiter closed the door.

"You see," observed the traveler,
  "Ere I can take a doze,
I'll have to ask a little help
  In getting off my clothes;
For I'm a trifle crippled,
  And can't pull off my hose."

"All right," replied the waiter,
  Who was a generous elf;
"I pities any man," said he,
  "As can't undress hisself.
"I'll very soon unrig you, sir,
  And lay you on the shelf."

"'Tis well," resumed the traveler,
  Who dropped into a chair,

"First, hang my wig upon yon peg
   (And he took off his hair),
I'm like a case of glass," said he,
   "And must be touched with care."

And as he spoke, he ope'd his mouth
   As though it were a trap,
And thrust his fingers in the hole, —
   The waiter heard a snap,
And out there rolled two sets of teeth,
   And fell into his lap.

"Now, waiter, just unscrew my arm,
   But do n't look so alarmed;
I'm helpless as a sailing ship
   Upon a sea becalmed;
And when my arm you've taken off
   You'll see that I'm disarmed."

The waiter, in astonishment,
   Upon the traveler gazed;
He thought so strange a stranger
   Must certainly be crazed;
But when he saw the arm come off
   He was still more amazed,

And seemed inclined to go away;
   "A moment more, I beg,"
Cried out the waggish traveler;
   "Help me unstrap my leg;"

The waiter's hair began to rise
    As he pulled off the peg.

"As sheep in summer," said the man,
    "Rejoice to lose their fleeces,
So when I doff my limbs at night
    My happiness increases;
Because I can not rest in peace
    Unless I rest in pieces."

Then he apostrophized his limbs
    In strange soliloquy;
"Alas!" said he, "one's in the earth,
    The other's in the sea;
But though I well remember them,
    They can't re-member me.

Now, bring me here that looking-glass,
    And I'll take out my eye;
Although I'm not a party man,
    A man of parts am I;"
And as he uttered this vile joke
    He laughed as if he'd die.

The waiter's hair now stood on end,
    He trembled with affright;
"Surely," thought he, "no mortal eyes
    E'er saw so strange a sight;
But the man of fractions sat
    And laughed with all his might.

"Now lay my fragments in that box
  Where they'll be out of sight;
Be careful not to drop the eye,
  And mind the teeth do n't bite.
My limbs go on my trunk by day,
  And in my trunk by night."

But fear held fast the waiter,
  He merely stood and stared;
To see such soul-appalling sights
  He had n't come prepared,
While the traveler only laughed the more
  To see the man so scared;

And, putting on a serious look,
  In solemn accents said,
"There's one thing more to do
  Before I get in bed;
Steady yourself against the wall
  And just unscrew my head."

THE EXECUTION OF ANDRÉ

HENRY PETERSON

THE hour of noon had been appointed for
Major André's execution. André rose from his
bed at his usual hour, and after partaking of
breakfast — which was supplied him, as had been

the custom, from Washington's own table — began to make his preparations for the solemn scene. His servant Laune had arrived from New York some days before with a supply of clothing; and André this morning shaved and dressed himself with even more than his usual care. He wore the rich scarlet uniform, faced with green, of a British officer, though without the customary sash and sword.

When his friend Pemberton entered, about eleven o'clock, he thought he had never seen a more splendid face and figure. The face was of a deadly paleness — the brow especially showing like a clear pale marble beneath the clustering masses of raven hair. The features appeared even more refined and intellectual than was their wont; and the beautiful expression which sat upon them and shone forth from his deep and melancholy eyes was such as naturally takes captive the hearts of men, and fills with devoted enthusiasm the souls of women.

"He is the handsomest man I ever saw!" exclaimed one of the officers in attendance, to Pemberton; "and the most gentle and winning."

"I am glad you have come in good time, Arthur," said André, with a serene composure. "You see I mean to die in the dress of a British officer."

Pemberton's heart was ready to burst, but he

knew his duty to his friend too well to allow his
sorrowful feelings to master him for a moment.

"Are you ready, Major?" said one of the
officers.

"I am ready," replied André proudly.

As André emerged from the prison into the
free, fresh air, he took a deep breath, and gazed
up into the beautiful blue sky above him, hazy
and golden with the glory he so much loved of an
October day.   He walked arm-in-arm between the
two officers, Pemberton walking near him.   A
captain's command of thirty or forty men marched
immediately around them, and André glanced ex-
pressively to Pemberton when he saw these, for
he thought they were the firing party, and that
his last request, namely, that he should be shot,
had been granted.

An outer guard of five hundred men also at-
tended, at the head of which rode nearly all the
principal officers of the army, with the exception
of Washington and his staff, who from a feeling of
delicacy remained indoors.   Large crowds of the
soldiery and of the citizens from the surrounding
country, also were present.

As André passed on, he retained his composure
in a wonderful degree, nodding and speaking
pleasantly to those officers with whom he was acquainted, especially to those who had constituted
the court-martial.

The gallows had been erected on the summit of an eminence that commanded a wide view of the surrounding country. It was also in full view of Washington's headquarters; but the doors and shutters of the latter were closed, not a soul was to be seen, save the usual sentinels pacing in front of the house.

As the mournful procession turned from the high road into the meadow, André first saw the gallows. He suddenly recoiled, and paused for a moment.

"I thought you meant to spare me this indignity!" he exclaimed, almost passionately.

"We have simply to obey our orders," replied one of the officers.

"Gentlemen, you are making a great mistake," cried Pemberton to a couple of officers who were riding near.

"If we are, we are doing it honestly, and because we think it our duty," replied one of them.

André moved on. "I must drink the cup to the dregs, it seems," he said with deep emotion. "But it will soon be over." The pleasant smile, however, had vanished from his face. It was evident that what he thought a needless indignity cut sharper than the sentence of death itself.

The gallows was simply a rude but lofty gibbet with a wagon drawn under it. Inside the wagon was a roughly-made coffin painted black. As

Andre stood near the wagon, awaiting some brief preparations, his agony seemed almost more than he could bear, his throat sinking and swelling as though convulsed, while he rolled a pebble to and fro under one of his feet. Laune, his servant, totally overcome, burst into loud weepings and lamentations. This seemed to rouse and restore his master, who turned to him and uttered some cheering and comforting words. All around there were solemn faces, and many were even in tears.

At a word from one of the officers, André flung his arms round Pemberton's neck and kissed him, and sprang lightly but with evident loathing into the baggage-wagon, standing upon the coffin. Then he looked around him — upon his executioner, with his blackened face; upon the saddened soldiery and the mournful crowd; upon the glorious landscape, resplendent with the hues of autumn, and melting gradually away into the hazy distance. The old, proud look came back into his face, and he seemed more like a hero, mounted in the car of triumph, and prepared to receive the acclamations of his followers, than a man about to suffer a shameful death.

The executioner approached him, but he waved him away with a grand disdain, and tossing his hat to the ground, removed his stock, opened wide his shirt-collar, and taking the noose, adjusted it himself properly about his neck. On his face was a proud disgust as he did this — as if he said, without useless words: "You have the power; and though you use your power meanly, I am man and soldier enough to submit to it!" Then he bound his handkerchief over his eyes.

The order of execution was read loudly and impressively by Adjutant-General Scammel. At its conclusion, Colonel Scammel informed the prisoner that he might speak, if he had anything to say.

Lifting the bandage from his eyes, and gazing around once more, as if that last look of earth and sun and sky and human faces was sweet indeed, André said, in a proud, clear voice:

"Bear witness, gentlemen, that I die in the service of my country, as becomes a British officer and a brave man."

The hangman now drew near with a piece of cord to bind his arms; but, recoiling from his snaky touch, André swept his hand aside, and drawing another handkerchief from his pocket, allowed his elbows to be loosely fastened behind his back. Then he said in a firm voice, "I am ready!"

Almost at the word the wagon was rolled swiftly away, and, with a terrible jerk and shock, the noble soul of John André was severed from the beautiful frame with which the Creator had clothed it.

And there was a solemn stillness through all
the multitude gathered around, broken only by the
sound of weeping.   For all felt that this was no
common man; and that he had done nothing
worthy of death.   Only that it was necessary that
he should die for the good of their country.

————

THE SIOUX CHIEF'S DAUGHTER

Lo gray hawks ride the rising blast;
Dark cloven clouds ride to and fro
By peaks pre-eminent in snow;
A sounding river rushes past,
So wild, so vortex-like, and vast;
A low lodge tops the windy hills;
A tawny maiden mute and still,
Stands waiting at the river's brink,
As weird and wild as you can think,
A mighty chief is at her feet;
She does not hear him wooing so —
She hears the dark wild water's flow;
She waits her lover, tall and fleet,
From far gold fields of Idaho,
Beyond the beaming hills of snow.

He comes!   The grim chief springs in air —
His brawny arm, his blade is bare.
She turns, she lifts her round brown hand;
She looks him fairly in the face;

She moves her foot a little pace
And says, with coldness and command,
"There's blood enough in this lorn land,
But see! a test of strength and skill,
Of courage and fierce fortitude;
To breast and wrestle with the rude
And storm-born waters, now I will
Bestow you both . . . Stand either side!
Take you my left, tall Idaho,
And you my burly chief, I know,
Would choose my right.   Now peer you low
Across the waters wild and wide.
See! leaning so this morn I spied
Red berries dip yon farther side.
See, dipping, dripping in the stream,
Twin boughs of autumn berries gleam!
Now this, brave men, shall be the test,
Plunge in the stream, bear knife in teeth
To cut yon bough for bridal wreath.
Plunge in! and he who bears him best
And brings yon ruddy fruit to land
The first, shall have both heart and hand."

Two tawny men, tall, brown and hewed
Like antique bronzes, rarely seen,
Shot up like flame.   She stood between
Like fixed impassive fortitude.
Then one threw robes with sullen air,
And wound red fox-tails in his hair;

But one with face of proud delight,
Entwined a crest of snowy white.

She stood between.   She sudden gave
The sign, and each impatient brave
Shot sudden in the sounding wave;
The startled water gurgled round:
Their stubborn strokes kept sullen sound.

Oh, then awoke the love that slept!
Oh, then her heart beat loud and strong!
Oh, then the proud love, pent up long
Broke forth in wail upon the air;
And leaning there she sobbed and wept
With dark face mantled in her hair.
Now side by side the rivals plied,
Yet no man wasted word or breath;
All was as still as stream of death.
Now side by side their strength was tried,
And now they breathless paused and lay
Like brawny wrestlers well at bay.
And now they dived, dived long, and now
The black heads lifted from the foam,
And shook aback the dripping brow,
Then shouldered sudden glances home,
And then with burly front, the brow
And bull-like neck shot sharp and blind,
And left a track of foam behind . . .
They near the shore at last, and now

The foam flies spouting from a face
That laughing, lifts from out the race.

The race is won, the work is done!
She sees the shining crest of snow;
She knows her tall brown Idaho.
She cries aloud, she laughing cries,
And tears are streaming from her eyes:
"Oh splendid, kingly Idaho!
I kiss his lifted crest of snow;
I see him clutch the bended bough!
'Tis cleft — he turns! is coming now!

My tall and tawny king, come back!
Come swift, O Sweet! Why falter so?
Come! Come! What thing has crossed your
       track?
I kneel to all the gods I know,
Oh come, my manly Idaho!
Great Spirit, what is this I see?
Why, there is blood? the wave is red!
That wrinkled chief, outstripped in race,
Dives down and hiding from my face,
Strikes underneath! . . . He rises now!
Now plucks my hero's berry bough,
And lifts aloft his red fox head,
And signals he has won for me.
Hist, softly! Let him come and see.

"Oh, come! my white-crowned hero, come.
Oh come! and I will be your bride,

Despite your chieftain's craft and might.
Come back to me! my lips are dumb,
My hands are helpless with despair;
The hair you kissed, my long, strong hair,
Is reaching to the ruddy tide,
That you may catch it when you come."

Now slow the buffets back the wave!
O God! he sinks! O Heavens! save
My brave, brave boy! He rises! See!
Hold fast, my boy! Strike! strike for me!
Strike straight this way! Strike firm and
        strong.
Hold fast your strength.   It is not long —
O God! he sinks! He sinks! Is gone!
His face has perished from my sight.

And did I dream, and do I wake?
Or did I wake and now but dream?
And what is this crawls from the stream?
Oh here is some mad, mad mistake!
What you! the red fox at my feet?
You first, and failing from a race?
What! you have brought me berries red?
What! you have brought your bridal wreath?
You sly red fox with wrinkled face —
That blade has blood between your teeth.

Lie still! lie still! till I lean o'er
And clutch your red blade to the shore . . .

Ha! ha! Take that! and that! and that!
Ha! ha! So, through your coward throat
The full day shines! . . . Two fox-tails float,
And drift and drive adown the stream.

But what is this? What sorry crest
Climbs out the billows of the west,
All weary, wounded, bent and slow,
And dripping from his streaming hair?
It is! It is my Idaho!
His feet are on the land, and fair
His face is lightning to my face,
For who shall now dispute the race?

The gray hawks pass, O love! and doves
O'er yonder lodge, shall coo their loves,
My love shall heal your wounded breast
And in yon lodge my hero rest.

THE PILOT'S STORY

W. D. HOWELLS

"THEY both came aboard there at Cairo, from
a New Orleans boat, ond took passage with us for
St. Louis. She was a beautiful woman, with just
blood enough from her mother, darkening her
eyes and her hair, to make her race known to a
trader. You would have thought she was white.
The man that was with her (you see such).

weakly good-natured and kind, and weakly good-natured and vicious; slender of body and soul; fit neither for loving nor hating. I was a youngster then, and only learning the river; not over-fond of the wheel. I used to watch them at monté, down in the cabin at night, and learned to know all of the gamblers. So, when I saw this weak one staking his money against them, betting upon the turn of the cards, I knew what was coming. They never left their pigeons a single feather to fly with.

"Next day I saw them together, the stranger and one of the gamblers; picturesque rascal he was, with long, black hair and mustaches, black slouch hat, drawn to his eyes from his villanous forehead. On together they moved, still earnestly talking in whispers, on towards the forecastle, where sat the woman alone by the gangway. Roused by the fall of feet, she turned, and, beholding her master, greeted him with a smile that was more like a wife's than another's; rose to meet him fondly, and then, with the dread apprehension always haunting the slave, fell her eye on the face of the gambler. Something was spoken so low, that I could not hear what the words were; only, the woman started, and looked from one to the other, with imploring eyes, bewildered hands, and a tremor all through her frame. I saw her from where I was standing, she

shook so. 'Say, is it so?' she cried. On the
weak white lips of her master died a sickly smile,
and he said, 'Louise, I have sold you.' God is my
judge! may I never see such a look of despairing
desolate anguish, as that which the woman cast
on her master; griping her breast with her little
hands, as if he had stabbed her; standing in
silence a space, as fixed as the Indian woman,
carved out of wood, on the pilot-house of the old
'Pocahontas'; then, with a gurgling moan, like
the sound in the throat of the dying, came back
her voice, that, rising, fluttered through wild
incoherence, into a terrible shriek, that stopped
my heart while she answered, 'Sold me! Sold
me! Sold —! And you promised to give me my
freedom! Promised me, for the sake of our little
boy in St. Louis! What will you say to our boy,
when he cries for me there in St. Louis? What
will you say to our God? He shall hear it! And
all of the angels in Heaven! Even the devils in
Hell! And none will believe when they hear it!
Sold me' fell her voice with a thrilling wail, and
in silence down she sank on the deck, and covered
her face with her fingers.

"Instantly, all the people, with looks of reproach and compassion, flocked round the prostrate woman. The children cried, and the mothers
hugged them tight to their breasts. But the
gambler said to the captain, 'Put me off there at

the town that lies round the bend of the river. Here, you! rise at once and be ready now to go with me.' Roughly he seized the woman's arm and strove to uplift her. She — she seemed not to heed him, but rose like one that is dreaming, slid from his grasp, and fleetly mounted the steps of the gangway, up to the hurricane deck, in silence, without lamentation; straight to the stern of the boat, where the wheel was, she ran, and the people followed her fast till she turned and stood looking them full in the face, and in the face of the gambler. Not one to save her, not one of all the compassionate people! Not one to save her, of all the pitying angels in Heaven! Not one bolt of God to strike him dead there before her! Wildly she waved him back, we waiting in silence and horror. Over the swarthy face of the gambler a pallor of passion passed, like a gleam of lightning over the west in the night time. White, she stood, and mute, till he put forth his hand to secure her; then, she turned and leaped, in mid-air fluttered a moment, down, — there, — whirling, — fell, like a broken-winged bird from a tree top, down on the cruel wheel, that caught her and hurled her and crushed her, and in the foam-ing water plunged her and hid her forever."

THE BLUE AND THE GRAY

ELLEN H. FLAGG

A waste of land, a sodden plain,
    A lurid sunset sky,
With clouds that fled and faded fast
    In ghastly phantasy;
A field upturned by trampling feet,
    A field up-piled with slain,
With horse and rider blent in death
    Upon the battle-plain.

Two soldiers, lying as they fell
    Upon the reddened clay, —
In daytime, foes; at night, in peace,
    Breathing their lives away.
Brave hearts had stirred each manly breast;
    Fate only made them foes;
And lying, dying, side by side,
    A softened feeling rose.

"Our time is short," one faint voice said.
    "To-day we've done our best
On different sides.   What matters now?
    To-morrow we're at rest.
Life lies behind.   I might not care
    For only my own sake;
But far away are other hearts
    That this day's work will break.

"Among New Hampshire's snowy hills
  There pray for me, to-night,
A woman, and a little girl
  With hair like golden light."
And at the thought broke forth, at last,
  The cry of anguish wild
That would no longer be repressed, —
  "O God! my wife and child!"

"And," said the other dying man,
  "Across the Georgia plain
There watch and wait for me loved ones
  I'll never see again.
A little girl with dark bright eyes
  Each day waits at the door;
The father's step, the father's kiss,
  Will never meet her more.

"To-day we sought each other's lives;
  Death levels all that now,
For soon before God's mercy-seat
  Together shall we bow.
Forgive each other while we may;
  Life's but a weary game;
And right or wrong, the morning sun
  Will find us dead the same."

The dying lips the pardon breathe,
  The dying hands entwine;

The last ray dies, and over all
  The stars from heaven shine;
And the little girl with golden hair,
  And one with dark eyes bright,
On Hampshire's hills and Georgia plain,
  Were fatherless that night.

THE SERMON

Louisa M. Alcott

SITTING in a station the other day I had a little sermon preached in the way I like, and I'll repeat it for your benefit, because it taught me one of the lessons which we all should learn, and taught it in such a natural, simple way, that no one could forget it. It was a bleak, snowy day. The train was late; the ladies' room dark and smoky, and the dozen women, old and young, who sat waiting impatiently, all looked cross, low-spirited, or stupid. I felt all three, and thought, as I looked around, that my fellow-beings were a very unamiable, uninteresting set.

Just then a forlorn old woman, shaking with palsy, came in with a basket of wares for sale, and went about mutely offering them to the sitters. Nobody bought anything, and the poor old soul stood blinking at the door a minute, as if reluctant to go out into the bitter storm again. She turned presently and poked about the room as if trying to find something; and then a pale lady in black, who lay as if asleep on a sofa, opened her eyes, saw the old woman and instantly asked in a kind tone, "Have you lost anything, ma'am?"

"No, dear. I'm looking for the heatin' place to have a warm 'fore I goes out again. My eyes is poor and I don't seem to find the furnace nowheres."

"Here it is," and the lady led her to the steam radiator, placed a chair, and showed her how to warm her feet.

"Well, now, is not that nice?" said the old woman, spreading her ragged mittens to dry. "Thank you, dear. This is comfortable, isn't it? I'm most froze to-day, bein' lame and wimbly, and not selling much makes me kind of down-hearted."

The lady smiled, went to the counter, bought a cup of tea and some sort of food, carried it herself to the old woman, and said as respectfully and kindly as if the poor woman had been dressed in silk and fur, "Won't you have a cup of tea? It's very comforting such a day as this."

"Sakes alive! Do they give tea to this depot?" cried the old lady in a tone of innocent surprise that made a smile go 'round the room, touching the gloomiest face like a streak of sunshine. "Well, now, this is just lovely," added the old lady, sipping away with a relish. "This does warm my heart!"

While she refreshed herself, telling her story meanwhile, the lady looked over the poor little wares in the basket, bought soap and pins, shoe-strings and tape and cheered the old soul by paying well for them. As I watched her doing this I thought what a sweet face she had, though I'd considered her rather plain before. I felt dreadfully ashamed of myself that I had grimly shaken my head when the basket was offered to me; and as I saw the look of interest, sympathy and kindliness come into the dismal faces all around me, I did wish that I had been the magician to call it out.

It was only a kind word and a friendly act, but somehow it brightened that dingy room wonderfully. It changed the faces of a dozen women and I think it touched a dozen hearts, for I saw many eyes follow the plain, pale lady with sudden respect; and when the old woman got up to go, several persons beckoned. to her and bought something, as if they wanted to repair their first negligence. That simple little charity was as good as a sermon to those who saw it, and I think each traveler went on her way better for that half-hour in the dreary station. I can testify that one of them did, and nothing but the emptiness of her purse prevented her from "comforting the heart" of every forlorn old woman she met for a week after.

PARRHASIUS AND CAPTIVE

NATHANIEL P. WILLIS

Parrhasius, a painter of Athens, amongst those Olynthian captives Philip of Macedon brought home to sell, bought one very old man; and when he had him at his house, put him to death with extreme torture and torment, the better by his example to express the pains and passions of his Prometheus, whom he was then about to paint.

THERE stood an unsold captive in the mart,
A gray-haired and majestical old man,
Chained to a pillar.   It was almost night,
And the last seller from his place had gone
And not a sound was heard but of a dog
Crunching beneath the stall a refuse bone,
Or the dull echo from the pavement rung,
As the faint captive changed his weary feet.

'Twas evening, and the half-descended sun
Tipped with a golden fire the many domes
Of Athens, and a yellow atmosphere
Lay rich and dusky in the shaded street
Through which the captive gazed.

The golden light into the painter's room
Streamed richly, and the hidden colors stole
From the dark pictures radiantly forth,
And in the soft and dewy atmosphere,
Like forms and landscapes, magical they lay.

Parrhasius stood gazing forgetfully,
Upon his canvas.   There Prometheus lay
Chained to the cold rocks of Mount Caucasus —
The vulture at his vitals, and the links
Of the lame Lemnian festering in his flesh;
And, as the painter's mind felt through the dim,
Rapt mystery, and plucked the shadows forth
With its far-reaching fancy, and with form
And color clad them, his fine earnest eye
Flashed with a passionate fire, and the quick curl
Of his thin nostril, and his quivering lip
Were like the winged god's breathing from his
      flight.

     "Bring me the captive now!
My hands feel skillful, and the shadows lift
From my waked spirit airily and swift
     And I could paint the bow
Upon the bended heavens — round me play
Colors of such divinity to-day.

     Ha! bind him on his back!
Look! — as Prometheus in my picture here!
Quick — or he faints! stand with the cordial near!
     Now bend him to the rack!
Press down the poison'd links into his flesh!
And tear agape that healing wound afresh!

     So — let him writhe!   How long
Will he live thus?   Quick, my good pencil now!

What a fine agony works upon his brow!
 Ha! gray-haired, and so strong!
How fearfully he stifles that short moan!
Gods! if I could but paint a dying groan!

 "Pity thee! So I do!
I pity the dumb victim at the altar —
But does the rob'd priest for his pity falter?
 I'd rack thee though I knew
A thousand lives were perishing in thine —
What were ten thousand to a fame like mine?

 Yet there's a deathless name!
A spirit that the smothering vault shall spurn,
And like a steadfast planet mount and burn —
 And though its crown of flame
Consumed my brain to ashes as it shone,
By all the fiery stars! I'd bind it on!

 Ay — though it bid me rifle
My heart's last fount for its insatiate thirst —
Though every life-strung nerve be maddened first,
 Though it should bid me stifle
The yearning in my throat for my sweet child,
And taunt its mother till my brain went wild —

 All — I would do it all —
Sooner than die, like a dull worm to rot —
Thrust foully into earth to be forgot!

O heavens — but I appal
Your heart, old man! forgive — ha! on your lives
Let him not faint! — rack him till he revives!

　　Vain — vain — give o'er!　His eye
Glazes apace.　He does not feel you now —
Stand back!　I'll paint the death-dew on his brow
　　　Gods! if he do not die
But for one moment — one — till I eclipse
Conception with the scorn of those calm lips!

　　Shivering!　Hark!　he mutters
Brokenly now — that was a difficult breath —
Another?　Wilt thou never come, oh, Death!
　　Look! how his temples flutter!
Is his heart still?　Aha! lift up his head!
He shudders, gasps, Jove help him! so, he's dead.

A SCENE ON THE BATTLEFIELD

HENRY W. GRADY

A SOLDIER lay wounded on a hard-fought field;
the roar of the battle had died away, and he rested
in the deadly stillness of its aftermath.　Not a
sound was heard as he lay there, sorely smitten
and speechless, but the shriek of wounded and the
sigh of the dying soul, as it escaped from the
tumult of earth into the unspeakable peace of the
stars.　Off over the field flickered the lanterns of

the surgeons with the litter bearers, searching that
they might take away those whose lives could be
saved and leave in sorrow those who were doomed
to die with pleading eyes through the darkness.
This poor soldier watched, unable to turn or speak
as the lanterns grew near.   At last the light
flashed in his face, and the surgeon, with kindly
face, bent over him, hesitated a moment, shook his
head, and was gone, leaving the poor fellow alone
with death.   He watched in patient agony as they
went on from one part of the field to another.   As
they came back the surgeon bent over him again.
"I believe if this poor fellow lives till sundown to-
morrow he will get well."   And again leaving him,
not to death but with hope, all night long these
words fell into his heart as the dews fell from the
stars upon his lips, "If he but lives till sundown,
he will get well."   He turned his weary head to
the east and watched for the coming sun.   At last
the stars went out, the east trembled with radiance,
and the sun, slowly lifting above the horizon,
tinged his pallid face with flame.   He watched it
inch by inch as it climbed slowly up the heavens.
He thought of life, its hopes and ambitions, its
sweetness and its raptures, and he fortified his soul
against despair until the sun had reached high
noon.   It sloped down its slow descent, and he
needed stronger stimulants to make him stand the
struggle until the end of the day had come.   He

thought of his far-off home, the blessed house resting in tranquil peace with the roses climbing to its door, and the trees whispering to its windows, and dozing in the sunshine, the orchard and the little brook running like a silver thread through the forest.

"If I live till sundown I will see it again. I will walk down the shady lane: I will open the battered gate, and the mocking-bird shall call to me from the orchard, and I will drink again at the old mossy spring."

And he thought of the wife who had come from the neighboring farmhouse and put her hand shyly in his, and brought sweetness to his life and light to his home.

"If I live till sundown I shall look once more into her deep and loving eyes, and press her brown head once more to my aching breast."

And he thought of the old father, patient in prayer, bending lower and lower every day under his load of sorrow and old age.

"If I but live till sundown I shall see him again and wind my strong arm about his feeble body, and his hands shall rest upon my head, while the unspeakable healing of his blessing falls into my heart."

And he thought of the little children that clambered on his knees and tangled their little hands into his heartstrings, making to him such music as the world shall not equal or heaven surpass.

"If I live till sundown they shall again find my parched lips with their warm mouths, and their little fingers shall run once more over my face."

And he then thought of his old mother, who gathered these children about her and breathed her old heart afresh in their brightness and attuned her old lips anew in their prattle, that she might live till her big boy came home.

"If I live till sundown I will see her again, and I will rest my head at my old place on her knees, and weep away all memory of this desolate night." And the Son of God who had died for men, bending from the stars, put the hand that had been nailed to the cross on ebbing life and held on the staunch until the sun went down and the stars came out, and shone down in the brave man's heart and blurred in his glistening eyes, and the lanterns of the surgeons came and he was taken from death to life.

THE YACHT RACE

"N. Y. HERALD"

IMAGINE two superb racing yachts, swaying and staggering before a wind which had the weight of half a gale in it, their swollen sails threatening each moment to bid farewell to creak-

ing boom and buckling spar. Picture, if you can,
the storm of foam which came boiling about the
flying yachts as, driving before wind and sea, they
rose buoyantly to the swells to sink stern first into
the sloping valleys that came racing after them.
Then home again, with flat sails as taut as drum-
heads and lee scuppers knee deep in foam, the one
straining spar and shroud and sail and stay in a
terrific effort to keep the vantage gained — the
other as desperately striving to overcome the lead.
'Twas well worth the ten misspent days which
excursionists had squandered on those other lifeless efforts at racing and which proved to be little
more than days of fog and calm and drift.

Straight out of the north a lively wind was
blowing when the two yachts arrived off the lightship. The wind had a twenty mile an hour gait,
and the Shamrock, as she dipped her green hull
into the sea, had a now-or-never look about her.
It was the wind that Sir Thomas had been looking
for, and in it all realized lay the Shamrock's last,
long, lingering hope of taking away the cup. In
all other sorts of weather she had been weighed
and found wanting. It remained to see what she
could do in a wind of the kind that was blowing
now.

The start was at the lightship, and the course
was a fifteen mile run to leeward and a beat back
to the finish line. Both boats were standing to

the northward under mainsail and jib when the preparatory gun was fired. The wind then was too brisk for the yachts to show clubtopsails, but their working topsails were up in stops and ready for setting. The Shamrock's was sheeted home three minutes after the preparatory gun was heard, the Columbia setting her staysail four minutes later.

At five minutes to eleven came the warning gun, and the two racers headed for the line, both jockeying for position, and neither gaining any decided advantage. The starting gun was fired, and the Shamrock stood across the line, showing mainsail, working topsail, jib and staysail. The challenger crossed at 11:00:34, followed one minute and one second later by the defender. The Shamrock lowered her spinnaker boom to starboard as she crossed the line, but Captain Hogarth did not get it set until a full half minute after the Deer Isle sailors had sent the Columbia's swelling to the wind. On the other hand, the Columbia had not set her working topsail, while that of the Shamrock was gradually drawing that vessel away from the Columbia.

Meanwhile the Shamrock's spinnaker was giving trouble, the sail hanging in stops a dozen feet or more from the topmast head. This disadvantage was evened by the queer capers which the Columbia's spinnaker cut. The pole seemed to be too light for the great weight of wind which the sail was carrying, and it frequently tipped at an angle so sharp that it seemed as though the spar would be up ended. Once it went so high into the air that it looked as though the pole had been broken or if the crew were making efforts to take in the sail.

Despite all handicaps of tipping booms and the absence of gaff topsail the American boat continued to overhaul the Shamrock. Then the Columbia broke out her topsail, and soon afterward the Shamrock's men had the same old familiar view of the Columbia's stern they had so often looked upon before.

The wind held true and strong, and the run down the wind was as pretty a yachting scene as was ever witnessed. The excursion fleet toiling along on either beam had all it could do to keep pace with the winged racers. The gallant American was still in the van as the two neared the turning point. The jib which the Shamrock had been carrying had been replaced by the largest in her sail locker, and for a time it seemed as though the Irish cutter would hold her own. But not for long. In spite of change of canvas, in spite of everything that Captain Hogarth could do, the Columbia steadily drew away from the Irish cutter. Nearing the outer mark both made preparations for turning it, the Columbia taking in her spinnaker as she brought the buoy broad off her starboard bow, the Shamrock doffing hers a half minute later. Luffing around the point, the Columbia stood away on the starboard tack, followed seventeen seconds later by the closely pursuing Shamrock.

The road home was the road of the rough, and immediately after heading into the wind both yachts began a lively dance over the tumbling seas. The defender was under mainsail, jib and staysail. The Shamrock under the same sail, carried a working topsail in addition. She took that in at twenty-six minutes to one, the strain being too great for her rigging. Over the decks of both cutters the spray flew in sheets, and the lower edges of their mainsails were kept dark with the flying clouds of spray.

Whenever one altered her course the other followed. The tacks were frequent and at irregular intervals, but each time the Shamrock spilled the wind out of her sails, spun around upon her heels and filled on the other tack her crew saw the Columbia still in the lead.

The Columbia gradually widened the gap and despite the Shamrock's attempt to overtake her swept grandly across the finish line at 40 minutes past two amid the shriek of whistles, followed 6 minutes and 34 seconds later by the Shamrock beaten at every point of sailing and in every sort of weather.